Another idea a ... adven...

Adventure Guide™ to

Florida's West Coast

Chelle Koster Walton

HUNTER
PUBLISHING

Hunter Publishing, Inc.
130 Campus Drive, Edison NJ 08818
(732) 225 1900, (800) 255 0343, Fax (732) 417 0482

In Canada
1220 Nicholson Rd., Newmarket, Ontario
Canada L3Y 7V1, (800) 399 6858

ISBN 1-55650-787-9

©1998 Chelle Koster Walton

Maps by Lissa Dailey

For complete information about the hundreds of other travel
guides and language courses offered by Hunter Publishing,
visit our Web site at:

www.hunterpublishing.com

Photo Credits
Cover, John J. Lopinot; 6, Patrick M. Rose; 30, 31, 39, 52, 54, Florida's
Pinellas Suncoast; 49, Tradewinds; 50, Don CeSar Resort; 60,
Tampa News Bureau; 61, Jeff Turnau; 65, Jeff Greenberg; 72, Busch
Gardens Tampa; 99, 100, 101, 106, 111, Sarasota Convention &
Visitors Bureau; 127, 157, Robert Overton; 129, 146, 150, 156, 166,
Lee County Visitors & Convention Bureau; 154, Sanibel Harbour
Resort; 159, 187, Florida Division of Tourism; 179, 180, Naples
Tourism Bureau; all others by author.

Contents

Introduction

Scope of This Book

For the purposes of this guide, the West Coast of Florida describes a slice of coastline along the Gulf of Mexico beginning in the north around the Tampa Bay area, and ending in the south at Naples and the Everglades. It encompasses the coastal portions of Pinellas, Hillsborough, Manatee, Sarasota, Charlotte, Lee, and Collier counties, including the Everglades. This region is cohesive in its types of vegetation, climate, and the presence of beachfront barrier islands, yet it is infinitely diverse.

History of Adventure

If you're looking for adventure, you're in the right place. West Coast Florida, as one of the nation's final frontiers, claims a history and heritage of rugged outdoorsmanship.

While the rest of the nation was busily traveling along paved roads and buying their supplies from general stores, in the farthest corners of Florida's Gulf Coast – down Naples way and in the Florida Everglades – folks were still trading with the natives for victuals and dredging enough land out of the swamps to build the Tamiami Trail. The West Coast of Florida was considered a wild, exotic place then, a place for safaris and catching giant silver fish – a place where prehistoric turtles, alligators, manatees, and horseshoe crabs still survived, where trees danced, birds dive-bombed, dolphins smiled, flowers bloomed at night, and winter never came.

The first white men traveled to western Florida for adventure. And they found it aplenty: half-naked natives, tricky waterways, impenetrable swamps, and enough fowl and fish to thicken seas, sky, and stews. In search of gold and youth, they chose to grumble, kill the natives, and curse the rest. They brought their own hogs, cows, and citrus to eat, then eventually left, discouraged by the persistent onslaughts of the resident Amerindian tribes – the Calusas in the south, the Tocobagas around today's Tampa and Sarasota. Evidence of important Amerindian centers of culture has been found on Marco Island, Mound Key, Pine Island, Useppa Island, Manasota Key, Terra Ceia, and Safety Harbor.

Juan Ponce de León himself was the first recorded European to set foot upon these shores, somewhere in Charlotte Harbor. Hernando De Soto landed at today's Fort Myers Beach or Bradenton, depending upon whom you believe. Ensuing parties established forts, missions, and colonies at Fort Myers Beach, Pine Island, and other strategic spots along the coast.

Legends fill the region's early timelines with dastardly pirates who came to prey upon ships sailing between the Caribbean and established towns in northern Florida. Much has been exaggerated, particularly the legend of Gasparilla, upon which a Tampa festival and a coastline attitude of devil-may-care thrive. The mottled backwaters of the West Coast undoubtedly harbor many a refugee from the law, but few as colorful as publicity agents have painted them.

More prevalent in the 17th through the 19th centuries were Spanish fishermen and gutsy farmers. Later, in the Charlotte Harbor area, commercial fishing developed into a thriving industry. Fishermen lived in stilt houses built on sand shoals from Placida to the Ten Thousand Islands. A handful of the historic shacks remain.

In many ways, fishing settled the West Coast. Farming proved less dependable, what with hurricanes and pests. Sugar plantations around Bradenton came and went with the wind. In later years, a reputation for great sportfishing brought well-heeled sportsmen to the coast, which eventually put the region on the map of the socially connected.

In the meantime, war introduced others to this balmy and palmy land. Florida, after being passed back and forth between Spain and England, became a US territory in the early 1820s. Shortly thereafter, Governor Andrew Jackson built forts on Tampa Bay and the Caloosahatchee River at today's Fort Myers to defend against the Seminole tribes he had angered. Later, Civil and Spanish-American War fortifications were built on Egmont and Mullet keys, at the mouth of Tampa Bay. In the wake of war came ex-soldiers and their families. Then came industry and tourism.

St. Petersburg was built in 1887 as a health resort, and Tampa, formerly Fort Brooke, gained a reputation as such. Railroads, cigar factories, and hotels started the twin cities down the path to becoming the region's metropolitan hub. Islands and coastal towns to the south remained the domain of the intrepid. It wasn't until big names like Ringling and Edison became associated with the region that people sat up and took serious notice.

They came to fish. They came to swim in the warm, gentle Gulf waves. They came to hunt, to escape, to winter. They came to stay. Since the

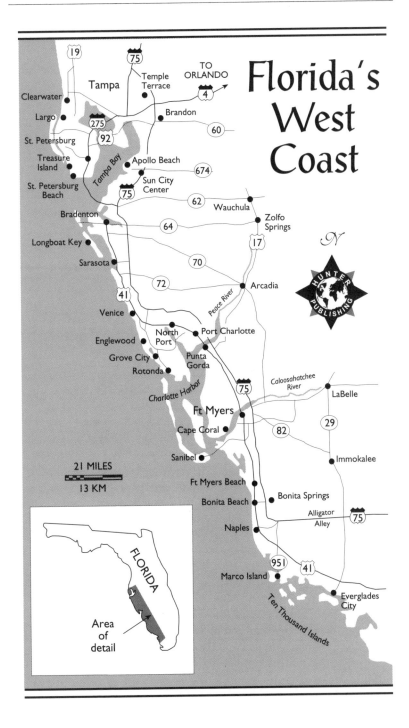

Florida's West Coast

1940s, the coast's population has built steadily. As more people came to reside permanently, cities developed along typical lines, adding services and culture to their slate of resorts, restaurants, and beachside facilities.

Adventure has always been part of what the coast offers. As ecotourism came into fashion, emphasis shifted to this aspect of vacationing. To the fishing charters, tour boats, parasailing concessions, and Hobie Cat rentals were added more bike trails, sea kayaking, and nature-oriented tours. More than any section of Florida, the West Coast has most firmly put its foot down about wanton development. This makes it especially desirable for adventurers seeking a return to what those first intrepid fishermen, hunters, and sailors found.

Largely gone are the untamed lands and rugged lifestyles that attracted adventurers a half-century ago. Still to be found throughout the region, however, are areas and activities that retain the flavor and fervor of Florida's derring-do days.

Natural Makeup

Heron.

With 170 miles of Gulf coastline, 400 miles of freshwater river, thousands of acres of mangrove estuary and untamed jungle, and the vast sawgrass plains of the Everglades, Florida's lower West Coast brims with opportunity for adventure on the land and on the water.

The diversity of its terrain and biological communities, when combined with the region's exotic, subtropical climate and ambiance, creates a destination that is both classroom and playground for outdoor enthusiasts. Where else can you camp among mangroves and canoe beneath roosting roseate spoonbills?

The island beach and marine communities, of course, are the most touted features of Gulf Coast Florida ecology. They introduce most visitors to the local environment with their shells, dolphins, pelicans, shorebirds, sting rays, tarpon, and loggerhead turtles; but they are only the start. Most intriguing to nature lovers are the undersung estuaries, the nurseries that build islands and nurture aquatic life. Haunting, steamy places, they harbor a species of tree that seems to dance on spindly legs – the mangrove. In its prop roots, dirt, barnacles, and other encrustrations collect to build shorelines and islands. Its leaf fall provides rich and fertile muck; its branches, nests for local and migrating birds. Here the food chain begins with the tiniest crabs and ends with the birds, fish, and manatees who come to munch on seaweed or lunch on a half-shell. The cycle is ancient, and one can sense that in the quietly regenerating world of the mangrove estuary.

Less brackish and freshwater systems are the domain of another ancient component of Florida wildlife – the alligator. Gnarly and tyrannasaurish, the American alligator survives and thrives in coastal rivers and particularly in the Everglades. With it co-exist cypress trees, turtles, bass, river otters, and fabulous birds, like the wood stork and great blue heron.

Salt marshes, scrublands, flatwoods, and high pine lands occupy different elevations between sea level and ridge land. On hammocks, high and dry, hard wood forests harbor the rarest of all Florida creatures, the panther, seldom seen in the wild. Its cousin the bobcat is less reclusive, its numbers less depleted. Black bears, white-tailed deer, squirrels, raccoons, oppossums, armadillos, and gopher tortoises roam the woodlands. Get closer and you'll find indigo snakes, anole lizards, skinks, tree frogs, ant lions, and love bugs.

Some locals are less friendly than others. Those you want to avoid include rattlesnakes, pygmy rattlers, jellyfish, fire ants, and sand fleas (no-see-ums). There are also noxious plants that can pose danger, particularly the detested pepper plant, an introduced tree whose berries can cause allergic reaction. Poison ivy and oak grow in the wilds. A mystery novel set on Sanibel Island describes murder by a different plant, the oleander, a limb of which was used by the murderer to roast a marshmallow for his victim.

Most native coastal plants are benign and serve to protect wildlife. Residents are becoming aware of that and there is a trend to plant wildlife-attracting gardens rather than exotic vegetation, which taxes the ecosystem. Cities, resorts, and commercial enterprises are planting sea oats, railroad vines, and other maritime vegetation to keep sands anchored to the beaches. Native grasses are used to attract gopher tortoises. Dead tree trunks provide homes for kestrels and other nesting birds, as well as food for pileated woodpeckers. Butterflies flock around certain native plants, to feed and lay their eggs.

On a larger scale, the region's many state and national parks and refuges began preserving habitat in its natural state back when land booms threatened Florida's fragile environment. Private enterprises have since joined the drive to save what is dwindling. Today, these preserves offer not only shelter to the threatened, but recreation to those who appreciate the region's distinct environment.

Government-Protected Parks & Refuges

Manatees.

The most extensive of the region's refuge lands in Everglades National Park were saved from disaster as they balanced on the brink, thanks to the efforts of Marjorie Stoneman Douglas. Her book, *The Everglades: River of Grass,* convinced the federal government to preserve the fragile wetlands in 1947.

The Florida Everglades and their accompanying Ten Thousand Islands contain 2,100 square miles, 99 miles of canoe trails, 600 types of fish, 350 species of birds, 60 species of amphibians and reptiles, 45 species of mosquitos, and 25 species of mammals. This guide covers the portion of the massive park that lies in Collier County and is accessible from the west, the part that includes Ten Thousand Islands.

Sharing the Everglades ecology, Big Cypress National Preserve, Fakahatchee Strand State Preserve, and Collier Seminole State Park offer a score of recreational opportunities in the near vicinity.

Another national preserve in the region takes up half of Sanibel Island. J.N. "Ding" Darling National Wildlife Refuge is also Everglades-like in its wetlands makeup. Egmont Key National Wildlife Refuge occupies the entire 398 acres of Egmont Key, which is approachable only by boat. So is the Pine Island National Wildlife Refuge, comprising out-islands in Pine Island Sound.

Much of what attracts adventurers to the region lies off briny shores, in the Gulf of Mexico, the world's largest gulf, or in the Intracoastal Waterway of bays and harbors between the mainland and barrier islands. Within the area we will be covering lie two of Florida's largest inlets: Tampa Bay and Charlotte Harbor. Marine life in the latter is preserved by the 7,667-acre Cape Haze Aquatic Preserve. The long

Caloosahatchee River provides watery passage between the Gulf and the great Lake Okeechobee. Other West Coast sea preserves include the Pine Island Sound Aquatic Preserve and Estero Bay Aquatic Preserve.

Florida maintains an excellent system of state parks, historic sites, and recreational areas. Several of the finest are covered this book, from the unbridged island refuge of Cayo Costa State Park to the unusual slice of nature and history preserved at Koreshan State Historic Site.

Many of the parks provide recreational opportunities that allow families to play while immersing themselves in nature. If you plan on exploring the parks to any extent, consider purchasing an annual family pass for $80 ($40 for individuals).

Endangered/Threatened Species

Florida is home to more than 100 fragile species. Almost 40 of these are listed on the US Fish and Wildlife Service list of endangered and threatened animals. Those found in West Florida include the Florida panther, West Indian manatee, wood stork, bald eagle, red-cockaded woodpecker, Florida scrub jay, roseate tern, American crocodile, Atlantic loggerhead turtle, Eastern indigo snake, and sand skink.

For information on protecting wildlife as a visitor and adventurer in Florida, see the section in Chapter II, *Guidelines for Wildlife Preservation.*

The People & Culture

Southwest Florida has built its population in great part from tourists who came and never left. The result is a rich blend of cultures.

The first tourists arrived before history books, probably from South America and the Caribbean. The Calusa and Tocobaga Amerindians did not survive the next incursion of visitors. The Spanish eventually decimated their numbers with bows, arrows, and disease. Spanish influence persisted, and the area's oldest families have names such as Padilla and Menendez, familial survivors from a time when Cuban fishermen set up camps on the islands and Cuban cigar-makers migrated from Key West.

Most of the latter settled in Tampa's Ybor City. They were joined by Germans, Italians, and other nationalities who came to work the cigar factories, making Ybor City still today one of the region's most colorful ethnic enclaves. The district is known for its restaurants, where a Cuban sandwich or bowl of rice and beans comes cheap and delicious.

Other early arrivals migrated from the north, among them the Seminole Amerindians, a branch of the Creek tribe, whose bloodlines reflected an intermingling of African and Spanish blood. The Seminole Wars forced them to Arkansas, except for those who took cover in the Everglades' forbidding wild lands. Seminoles and an offshoot tribe known as the Miccosukees still live in the Everglades and on other tribal lands around Tampa. In the Everglades, most live in chickee huts, pole structures topped with thatched roofs. The Native Americans subsist on fishing, farming, and tourism, selling their colorful weaving and raking in the proceeds from bingo and a casino in nearby Immokalee.

Settlers from Georgia and Alabama came to be known as Crackers, a term also associated with the region's early cattle drivers, who "cracked" their whips to herd wild cows. Crackers contributed Deep South cuisine, folk medicine, and a simple style of architecture known as the Cracker house, which recently came into fashion as "Old Florida" architecture. They settled and farmed mostly in the interior sections of the region, where to this day their lifestyles whistle Dixie and folks speak with "south in the mouth."

The Seminole Wars, and later the Civil War, further stocked the slowly growing population with American soldiers who fell in love with the pleasant climate and lush surroundings. Land booms of the pre- and post-Depression eras brought northerners from far reaches. First came the well-to-do in search of adventures in the untamed wilderness. Among them were President Teddy Roosevelt, Zane Grey, Shirley Temple, Hedy Lamarr, Charles Lindbergh, Thomas Edison, John Ringling, and Henry Ford. Giants from the industrial world followed, often buying up land to insure the exclusivity of the region. They left behind a standard for nature appreciation and beautiful architecture. Others, such as Henry Plant and Barron Collier, saw the opportunity to develop the land, and so built railroads, roads, ports, resorts, and hotels.

Once the word got out, another sort of adventurer, known then as the "Tin Can Tourist," arrived in motor homes. They precursed Florida's reputation as RV heaven.

Much of Southwest Florida's population in the past three decades came from the Midwest, bringing along their meat-and-potatoes cuisine and steady work ethics. At the onset of that era, the population was dominated by retirees and seasonal residents. The late 80s and early 90s have seen the population homogenize somewhat, with folks coming from all parts of the United States, all age groups, and all walks of life.

The Hispanic population again grows as immigrants who had moved north discover in West Coast Florida the sort of climate they once left behind in their homelands. Cape Coral, one pocket of Hispanic ethnicity, enjoys the celebrated cuisine and festivities indigenous to the culture. The town is also known for its German and Italian populations.

Young families have found an ideal atmosphere for their children in West Coast Florida – a playground open all year 'round.

Today's West Coaster is said to have a calmer attitude than the East Coaster – more like the Gulf than the sea. Laid-back is the term most commonly applied. The pace is slower, the surroundings more natural. That's where the generalities end. From the sophisticated Tampa metropolis to the Everglades backwoods Seminole, the West Coast embraces a range of people as diverse as its terrain.

Explanation of Sections

This book divides the West Coast into six sections. It begins in the north with Pinellas County, known in tourism jargon as the Suncoast. The chapter encompasses Clearwater, St. Petersburg, and their barrier island chain.

Tampa, as metropolitan core of the West Coast, has its own chapter, then we move south to Bradenton, Sarasota, their islands, and Venice.

The little known county named Charlotte has one chapter. Then we cover Lee County, promoted as Lee Island Coast, from Fort Myers south to its famous island pair Sanibel and Captiva.

Collier County, one of Florida's largest, includes its main town and governmental seat, Naples, as well as Marco Island, the Ten Thousand Islands, the western half of the Florida Everglades, and its surrounding parks and preserves.

Each chapter begins with a brief overall history and information that will make finding your way around easier. Then it is divided by cities or areas within the sub-region, their sights, adventure opportunities, restaurants, hotels, and other attractions.

Before we begin our adventure down the path once followed by conquistadores and pirates, let's nail down some of the practical details.

Chapter II

Information

Transportation

If you are traveling by air, four international airports and various local runways serve your needs. The largest airport is in Tampa; others are in St. Petersburg, Sarasota-Bradenton, and Fort Myers. Major domestic airlines serve all four. International flights arrive principally from Canada, Germany, and the United Kingdom. Each chapter gives specific airport and airline information.

Motorists make inroads on Interstate 75, the coast's zippy north-south artery, and Interstate 4, which hits Tampa from the east. Tamiami Trail, Highway 41, is the more leisurely way to explore the coast. In winter's high-season, traffic can get a bit frustrating as The Trail makes its way through towns that seem to grow together at the seams. Yet The Trail, the coast's earliest land route, has a story to tell, if you take the time to stop, look, and listen.

Note: Florida has a seat belt law, so buckle up.

Before folks traveled from town to coastal town on the Tamiami Trail, they followed water routes – rivers, bays, and the Gulf. Water transportation is still the preferred mode for adventurous West Coasters. The Intracoastal Waterway, runs between the mainland and the islands from Pinellas County to the Everglades, helping keep boaters afloat. These shoal-ridden waters can be tricky. Trickiest of all are the skinny waters around Ten Thousand Islands and in the Everglades; in fact, the natives had to invent new means of transportation to get around. The swamp buggy was Naples-born and remains a symbol of frontier adventure. The shallow-draft airboat, described below in *Boating & Fishing*, is another invention created by necessity.

Weather/How to Pack

Weather is one of the region's top selling points, particularly in winter when you can celebrate the great outdoors free from fear of freezing. Temperatures along the entire subtropical coast, which encompasses two degrees in latitude, are generally balmy throughout the winter months, although snow has been sighted as far south as Fort Myers. The average winter temperature in Tampa is 62.5°; in the southern extremes, the average is 67.5°. From November through February, definitely pack your swimsuit (Gulf temperatures rarely dip below 60°), but don't forget a warm jacket, long-sleeved shirts, and slacks. If you'll be traveling by water, mittens, hats, and scarves may prove valuable.

Summer comes early to the Gulf Coast. Those who don't know better believe the weather skips right over spring, but residents have learned otherwise. In spring, as in fall, changes are subtle. No spring showers here, generally; a torrent of flower blossoms is more indicative of the season. Fall means a crispness to the normally moist air, and a long-awaited reprieve from summer swelter. During March, April, October, and November, you won't need heavy clothes, but you should still pack shirts with long sleeves, sweaters, sweatshirts, jeans, and slacks.

Summer is great for watersports. Hiking, biking, and other dry activities are best planned for early morning. Work into exercise gradually if you're not used to the heat and humidity. Summer average temperatures range from 81.4° in Tampa to 81.9° in the south. Gulf temperatures reach 86°.

When planning your summer trip to Florida's West Coast, take into account that June officially begins hurricane season. Hurricanes usually don't track into the Gulf until the fall months, but there are no hard and fast rules with Mother Nature. Warnings come well in advance of a major storm. Afternoon summer storms are the norm, so schedule your activities accordingly. Pack your coolest duds for the summer months, May through September. Plan on living in a swimsuit during daylight hours, and in light cotton shorts, shirts, skirts, and dresses at night. If you'll be hiking in wooded areas, or even on the beach at sunset, bring something light to cover your arms and legs against mosquitos and no-see-ums. A hat with a brim will protect your face and scalp from the sun.

No matter what time of year you visit, bug repellent and sunscreen are necessities. In Tampa, St. Petersburg, Sarasota, and Naples, you may have occasion to dress formally for theater or dinner, but in general, restaurants declare a casual dress code. For the adventurer, surf walkers, sneakers, and deck shoes are more essential than high heels or wing tips.

Don't forget to pack some common sense. Keep a level head about potential crime, sunburn, over-exertion, over-exposure, and dehydration, and your vacation to West Coast Florida will be a happy one.

Guidelines for Wildlife Preservation

Regulations and guidelines apply for the protection of wildlife and habitat.

SHELLING

Live shelling is prohibited in state and national parks, in refuges, and on Sanibel Island. In these areas, do not keep any shell with an animal in it, whether or not you believe the animal is dead. Gently return a live shell to the water; do not fling it.

Lee and Collier counties limit live shelling to two per species per person per day.

Live shells must be properly cleaned or they will smell like dead fish in a day or two. If you don't know what you're doing, don't collect the shells only to toss them from the car window down the road.

A fishing license is required for collecting live shells in Florida.

FEEDING

Don't feed wild animals. This includes everything from those harmless seagulls on the beach to that very harmful alligator behind the fence. Feeding alligators is illegal in Florida and noncompliance is punishable by a hefty fine. More importantly, by feeding an alligator, you are teaching it not to fear man. That's when toddlers get grabbed off bank shores or fishermen's feet become 'gator bait.

Feeding birds on the beach not only causes a nuisance, it again overrides their instincts and the birds forget how to feed themselves.

Do not throw fish to pelicans, no matter how much they beg and how cute they are. Large bony fish can cause bill and throat punctures. Be careful when you cast around gathered pelicans. They often swallow bait, hook and all. If this happens, gently reel in the bird, cover its head with a towel or shirt, and carefully clip and extract the hook, trying to back it out rather than running the barb through the bird's skin.

If you're camping or picnicking, you may find yourself inadvertently feeding raccoons and squirrels. At night, put all of your food, including supposedly sealed coolers and bags of garbage, inside a vehicle or trash bin.

Be careful not to throw food or food litter out the car window. This attracts animals to roadways, where they can be run down.

HARMFUL LITTER

Discarded fishing filament, plastic shopping bags, and beverage six-pack rings can cause damage to pelicans and marine life. Toss them in a trash receptacle.

SEA TURTLES

Loggerhead turtles come to nest on our beaches during the summer. Do not disturb their nests, which are marked by turtle night patrols. Turn off lights facing the beach; they disorient nesting and hatching turtles.

MANATEES

Manatees fall tragically victim to careless boaters. Observe manatee zone signs by slowing down to no-wake speed. Take the slack time to watch for the fascinating mammals as they surface for air. If you spot an injured manatee, call the Manatee Hot-Line at ☎ 800-342-1821.

OTHER BOATING/FISHING GUIDELINES

Stay in the marked channels when boating. This not only protects you and your vessel, but also the fragile grass flats that feed our fish.

Most local guides and fishermen practice catch-and-release, and will urge you to do so as well. Certain fish, such as tarpon, require a special permit to kill.

VEGETATION

It is illegal to pick sea grass, which keeps our beaches in place. Mangroves are also protected by the law; don't trim or cut them down.

Sights & Attractions

Although this book focuses on adventure and outdoor activities, it gives visitors alternatives for sightseeing and playing indoors. I pay particular attention to those attractions that lean on nature. Beaches and parks that offer a wide variety of open-air fun are first listed under *Sights & Attractions*, then repeated under applicable activities.

West Coast beaches and state parks are centers of regional adventure. Beaches have restrooms unless otherwise noted. Most prohibit alcohol, pets, open fires, and glass containers. State parks also prohibit pets. Admission fees and hours change constantly at Florida attractions, often according to seasons. Call ahead to confirm.

Fishing

Since the days of Teddy Roosevelt and before, fishing has been the lure for adventure-seekers headed to Florida's West Coast. For early residents, fishing was a way of life and commercial fishing, due to net banning, is just beginning to die out in the last hold-out fishing communities, such as Pine Island (Chapter VII) and Cortez (Chapter V).

Recreational fishing still thrives; many once-commercial fishermen have turned to guiding. To make sure it continues to thrive, the state enforces licensing, season, number, and size regulations.

Non-Florida residents age 16 or older must obtain a saltwater fishing license to cast from shore or any pier or vessel not covered by its own license. Most charter boats carry vessel licenses that cover all passengers. Florida residents fishing from land or a landbound structure also are required to purchase a license. Inexpensive short-term licenses are available for residents and non-residents.

Prices For Saltwater Fishing Licenses

Non-residents	
three-day	$6.50
seven-day	$16.50
one-year	$31.50
Residents	
10-day	$10.00
one-year	$30.00

You can buy saltwater fishing licenses at some local bait shops, Kmarts, marinas, or tax offices. Surcharges apply. For more information, contact the **Department of Natural Resources, Florida Marine Patrol, Support Services**, 3900 Commonwealth Blvd, Tallahassee, FL 32303; ☎ 904-488-5757.

Nonresidents must purchase a separate license for freshwater fishing. It costs $30 per year or $15 for seven days. For information, contact the **Florida Game and Freshwater Fish Commission**, 620 S Meridian Street, Farris Bryant Building, Tallahassee, FL 32399-1600, ☎ 904-488-1960 or 800-282-8002.

For guidelines on species size and season, visit local bait shops, which are listed in chapters under this category.

Along the West Coast, you have several types of fishing. In the sea, where some 300 species of fish live, there is, first of all, **backwater fishing**, also known as flats fishing. It takes place in bays, estuaries, mangrove areas, oyster bars, and Intracoastal waters near shore. The region's excellent backwater fishing has spawned a recent interest in fly fishing. Most backwater fishing uses light tackle. Backwater catches include tarpon, mangrove snapper, sheepshead, ladyfish, nurse sharks, sea trout, snook, and redfish. You can do this kind of fishing from piers, docks, seawalls, and leeside shores, or by boat. Backwater fishing charters are numerous throughout the coastal region, and are generally cheaper than deep-water excursions, about $200-$300 per half-day for six people.

Open water fishing can be intimidating for the first-timer. If you're serious about catching fish, hire a guide. If you set out on your own, look for fast-moving waters in passes and rivers, and for shady spots, mangroves, and bridges, where fish lay up in the heat of the day. Seek advice at the local bait shop concerning tides, type of bait, and prescribed line weight.

Charters and party boats take you offshore to catch grouper, red snapper, king mackerel, and other whoppers that lurk in deep seas. Party boats, also called head boats, are the less expensive option, costing $25-$30 per person. The fee normally includes bait, tackle, license, and cleaning. It is customary to tip the crew.

Surf fishing is another option and can be done from most beaches – again, with the best success in passes between islands or at the end of islands.

Freshwater fishing yields bass, perch, catfish, and other catches. The West Coast has its share of rivers and small lakes for fishermen.

Boating

 All motor-powered boats used in Florida must be registered at the local county tax collector's office. If currently registered out of state, boats need not be registered in Florida for stays of 90 days or less.

Whether you own or are renting a boat, you should use a chart of local waters. Many rental concessions provide them. West Coast waters are challenging, riddled with shoals, oyster beds, and grass flats. If you're not practiced at boating and chart-reading, consider hiring a guide with local knowledge to take you out for the first time or two.

Island-hopping along the coast is one of the region's greatest adventures and pleasures. Unbridged islands from Caladesi (Chapter III) in the north to Ten Thousand Islands in the south (Chapter VIII) offer beaches, restaurants, bird-watching, shelling, and other activities enhanced by the thrill of being cut loose from mainland bustle and tempos.

You won't have any problem finding charters along the coast, for everything from island-hopping and fishing to sightseeing, shelling, and dolphin spotting. Private charters by motor or sail can be easily tailored to your interests, and usually hold four to six people. For a half-day, that will typically run you $200 to $300; for a full day, $300 to $450.

Larger tour boats have a set agenda and hold a party of people for sunset, mansion-gazing, island lunching, and other special interests. In some places, you'll find huge cruise ships or showboats with dinner, shows, gambling, and dancing. Prices vary greatly. Several options are given in every chapter. In the Everglades and other shallow water areas, air boat tours make it easiest to get around. Tours cost about $10-$15 per person. Reservations are usually required for charters and tours.

Powerboat rentals will cost you anywhere from $50 to $250 for a half-day, which amounts to four hours, either morning or afternoon. Daily rates usually cover eight hours. Some places will rent them by the hour, some by the week. Rental rates vary according to boat and engine size. The chapters give a range of rates as a guideline to renters. Be sure to ask whether quoted rates include gas, oil, and tax. They usually don't, with the exception of pontoons.

The most popular type of boat, especially for open water fishermen, has a center console. Freshwater anglers often use flat-bottomed bass boats. Bowriders are better suited to passenger travel. Pontoon and deck boats are flat boats set aboard floats and are practical for large groups and for use in shallow waters, such as around Ten Thousand Islands.

Sailboats for rent are scarcer. Many resorts and some beach concessions have small Hobie Cats and Sunfish, which run about $60 for a half-day. Lessons are available in some locales, as part of a rental or part of a cruise.

Waverunners and jet skis, known under the umbrella of personal watercraft, are usually rented by the hour for about $50 and charge an extra fee for passengers. Some concessions offer tours.

The best way to get close to nature while on the water is by canoe or kayak. Sea kayaking is enjoying a surge in popularity on Florida shores, and you're likely to find rentals, lessons, sales, and tours available no matter where you land. You can rent a single or tandem. Rates run around $20 for two hours.

The Everglades (Chapter VIII), Peace River (Chapter VI), Myakka River (Chapter V) and Hillsborough and Alafia rivers (Chapter IV) provide excellent canoeing and kayaking trails.

INFORMATION

For more information on canoeing and kayaking, contact the **Florida Department of Environmental Protection**, Office of Greenways and Trails, 325 John Knox Rd, Bldg. 500, Tallahassee, FL 32303-4124, ☎ 904-488-3701. Ask for a free copy of "Florida Recreational Trails System – Canoe Trails" and its *Canoe Liveries and Outfitters Directory*.

Other resources in the area include **Florida Professional Paddlesports Association**, P.O. Box 1764, Arcadia, FL 34265, ☎ 941-494-1215; **Florida Competition Paddlers**, 4546 Huntington Street SE, St. Petersburg, FL 33707; and **Florida Sea Kayaking Association**, 626-45th Ave S, St. Petersburg, FL 33705-4418, ☎ 813-864-2651.

Sailboarding, parasailing, and water-biking are all part of the resort water scene. The larger resorts and some beaches offer these and other rentals.

Surfing, snorkeling, and scuba diving are found on the West Coast, but are generally better on Florida's East Coast.

Hiking

Nature trails in state and other parks provide opportunity for short, scenic hiking in the sunshine. Be sure to take water. Plan for the heat and, if you're hiking on the beach, the soft surface. All of these factors make hiking parts of the coast quite strenuous.

Biking

Bike paths and lanes accommodate casual cyclists; more serious bikers take to quiet back roads throughout the region.

Bike paths are separated from traffic by distance and, ideally, a vegetation buffer. The best ones leave the roadside altogether to penetrate natural environments unreachable by motor vehicles. Lanes, on the other hand, are a part of the roadway designated for bike traffic.

Where neither lanes nor paths exist, bikers must share the road with vehicular traffic. Florida law considers a bicycle a vehicle, so its operator must follow all the rules of the road upon entering the flow of traffic.

In resort communities, you can usually rent a bike at your hotel or at bike shops. Some have only basic equipment, others carry a variety of bikes and paraphernalia. Rates are usually offered by the hour, half-day, day, and week.

TIP   *Florida law requires that bike riders under age 16 wear helmets.*

Hunting

Florida's days as the great hunting ground are gone. But the Everglades (Chapter VIII) and a region in the Charlotte Harbor area (Chapter VI) keep hunters happy still.

Where to Eat

Seafood is the pride of West Coast Florida cuisine. Influenced by Deep South, Cajun, Caribbean, Latin, Midwestern, and continental styles, restaurants dish up infinite variety and creativity.

In the fish houses you'll find classic Florida cuisine – raw oysters, steamed clams, fried grouper and shrimp, broiled snapper, and chilled stone crab claws. At the other end of the scale, fine restaurants create masterpieces in the art of cultural mix-and-match. Most *au courant* is the Floribbean style that stews together Florida and West Indian cookery, and Mediterranean cuisine, mixing local fresh produce with exotic preparations. Ethnic eateries from northern Italian to Thai demonstrate the cultural influences that make up the West Coast's melting pot.

The chapters' dining sections give a quick overview of that area's restaurant scene, then short descriptions of a few favorites in different categories. In each, I describe a price range for the meals served. These round off prices to the nearest dollar and leave out dishes that stray too far up or down from the average. Nightly specials and that one expensive surf-and-turf platter, for instance, do not figure into the range.

Where to Stay

The West Coast of Florida is the land of resorts in all shapes, sizes, and price ranges. Some areas are more expensive than others. You'll find the best bargains in the Pinellas and Charlotte Harbor areas.

Rates throughout the area change seasonally. Some resort rate cards reflect as many as six different seasons: Christmas (high), January (shoulder), February-Easter (high), Easter-May (shoulder), Summer, and Fall (low). Smaller places stick to two or three seasons: high (mid-December-Easter), low (Easter-September or mid-December), and possibly shoulder (summer).

I generally quote a range of rates for high and low season. In-season rates often begin at the lowest January shoulder rate and end at the highest winter rate. Off-season rates begin with the lowest fall rate and top off with summer's highest rates. Of course, these rates are subject to availability and special package offers. Always ask about specials, and about corporate, AAA, or other discounts that may apply.

Rates quoted in the chapters are for double occupancy, except where noted. There is usually a charge for extra persons; not always for children, however. Most accommodation rates are based on the European Plan, with no meals, except for B&Bs and certain others noted within their description. Many of the listed accommodations have kitchen facilities, whether basic or full, which can save you on dining bills.

Price ranges described for each property often do not take into account penthouses and other exceptional, high-priced accommodations.

 Florida adds a 6% sales tax to room rates (in Tampa it's 7%), plus most counties add a 5-7% bed tax, which goes toward maintaining and improving beaches, parks, and other tourist-impacted areas.

Camping

The best wilderness camping is found in the coast's state parks. See individual chapters for particulars or contact the **Department of Environmental Protection, Office of Recreation & Parks**, Mail Station 535, 3900 Commonwealth Blvd, Tallahassee, FL 32399-3000, ☎ 904-488-9872.

 *The **Florida RV Trade Association** at 401 N Parsons Ave, Ste. 107, Brandon, FL 33510, ☎ 813-684-7882, can help you locate certified campgrounds, resorts, and dealers.*

Nightlife

West Coast Florida pales in comparison to its East Coast counterparts when it comes to culture and nightlife. Don't despair, however, if you're an adventurer who likes to use the night-time hours to test the good-time waters. If nightlife is a priority, plan your destination along the coast's northern sections – in Tampa, St. Petersburg and vicinity, and Sarasota. These, along with Fort Myers Beach, are the hot spots, and you'll find plenty of after-dark action.

Sarasota's brand of nightlife appeals to a high-brow crowd as well as pub-crawlers. It's known for its theater. Tampa and St. Petersburg have something for everyone. Fort Myers Beach is strictly for bar-hopping, but there's plenty of that.

Tourist Information

For general travel information about Florida, contact the **Florida Division of Tourism**, 432 Collins Bldg., 107 W Gaines Street, Tallahassee, FL 32399-2000, ☎ 904-487-1462.

Recommended Reading

BEACHES

Walton, Chelle Koster. *Frommer's Best Beach Vacations Florida*. New York: Macmillan, 1995. 266 pp, maps.

ENVIRONMENT

Campbell, George R. *The Nature of Things on Sanibel*. Fort Myers: Press Printing, 1978. 174 pp, illustrations, index.

Douglas, Marjory Stoneman. *The Everglades: River of Grass*. St. Simons, GA: Mockingbird Books, 1947. 308 pp.

WATERSPORTS

Fuery, Captain Mike. *South Florida Bay and Coastal Fishing*. Captiva: Sanibel Sandollar Publications, 1987.

Hidden Florida. Berkeley: Ulysses Press, 1997. 529 pp, maps, index.

Lenfestey, Tom. *A Gunkholer's Cruising Guide To Florida's West Coast*, St. Petersburg: Great Outdoors Publishing, 1991. 156 pp, nautical charts, illustrations, index.

O'Keefe, Timothy M. and Larry Larsen. *Fish & Dive Florida and The Keys*, Larsen's Outdoor Publishing, 1992. 191 pp, photos, index.

Trupp, Phil. *Diver's Almanac: Guide to Florida & the Keys*. Triton Publishing, Inc., 1991. 236 pp, color maps and photos.

Walton, Chelle Koster. *Florida Island Hopping: The West Coast*. Sarasota: Pineapple Press, 1995. 324 pp, photos, index.

Young, Claiborne S. *Cruising Guide to Western Florida*, Pelican Publishing, 1992.

WHERE TO STAY & EAT

Frommer's America on Wheels: Florida. New York: Macmillan, 1995. 260 pp, ratings, color maps, coupons, index.

HISTORY

Beater, Jack. *Pirates & Buried Treasure.* St. Petersburg: Great Outdoors Publishing, 1959. 118 pp, illustrations.

Bickel, Karl A. *The Mangrove Coast: The Story of the West Coast of Florida.* New York: Coward-McCann, 1942. 332 pp, photos, index.

Briggs, Mildred. *Pioneers of Bonita Springs (Facts and Folklore).* Florida, 1976. 100 pp, photos.

Board, Prudy Taylor and Esther B. Colcord. *Historic Fort Myers.* Virginia Beach: The Donning Publishers, 1992. 96 pp, photos, index.

Brown, Loren B. "Totch." *Totch: A Life in the Everglades.* University Press of Florida, 1993. 269 pp, photos.

Captiva Civic Association. *True Tales of Old Captiva.* 1984. 353 pp, photos.

Dormer, Elinore M. *The Sea Shell Islands: A History of Sanibel and Captiva.* Tallahassee: Rose Printing Co., 1987. 273 pp, illustrations, index.

Fritz, Florence. *Unknown Florida.* Coral Gables: University of Miami Press, 1963. 213 pp, photos, index.

Jordan, Elaine Blohm. *Pine Island, the Forgotten Island.* Pine Island: 1982. 186 pp, photos.

Gonzalez, Thomas A. *The Caloosahatchee: History of the Caloosahatchee River and the City of Fort Myers Florida.* Fort Myers Beach: Island Press Publishers, 1932. 134 pp.

Grismer, Karl H. *The Story of Fort Myers.* Fort Myers Beach: Island Press Publishers, 1982. 348 pp, photos, index.

Grismer, Karl H. *The Story of Sarasota.* Tampa: The Florida Grower Press, 1946. 376 pp, photos, index.

Jahoda, Gloria. *River of the Golden Ibis.* New York: Holt, Rinehart & Winston, 1973. 408 pp, illustrations.

Marth, Del. *Yesterday's Sarasota.* Miami: E.A. Seemann Publishing, Inc., 1973. 160 pp, photos.

Matthews, Janet Snyder. *Edge of Wilderness: A Settlement History of Manatee River and Sarasota Bay.* Sarasota: Coastal Press, 1983.

Newton, James. *Uncommon Friends.* New York: Harcourt, Brace, Jovanovich, 1987. 368 pp.

Pacheco, Ferdie. *Ybor City Chronicles.* Gainesville: University Press of Florida, 1994. 301 pp, illustrated.

Peeples, Vernon. *Punta Gorda and the Charlotte Harbor Area*. Norfolk: The Donning Co., 1986. 208 pp, photos, index.

Pizzo, Anthony P. *Tampa Town 1824-1886*. Miami: Hurricane House, 1968. 89 pp, illustrations.

Schell, Rolfe F. *De Soto Didn't Land at Tampa*. Fort Myers: Island Press, 1966. 96 pp, illus.

Schell, Rolfe F. *History of Fort Myers Beach*. Fort Myers Beach: Island Press, 1980. 96 pp, photos, index.

Tebeau, Charlton W. *Florida's Last Frontier: The History of Collier County*. Coral Gables: University of Miami Press, 1966. 278 pp, photos, index.

Zeiss, Betsy. *The Other Side of the River: Historical Cape Coral*. Cape Coral, 1986. 206 pp, photos, index.

FICTION/LITERATURE

Lindbergh, Anne Morrow. *Gift from the Sea*. New York: Pantheon, 1955, 142 pp, illustations.

MacDonald, John D. *The Empty Copper Sea*. New York: Fawcett Gold Medal Books, 1978, 245 pp.

White, Randy. *Heat Islands*. New York: St. Martin's Press, 1992. 307pp.

White, Randy. *Sanibel Flats*. New York: St. Martin's Press, 1990. 307pp.

Chapter III

St. Petersburg-Clearwater

Area code: 813

The West Coast's largest and most popular sun-spotlit playground is contained in Pinellas County and has been dubbed the Pinellas Suncoast. From Clearwater Beach in the north to St. Pete Beach in the south, it is one long fling of sand-lined islands where fun-in-the-sun and full speed adventure reign. The not-a-care-in-the-world beaches give the region a playful, somewhat boisterous reputation, but, as you will find in this chapter, there's something for everyone here. Far flung, remote islands offer the flip side to all that action. These are hide-outs for wildlife and for reclusive beachers. Downtown St. Petersburg, with its Dali and other museums and trendy clubs, satisfies more high-brow vacation requirements. The Clearwater area holds all sorts of pleasant surprises: a 47-mile bike trail, a natural mineral spa, one of the state's oldest surviving wooden hotels, a marina-full of high sea adventures, and a highly respected marine biology facility.

St. Petersburg, the region's metropolitan center, along with its environs, has long been the destination for winter refugees seeking restored health. Downtown became known for its population of retirees, but in more recent years has injected youthful life into its withering reputation. Its sling of islands, conversely, built a reputation for frivolity, even back when Scott and Zelda danced at the landmark Don CeSar Hotel. Because the islands have been hosting beachers for so many years, they have a faded-glory feeling. That too is changing as the county pumps more and more dollars into beautifying park and beach areas. Huge centers of water recreation, most notably Clearwater Beach Marina and John's Pass Village at Madeira Beach, make this sunshiny land legendary for its boating, fishing, and beaching. The sum total of Pinellas County covered in this chapter confines itself to a fat peninsula separated from mainland and the city of Tampa by deep, wide Tampa Bay. Sandwiched between it and the Gulf of Mexico, the region is all but surrounded by on-the-water opportunities. Despite its metropolitan and developed beach nature, it has plenty of wild spaces and recreational adventures to offer landlubbers as well.

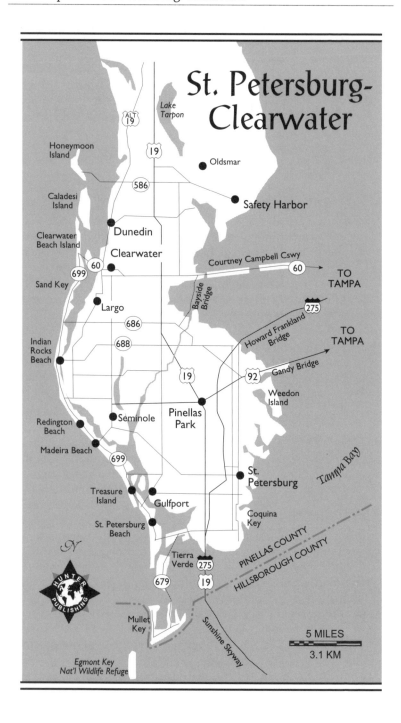

St. Petersburg-Clearwater

Lake Tarpon

Honeymoon Island

Oldsmar

Caladesi Island

Safety Harbor

Clearwater Beach Island

Dunedin

Clearwater

Courtney Campbell Cswy

TO TAMPA

Sand Key

Largo

Bayside Bridge

Howard Frankland Bridge

TO TAMPA

Indian Rocks Beach

Weedon Island

Gandy Bridge

Redington Beach

Seminole

Pinellas Park

Madeira Beach

St. Petersburg

Tampa Bay

Treasure Island

Gulfport

Coquina Key

St. Petersburg Beach

PINELLAS COUNTY

Tierra Verde

HILLSBOROUGH COUNTY

Mullet Key

Sunshine Skyway

5 MILES

3.1 KM

Egmont Key Nat'l Wildlife Refuge

Transportation, Etc.

Two international airports serve the Tampa Bay area, one in Tampa, the other in Clearwater. **Tampa International Airport,** ☎ 396-3690, receives more flights, especially from international destinations. Major domestic airlines include **American,** ☎ 800-433-7300; **Continental,** ☎ 939-9524 or 800-525-0280; **Delta,** ☎ 800-221-1212; **Northwest,** 800-225-2525, **TWA,** ☎ 800-221-2000, **United,** ☎ 800-241-6522; and **USAir,** ☎ 800-428-4322. **Air Canada,** ☎ 800-776-3000 and **British Airways,** ☎ 800-247-9297, are among international airlines that land in Tampa.

St. Petersburg/Clearwater International, ☎ 535-7600, principally serves charters and shuttles.

BATS City Transportation System, ☎ 367-3086, operates buses throughout St. Pete Beach. **Pinellas Suncoast Transit Authority,** ☎ 530-9911, services St. Petersburg and the rest of the county.

Rental cars are available at the airport and other locations throughout the area, including **Avis,** ☎ 367-2847 or 800-331-1212; **Hertz,** ☎ 800-654-3131, **National,** ☎ 800-227-7386, **Pinellas,** ☎ 535-9891 or 800-526-5499, and **Budget,** ☎ 800-527-0700.

Several taxi companies provide transportation to and from the airport, including **United Cab Company,** ☎ 253-2424, **Pinellas County Yellow Cab,** ☎ 799-2222, **The Limo Airport Connection,** 572-1111 or 800-282-6817, and **Red Line Limo,** ☎ 535-3391 or 800-359-LIMO.

Interstate 275, which merges into Interstate 75 from the north and south and into Interstate 4 (and Orlando) from the east, is the major thoroughfare of the St. Petersburg-Clearwater area. At its south end lies the dramatic Sunshine Skyway Bridge; at its north, Howard Frankland Bridge (Interstate 275) crosses to Tampa. In between, the Gandy Bridge (Highway 92), connects St. Petersburg to downtown Tampa. Courtney Campbell Causeway (Route 60/Memorial Highway), north of Interstate 275, connects Clearwater to north Tampa. Highway 19 runs north-south on the east side of the Pinellas County Peninsula. Nearer to the islands, Alternate Highway 19 takes you along the county's northern shores.

For information on Pinellas County, contact **St. Petersburg/Clearwater Convention & Visitors Bureau**, 14450 46th St. N, Clearwater, 34622; ☎ 464-7200.

Events

The **J22 Mid-Winter Regatta**, ☎ 822-3873, is one of several sailing events held in St. Petersburg; this one starts the end of February.

Clearwater Beach, known for its beach volleyball action, hosts the **Miller Lite Professional Men's Beach Volleyball Tournament**, ☎ 461-0011, in April and the **Pro Beach Volleyball Hall of Fame Challenge** in May.

Madeira Gulf Beaches Triathalon, ☎ 391-7373 or 800-944-1847, takes place in May.

Clearwater Jazz Holiday, ☎461-5200, the largest free jazz festival in the southeastern US, brings music-loving crowds to Clearwater in October.

John's Pass Seafood Festival in Madeira Beach, ☎ 397-1571, is a huge affair in October.

The holiday **Lighted Boat Parade**, ☎ 363-9245, is a twinkly event in December that begins in Pass-A-Grille on St. Pete Beach.

Clearwater/Clearwater Beach

Often overshadowed by the more household names of St. Petersburg and St. Pete Beach, the Clearwater area is really the place to head if you're serious about spending days on and in the water. Its beach facilities are top-notch and its marinas are beehives of sail-away activity.

Clearwater itself is principally big-city. Its main concession to tourism is a 100-year-old grande dame of a wooden hotel. On its eastern coast, fronting Tampa Bay, the community of Safety Harbor is the county's birthplace – a quiet spot for boaters, picnickers, and spa-goers.

Clearwater Beach occupies all of Clearwater Beach Island, as well as part of neighboring Sand Key.

BASICS

Gulf to Bay Boulevard (Route 60) is the major road running east-west. It connects to the Courtney Campbell Causeway and Tampa at its eastern extreme, penetrates downtown Clearwater (where its name changes to Cleveland Street) and, at its western extreme, crosses Memorial Causeway to Clearwater Beach. It intersects with Gulfview Boulevard (Route 699), the island's major road. South of the Clearwater Pass Bridge, the road's name changes to Gulf Boulevard. Mandalay Avenue is the northern extension to Gulfview Boulevard, where you'll find most of the shopping.

 The Clearwater area is closely policed. Mind the speed limit signs (25 MPH on the beach), and be sure to feed your meter.

INFORMATION

Clearwater Yellow Cab, ☎ 799-2222, provides transportation to and from the Tampa and St. Petersburg/Clearwater airports.

The Jolley Trolley, ☎ 445-1200, travels around Clearwater Beach and downtown Clearwater. Tours begin and end at the Clearwater Beach Memorial Civic Center on Causeway Blvd, with pickups every 30 minutes daily. Fare is 50¢ each.

For more information on the area, contact the **Greater Clearwater Chamber of Commerce,** 1130 Cleveland Street, Clearwater, FL 34617, ☎ 461-0011, open 8:30-5 Monday-Friday; or visit the **Clearwater/Pinellas Suncoast Welcome Center** at 3350 Courtney Campbell Causeway Blvd, ☎ 726-1547, open daily from 9 to 5.

SIGHTS & ATTRACTIONS

North of Clearwater Beach, an assemblage of unhooked islands provides destinations for birders, shellers, canoeists, and beachers. The largest, **Caladesi Island State Park**, is the most developed. It's most visited because of its absolutely gorgeous beach, white and fine as baby powder. Visitors can get to the beach in several ways. They can actually walk there, and this is a little known fact. From the northernmost beach access on Clearwater Beach, it's less than a mile walk. Some say it's best to attempt it only at low tide, others say the split between the two islands is always passable. You must be prepared and in good shape to do this, because it's another couple of miles to park concessions once you get on the island, and the soft sand doubles the distance as far as your legs are concerned. Other options are listed below under *Fishing & Boating*. The park contains a nature trail, picnic area, concessions, boat docking, and a wide apron of beach.

The **Clearwater Marine Science Center Aquarium Museum** at 249 Windward Passage, off Memorial Causeway, ☎ 441-1790, conducts research and rehabilitates marine mammals, river otters, and sea turtles. A touch tank, aquariums, and other tanks hold local and exotic sealife, including mangroves, seahorses, baby sharks, dolphins, playful otters, Kemps Ridley sea turtles, and a 320-pound loggerhead turtle named Mo. Admission is $5.75 for adults, $3.75 for kids three and older. Hours are Monday-Friday 9-5; Saturday 9-4; and Sunday 11-4.

Clearwater Beach has some of the widest, most gorgeous beaches in the area, offering outdoor entertainment in a variety just as wide. **Gulfview Beach**, at the intersection of Causeway and Gulfview boulevards, is most active, with its **Pier 60** (see *Fishing & Boating*, below), ☎ 462-6466, and continuous volleyball, for which Clearwater Beach has a reputation. You'll also find lifeguards, concessions for food, beach supplies, watersports rentals, and a new, sheltered playground with very cool equipment. Each night before sunset, artisans and performers put on a show. You pay about $1 an hour to park in large lots at each end of the beach.

For more quiet with your beach scene, spread your beach blanket at the **passive beach area**, between Rockaway Street and Bay Esplanade. It also has volleyball nets, but not all of the sports rentals and family activities of Gulfview.

Across the south-end bridge to Sand Key lies Clearwater Beach's most highly rated recreational area, **Sand Key Park**. Its 65 acres contain lots of green spaces with picnic areas and playgrounds. The wide, sugarsand beach is patrolled by lifeguards and offers watersports rentals. Parking is by meter at 25¢ for 20 minutes.

Sanf Key Park, Clearwater.

Marina on the Pinellas Sun Coast.

FISHING & BOATING

The possibilities for on-the-sea adventure are practically endless on Clearwater Beach.

Fishing enthusiasts dangle their bait from **Pier 60** on Gulfview Beach (see *Sights & Attractions,* above), at the intersection of Causeway Blvd and Gulfview Blvd, ☎ 462-6466. It contains all the shops and facilities necessary for a successful day of fishing; you provide the catches. Admission for walking on or fishing from the pier runs $2.50-$5.35. You can rent fishing rods for $14.

You'll find a boat ramp into Clearwater Harbor at **Clearwater Beach Recreation Center** on Bay Esplanade, and into Tampa Bay in Safety Harbor at **Philippe Park**, 2355 Bayshore Drive, with extensive picnic facilities and at **Marina Park**, with limited picnic facilities and docking.

For half- and full-day fishing charters, check at the **Clearwater Beach Marina**, 25 Causeway Blvd, ☎ 462-6954. Guides and party boats line the dock; you can just walk around and "shop" for the one that fits your needs. A bait house, shops, and a restaurant complete the complex.

For deep-sea fishing, **The** *Double Eagle III* **and** *II* at Clearwater Beach Marina, ☎ 446-1653, charges $24 for adults and $20 for children (tackle included); for all day, $39 and $34. Ride aboard modern catamarans.

Clearwater Beach Water Sports Center at Clearwater Beach Marina, slip 23, ☎ 443-6685, does half-day, six-hour, and all-day fishing charters, at $300-$500. Night shark fishing excursions cost $260. Power boat rentals range from $120 for two hours to $270 all day, gas and oil included. All prices subject to tax. They also rent deck boats.

For another option in boat rentals, stop at **Budget Boat Club Rental**'s marina kiosk, slips 23 and 24, ☎ 443-6685. It rents motorboats 17 to 20 feet in length, for $20 an hour, based on an eight-hour rental. Ski, tube, or knee board packages cost an extra $15. Fuel and sales tax are extra.

For deep-sea fishing, board the *Mar-Chelle II* at the Clearwater Beach Marina, slip 21, ☎ 442-3770, for half-day trips costing $25 for adults, $15 for children.

Many day boating trips launch from Clearwater Beach Marina, headed to Caladesi Island (see *Sights & Attractions,* above), Sarasota, and points beyond. The latest popular thing is dolphin encounter cruises. You are not allowed to feed dolphins on these trips, however.

The **Clearwater Ferry Service**, located at Drew Street Dock in Clear-water, ☎ 442-7433, picks up from Clearwater Beach at Sea Stone Resort (see *Where to Stay,* below), the Recreation Center on Bay Esplanade, and the Clearwater Beach Marina for trips to the mainland, to Caladesi Island (see *Sights & Attractions,* above), and dolphin habitat. Fares begin at $9.35 for adults, $5.40 for children (ages three-12), plus tax. Call for schedules and reservations.

For something much faster, *Sea Screamer* at marina slip 10, ☎ 447-7200, charges $11 for adults, $7 for children age 12 and under, plus tax. The hour-long tour takes in dolphins and the beaches.

The Show Queen, ☎ 461-3113, hosts narrated luncheon trips and dinner sunset cruises aboard a three-deck riverboat. Daytime fares are $8.95 adults, $5.95 children; evening, $10.95 and $8.95; sunset, $20.95-$24.95 and $10.95-$13.95. Children ages three and under ride free. Tax and gratuities are extra.

If you have kids, your best bet on the high seas is **Captain Memo's Pirate Cruise** at the marina, ☎ 446-2587. Dressing as pirates, face-painting, water-pistol battles, and cannon-shooting are part of the regime. It sets sail three times daily, including sunset. Day cruises cost $25 for adults, $15 for children, and include complimentary beer, wine, and beverages.

Starlite Princess at the marina, ☎ 462-2628, hosts luncheon, sightsee-ing, Dixieland Jazz, and Favorite Oldies cruises. Tickets cost $8.90-$11.70; meal is extra. Children pay $6.05-$8.20. Tax is not included.

Southern Romance at the marina, ☎ 446-5503, does two-hour sailing trips four times daily. Cost is $20 for adults, $10 for children.

Zenith Yacht Charters at 850 Bayway Blvd, Slip 38, ☎ 442-3273, sets sail for half-day ($25 each), full-day ($65 each), and sunset ($35 each) charters.

On **Windjammer Cruises'** *Tradewinds* at the Clearwater Marina, ☎ 581-4662, willing passengers can learn to handle the helm, trim the jibs, and raise the sails of a 60-foot three-masted racing schooner. The two-hour cruise departs daily and costs $22 per adult, $12 per child.

For a sea-kayaking adventure, contact the all-around experts at **Agua Azul Kayaks** at 17952 Hwy. 19 in Clearwater, ☎ 530-7555. They sell and rent kayaks, instruct, and conduct tours. Single rentals cost $12.50 per hour, $35 per day. Tandems also available. Four-hour tours to Caladesi Island cost $42 per person, including equipment, food, and drink.

SNORKELING & SCUBA

Rock ledges, underwater sinkholes, artificial reefs, and submerged vessels provide variety in local waters, where visibility can reach 60 feet. Most sites are well off shore. The Clearwater Reef is one of the area's largest and most popular artificial reefs.

Clearwater Beach Water Sports Center at Clearwater Beach Marina, slip 23, ☎ 443.6685, hosts 2½-hour snorkeling trips for $36 per adult, $26 per child.

OTHER WATER ADVENTURES

Parasails are a gay and common sight along Clearwater's beaches. You'll find concessions at the Clearwater Beach Marina (see *Fishing & Boating*, above). They generally charge according to height of ride, something like $35 for 600 feet, $45 for 800 feet, and $55 for 1,000 feet. Some include an optional free fall, for the ultimate thrill. Try **Joy Ride Parasail** at slip 22, ☎ 447-0969.

For water-skiing and kneeboard pulls, contact **Clearwater Beach Water Sports Center** at Clearwater Beach Marina, slip 23, ☎ 443-6685. Open daily, prices vary. Ski boat rentals, with equipment included, cost $210 for a half-day, plus tax.

HIKING & BIKING

On Caladesi Island, a three-mile trail leads through scrub and beach communities. Paved with soft sand, it takes longer than you'd think and can be hard on leg muscles. Wear shoes with support.

Joggers, skaters, and bicyclists take to the 47-mile **Pinellas Trail**, ☎ 464-4751, which begins in downtown St. Petersburg and heads north through Clearwater and beyond along an old railroad route.

On Clearwater Beach, you can rent a ride at **Transportation Station**, 645 Bayway Blvd, and other locations, ☎ 443-3188. It has a full complement of bikes and equipment, from racers to tandems and child trailers; also in-line skates. Hourly rates begin at $5 for bikes and skates, with daily and weekly discounts. Open 9-dusk daily.

WHERE TO EAT

When compared to prices in Tampa and on islands to the south, restaurants in Pinellas are refreshingly reasonable. And the seafood is about as fresh as it gets, short of catching it yourself.

Seafood & Sunsets at Julie's, across the street from Gulfview Beach at 351 S Gulfview Blvd, ☎ 441-2548, is, as its name implies, a great place to catch the sunset and fresh-from-the-fish-market specialties. The atmosphere is fun and funky, à la Key West. It's open daily for lunch ($2.50-$7) and dinner ($8-$14).

Beachgoers will also find **Frenchy's Rockaway Grill**, 7 Rockaway Street, ☎ 446-4844, convenient, tropical, and lively. Seafood again, and the very freshest, prepared grilled, blackened, and jerk-style. There is live music. It's open daily for lunch and dinner; prices for sandwiches, salads, and dinners run $5-$15.

For something more formal, **Bob Heilman's Beachcomber** at 447 Mandalay Ave, ☎ 442-4144, is a popular choice for American cuisine in both its classic and creative forms. Back-to-the-farm chicken with all the fixings is an all-time favorite. Seafood and prime meat dishes run a gamut from Everglades frog legs to Wisconsin veal piccata. People dress up and the setting is on the elegant side – a refined respite from the beach bustle. Prices are surprisingly affordable. Lunches are $5-$7 for sandwiches and salads, $12-$15 for "executive lunches." Dinners are $14-$24. Open for lunch and dinner daily. Dinner reservations recommended.

WHERE TO STAY

To stay in grand style, revel in the old-Florida aristocracy of **Belleview Mido Resort Hotel** at 25 Belleview Blvd in Clearwater, ☎ 442-6171 or 800-237-8947. One of the state's few surviving wooden hotels, it was built in the 1890s with wide verandas, distinctive gables, and Victorian airs. Recent renovations have modernized its 310 rooms, swimming pool with waterfalls, spa, and gracious lobby-dining areas. Rates in season are $200-$500 for a bedroom, suite, or one- or two-bedroom suite; in off-season, $170-$450. Packages are available.

Across the peninsula on Tampa Bay, **Safety Harbor Resort and Spa** at 104 N Bayshore Drive, ☎ local 726-1161 or 800-237-8772, is the historic pride of the bay coast. The low-slung, Mediterranean villa-style property has one of Florida's best spa and gym facilities. Rates for rooms and suites in winter are $149-$219; in off-season, $129-$179. Packages available.

On Clearwater Beach, you have many choices, in all price ranges and sizes, beach-side, bay-side, or in-between.

Hostel members are welcomed at the Sands Motel's **Clearwater Beach International Hostel**, 606 Bay Esplanade Ave, ☎ 443-1211. Besides its dorm accommodations, it has some shared apartments with adjoining bathrooms. Communal kitchen, picnic, and laundry facilities are provided, as well as free bike and canoe use, and games. The beach is a 15-minute walk away. There's no curfew. This is the only international hostel on Florida's West Coast. Member fees are $12, including tax. Non-member rates also available.

Best Western Sea Stone Resort at 445 Hamden Drive, ☎ 441-1722 or 800-444-1919, is water-oriented, located at the edge of a harbor with its own marina, watersports rentals, pool, Jacuzzi, restaurant, and lounge. In its rooms, suites, and plush public spaces, you are sheltered from the hustle-bustle in this part of the island. The beach is close by. Rates in winter start at $119 for rooms, $179 for suites; in summer, $89 and $129. They change according to availability and special promotions.

For a charmingly different beach lodging experience, rent an efficiency or one- or two-bedroom apartment at **Haddon House Inn**, 14 Idlewild Street, ☎ 461-2914. Many of the units reside in the property's two 100-year-old homes, located on the quiet, north end of the beach. All have full kitchen facilities and use of a heated pool. A pool-beach deck mimics Caribbean style with a tin roof and gingerbread trim. It's a colorful place with lush vegetation and a white picket fence. High-season rates range $60-$125; low season, $55-$90.

High-rising **Radisson Suites Resort of Sand Key** at 1201 Gulf Blvd, ☎ 596-1100 or 800-333-3333, across from Sand Key Park on the bay, caters to families. Waterfalls give its pool an exotic feel. A beach shuttle delivers you Gulf-side. Suite rates throughout the year run $149-$199 including breakfast. European plan and packages also available.

NIGHTLIFE

Whether you're on spring break, retirement, or somewhere in between, Clearwater can entertain your evening hours.

Ruth Eckerd Hall at 1111 McMullen Booth Rd, Clearwater, ☎ 791-7400, presents the top traveling entertainment in an acoustically sound environment – from Broadway shows to country singers and wekend family theater. Call for ticket prices.

Musicana Dinner Theater, 560 McMullen Booth Rd, Clearwater, ☎ 791-3204, is the place for dining, dancing, and shows Tuesday-Sunday evenings, and Sunday matinee. Prices vary according to meal options.

Several restaurants and bars keep the beach hopping with live music, especially in spring and summer. For night-time action, start at **The Beach Bar** at 454 Mandalay Ave, Clearwater Beach, ☎ 446-8866, and follow the crowds.

Sand Key Communities

Twelve-mile-long Sand Key begins in the north at the bridge to Clearwater Beach, which occupies a few miles at the island's top. South from there, a series of communities in varying degrees of commercial development stretch to John's Pass and Sand Key's most developed and water-adventuresome town, Madeira Beach. A few of the towns through which you pass, such as Belleair Beach, are blink-of-an-eye residential settlements. Others, such as Redington Beach, Redington Shores, and Indian Rocks Beach, offer visitors beach and old-island character, as well as a slew of fun-time activities, particularly fishing.

This stretch of island isn't among the best beaches of the Pinellas Suncoast. In the more private communities, there are no public accesses. In Madeira Beach, beaches have a distinctly metropolitan feel.

BASICS

Gulf Boulevard (Route 699) runs down the middle of 12-mile long Sand Key. Four bridges cross from Sand Key to the mainland. They are located (from north to south) in Belleair Shores at West Bay Drive (Route 686), in Indian Rocks Beach at Walsingham/Ulmerton Rd (Route 688), in Indian Shores at Park Boulevard (Route 694), and in Madeira Beach at 150th Avenue, which intersects with Seminole Boulevard (Route 595) and Alternate Highway 19 on the mainland.

INFORMATION

Gulf Beaches Chamber of Commerce at 105 Fifth Ave, Indian Rocks Beach, FL 33708, ☎ 595-4575 or 800-944-1847; or at 501 150th Ave, Madeira Beach, FL 33708, ☎ 391-7373 or 800-944-1847. Both offices open daily 9-5.

INDIAN ROCKS BEACH/ INDIAN SHORES ATTRACTIONS

In Indian Rocks Beach, between 15th and 27th avenues and First and Eighth avenues, you'll see public beach accesses about every block or so. Parking has been limited in the past, but recently the county built a large lot and facilities at 18th Street. This is a good spot for surfers and surf-fishers.

At Indian Shores, **Tiki Gardens Beach Access** provides ample parking spaces in a lot across the street. The fee is $1 per hour.

A collection of local historical memorabilia is found in a vintage home known as the **Indian Rocks Area Historical Museum** at 1507 Bay Palm Blvd, ☎ 595-2517. It is open only on Tuesday 9:30-11 and Saturday 1-4. Admission is free or by donation.

Suncoast Seabird Sanctuary at 18328 Gulf Blvd in Indian Shores, ☎ 391-6211, is the largest wild bird hospital in North America. In a zoological setting on the Gulf, it nurses more than 40 species – owls, hawks, sandhill cranes, pileated woodpeckers, wood storks, and lots of pelicans. It is open daily 9-dark. One-hour tours are conducted every Tuesday at 2. Admission is free, but donations are appreciated.

MAINLAND ATTRACTIONS

From the Indian Rocks Bridge (Walsingham Rd), head east to the town of Largo, where you can explore the history of Pinellas County in a 21-acre historic village known as **Heritage Park** at 11909 125th Street N, ☎ 582-2123. The park holds the county's oldest existing structures, including family homes, a one-room schoolhouse, a railroad depot, a blacksmith shop, **the Pinellas County Historical Museum**, and more than a dozen other historic places. Tour guides and artisans dress the part of turn-of-the-century pioneers and demonstrate period crafts. Visit for free Tuesday-Saturday 10-4 pm or Sunday 1-4. Tours run from 10-3:30 Tuesday-Saturday and 1-3:30 Sunday.

MADEIRA BEACH ATTRACTIONS

At Sand Key's south end, Madeira Beach, variously known as Mad Beach, is where the action happens, but more so in and around marinas than on the town's claustrophobic beaches. Most of the activity centers around **John's Pass and Village**, where a fishing charter industry has grown into a shopping and restaurant district with a shanty fish house motif.

FISHING & BOATING

Grouper is the password here. **John's Pass** (see *Sights & Attractions,* above) claims it is the grouper-catchingest place in the world. Try your luck on a deep-sea fishing charter. Other favored catches include pompano, snapper, snook, redfish, and tarpon.

Locals recommend the **Redington Long Pier** at 17490 Gulf Blvd in Redington Shores, ☎ 391-9398, for the best fish action onshore. It extends more than 1,000 feet into the Gulf and offers a snack bar, bait and tackle, shelters, and restrooms. It costs $6 for adults and $5 for children to fish off the pier, 50¢ to walk on. There's a two-pole maximum and no shark fishing is allowed.

Across the street, you'll find a more extensive stock of fishing supplies and bait at the **Dogfish Tackle Company**, 17477 Gulf Blvd, ☎ 392-6644.

Head to **Hubbard's Marina** at 150 128th Ave in John's Pass Village, ☎ 393-1947 or 800-755-0677, and embark on a deep-water trip that lasts anywhere from five hours to three days. Rates begin at $29.43 all-inclusive for adults, half-price for kids aged 11 and under.

Boardwalk at John's Pass Village.

For bait, fuel, fishing licenses, rod rentals or sales, and other fishing accessories, stop by **Don's Dock** at 215 128th Ave E, John's Pass, ☎ 391-3223.

Shell Island Adventure, ☎ 399-9633, departs out of Hubbard's Marina for five-hour beach and barbecue cruises to unbridged Shell Island (see St. Pete Beach *Sights & Attractions*, below). Cost for cruise and lunch is $26.90 for adults, $14.95 for children aged 2-12. Snorkel gear rentals are $5, boogie boards are $3. Other adventure cruises include a dolphin watch and an Egmont Key Tour (see St. Pete Beach *Sights & Attractions*, below). The boats have restrooms and covered seating.

You can launch your own craft at **Park Boulevard Boat Ramp**, near the Indian Shores Causeway.

Bayway Adventures at 17811 Gulf Blvd, Redington Shores, ☎ 397-5171, rents power boats at $79-$109 for a half-day, $139-$179 for a full day. Waverunners rent for $40 the first hour. It is open daily 8-6.

Europa SeaKruz at John's Pass Village, ☎ 393-5110 or 800-688-7529, is the premier dining-dancing-gambling cruise into the Gulf of Mexico. Six-hour day or evening excursions cost $27-$32 for adults, $12 for children under age 18.

SNORKELING & SCUBA

The wreck of a 100-foot-long vessel in 80 feet of water and a 110-foot Coast Guard cutter supply divers with underwater sights. There are also some cave-like ledges to explore, plus various other reefs and wrecks lie several miles from land, in water up to 45 feet deep.

Indian Rocks Tackle & Dive Center at 1301 N Gulf Blvd, ☎ 595-3196, offers PADI instruction and has complete diving services. It's open 9-5:30 Monday-Saturday.

At the south end of the island, check with **Mad Beach Dive Center** at 13237 Gulf Blvd, Madeira Beach, ☎ 398-6875. Hours are 9-5 Sunday, 9-6 the rest of the week.

OTHER WATER ADVENTURES

Windsurfers favor the beach on the causeway from Belleair Beach to the mainland.

Try **Gilligan's Waverunner Rentals** at 209 John's Pass Boardwalk in Madeira Beach, ☎ 397-0276, for waverunners, pontoons, and fishing boats for use in the Intracoastal Waterway.

HIKING & BIKING

Bikers America at 19709 Gulf Blvd in Indian Shores, ☎ 593-0665, delivers and picks up free on multi-day rentals. Daily rates for bikes are $22-$28, $20 for in-line skates. Hourly and weekly rates available. It's open every day.

WHERE TO EAT

Sand Key has some of the best seafood you'll ever find, and at tasty prices. Check out the fish markets for do-it-yourself seafood feasts.

Crabby Bill's at 401 Gulf Blvd in Indian Rocks Beach, ☎ 595-4825, gave birth to a Florida chain. The fare is simple and fresh: fried oyster sandwiches, crab cakes, catfish, and key lime pie – served on long picnic tables amid sign-plastered walls. The same menu holds daily through lunch and dinner, priced at $3-$13.

For something special, **The Lobster Pot Restaurant** at 17814 Gulf Blvd in Redington Shores, ☎ 391-8592, combines fish-house casualness with finely executed cuisine. Lobster dominates in varieties un-dreamed-of, followed in eminence by grouper. It's open daily for dinner, priced at $13 and up. Reservations recommended.

Friendly Fisherman Seafood Restaurant at 150 John's Pass Board-walk on Madeira Beach, ☎ 391-6025, should be the Florida fish house prototype, with its casual attitude, water view, and just-caught fish. You can even bring in your own catch to be cleaned and cooked to your specifications. It's open daily for breakfast, lunch, and dinner. Luncheon platters range from $5-$8, dinner platters $11-$15.

WHERE TO STAY

There are any number of places to stay along the stretch of Sand Key, in unlimited variety. Most have their own distinct personality and are not part of any chain. Rates are relatively low.

Top-end is the **North Redington Beach Hilton** at 17120 Gulf Blvd, ☎ 391-4000. High-rise in style, its 125 rooms are set on the beach, where a pool, restaurant, and tiki bar complete the amenities. Rates vary according to availability, but generally run $185-$215 in season, $155-$195 in the off-season.

For something more intimate and affordable, try **Villa St. Tropez**, located across the street from the Indian Rocks beach access at 1713 Gulf Blvd, ☎ 596-7133. Its cheerful cottages hold nine one-bedroom apartments and efficiencies, which range $43-$50 in season, $33-$44 May through December. All have full kitchens, plus there are barbecue grills for guests' use.

CAMPING

RVers can stay at **Indian Rocks Beach RV Resort**, 601 Gulf Blvd, ☎ 596-7743 for $25-$35 a night or $150-$220 a week. It has an on-property fishing bayou, swimming pool, and full hook-ups.

NIGHTLIFE

There's fun to be had once the sun sets on local beaches. Here are a couple of places to try. Follow your ears to the music and fun, or refer to local Friday newspaper inserts.

Alley Cats Café Beachside at 2721 Gulf Blvd on Indian Rocks Beach, ☎ 595-7877, hosts contemporary bands.

For something more mature, check out the lounge at **The Wine Cellar** at 17307 Gulf Blvd in North Redington Beach, ☎ 393-3491, which features live jazz, blues, and easy-listening tunes.

Treasure Island

Treasure Island, despite its rich-sounding name, is the Suncoast's best value. It's low on character, except for its Sunset Beach district, yet offers the same white sand beaches and watersports thrills as its neighbors.

BASICS

Central Avenue connects Treasure Island to Highway 19 and downtown St. Petersburg. There's a 50¢ toll to cross the Treasure Island Causeway, which becomes 107th Avenue on the island. Gulf Boulevard (Route 699) runs the length of the island, connecting it to Sand Key in the north. At the south end, Blind Pass Rd leads to Long Key/St. Pete Beach.

INFORMATION

The **Treasure Island Chamber of Commerce** is located at 152 108th Ave, Treasure Island, FL 33706, ☎ 367-4529 or 800-944-1847, and is open Monday-Friday 9-5.

SIGHTS & ATTRACTIONS

Treasure Island is perhaps the blandest of the region's beaches – behind the times but not far enough to have a lot of character. The exception is **Sunset Beach** on the island's south end, where you'll find a mish-mash of architectural styles, from historic cottages to funky bars to majestic modern homes. The beach bars are a fun place to visit day or night.

FISHING & BOATING

You can fish along the seawall at **Treasure Island Golf, Tennis & Recreation Center**, 10315 Paradise Blvd, ☎ 360-6062.

At Kingfish Marina, on the south side of John's Pass, **John's Pass Seafood Co.,** ☎ 360-6907, sells bait and fishing supplies.

Island Marine at 11045 Gulf Blvd, ☎ 367-2132, does fishing charters, and sells bait and tackle, and also rents fishing and pontoon boats. Half-day boat rental rates range from $80-$140; full-day $135-$200.

Rent a rod and reel for $7.50 a half-day, $10 all day. Two- and three-person waverunners rent for $40-$50 per hour.

On the south side of St. John's Pass, Treasure Island supplies water-sports action with boat and jet ski rentals. **Ocean Adventures** at John's Pass Marina, 12795 Kingfish Drive, ☎ 363-1131 or 800-363-1131, rents Grady White boats equipped with fishing electronics. Half-day rates are $169-$239; full-day, $229-$329, gas, oil, and tax extra. Packages are available for water skiing, fishing, snorkeling, and other adventures.

There's a free boat ramp on the bay side near the south end of Treasure Island. Watch for the sign.

Empress Cruise Lines, Kingfish Wharf at John's Pass, ☎ 895-DEAL, gives you dining, dancing, and full casino games during two daily cruises. A six-hour cruise for adults costs $13; for seniors, $10; and for children under age 4, free.

SNORKELING & DIVING

The Treasure Island Artificial Reef and a barge wreck provide places of interest for divers offshore.

Call **Treasure Island Divers** at 111 108th Ave, ☎ 360-3483, for scuba charters and equipment sales and rentals. It charges $50 for a two-tank dive 10-20 miles from shore. PADI certification courses are also offered.

HIKING & BIKING

Island Marine (11045 Gulf Blvd, ☎ 813-367-2132) rents bicycles for $5 per hour, $15 per day (24 hours).

WHERE TO EAT

You won't find much in the way of fine dining on Treasure Island. Check out the small beach bars along Sunset Beach for casual, scenic eats.

Sunset Beach Café at 9701 First Street E, serves typically inexpensive, casual fare daily for lunch and dinner. Sandwiches, salads, and seafood and steak dinners are $6-$14.

Beach Nutts at 9600 W Gulf Blvd, ☎ 347-7427, is a swinging place on Sunset Beach, with seafood specials such as live lobster dinner for

$11.95. It features live music nightly and serves seafood and American cuisine daily for lunch and dinner.

WHERE TO STAY

Like all of the Suncoast beaches, Treasure Island is lined with hotels, motels, cottages, and resorts of all sizes and types. Most are either on the Gulf or the bay. Prices are low. For example, you can stay at the **Buccaneer Beach Resort Motel** (doesn't that have an adventurous ring?), 10800 Gulf Blvd, ☎ 367-1908 or 800-826-2120, for $70-$95 in winter, $42-$70 in off-season. Accommodations include motel rooms with refrigerators, mini-efficiencies, efficiencies, and one-bedroom apartments. It has volleyball and shuffleboard, a pool, and a beach, and is located centrally to watersports activities and restaurants.

NIGHTLIFE

One thing Treasure Island does have is after-dark activity.

Gators at John's Pass, 12754 Kingfish Drive, ☎ 367-8951, is decorated with alligator and Florida Gator team paraphernalia. Even the French fries are shaped like 'gators. It hosts live entertainment on weekends.

The Dead Beats Club at 245 108th Ave, ☎ 367-3400, hosts rock and roll artists Wednesday through Saturday nights.

On stilts, **Beach Nutts** at 9600 W Gulf Blvd, ☎ 367-7427, features live music every night, with outdoor seating overlooking the beach.

The funkiest structure in Sunset Beach, **Bedrox Night Club** at 8000 W Gulf Blvd, ☎ 367-4114, actually looks prehistoric. It is near the public beach access and features live contemporary music.

St. Pete Beach & Lower Islands

St. Pete Beach occupies a 7½-mile island known as Long Key. Of all the area's islands, Long Key beach has kept its intriguing history the most well-preserved. Its greatest landmark is the fantasy-pink Don CeSar Resort, playground of 1920s glitterati such as F. Scott Fitzgerald and Al Capone. It majestically crowns St. Pete Beach's southern threshold. The island's southernmost community of Pass-A-Grille fills its history pages with adventuresome tales of French fishermen and 20th-century drug smugglers.

South of Long Key, the islands get smaller and more remote. Tierra Verde holds a marina community at the doorstep to Fort De Soto County Park, which occupies five small keys, where once war strategies were planned.

Unreachable by land, Egmont Key was site of Fort De Soto's sister fortifications. Today it is a refuge for wildlife and weekenders alike. Shell Key has its namesake shells and birds to attract day trippers to its pristine shores.

BASICS

From the south, take Interstate 275 off of Interstate 75 to the Sunshine Skyway. Turn east on Pinellas County Bayway (54th Avenue/Route 682), toll 50¢, which goes directly to St. Pete Beach. Pinellas Bayway (Route 679) splits off at Isla Del Sol to take you to Tierra Verde and Fort De Soto Park. Roadways are well-marked.

From downtown St. Petersburg, take Central Avenue west about nine miles, turn south on Pasadena Avenue and proceed to the St. Pete Beach Causeway/75th Avenue. Follow Route 699 down from the islands to the north. Blind Pass Rd crosses from Treasure Island to St. Pete Beach, and connects to Gulf Boulevard, which runs the island's length as the major thoroughfare. In Pass-A-Grille, Gulf Boulevard splits into Gulf Way and Pass-A-Grille Way, the bayfront route. Eighth Street is the historic section's main drag.

You can reach Egmont and Shell keys via shuttles, charters, and boat rentals (see *Fishing & Boating,* below).

INFORMATION

For more information, contact the **St. Pete Beach Area Chamber of Commerce,** 6990 Gulf Blvd, St. Petersburg Beach, FL 33706; ☎ 360-6957 or 800-944-1847, open Monday-Friday 9-5.

ST. PETE BEACH SIGHTS & ATTRACTIONS

South of the majestic Don CeSar Resort, you'll discover historic **Pass-A-Grille.** Browse between Eighth and 10th avenues, where old-island homes, and galleries and shops in historic buildings take you back to yesteryear. Of special interest, **Evander Preston Contemporary Jewelry** at 106 Eighth Ave, ☎ 367-7894, is the studio and gallery of a local character. Besides his own artistic jewelry, you can see his private eclectic collection of art, which ranges from a John Lennon work to a 1986 Harley Davidson. It's open daily.

Nearby, **Gulf Beaches Historical Museum** at 115 10th Ave, ☎ 360-2491, resides in a historic church near the beach. Through pictures and artifacts, it tells the story of settlement in these parts. Admission is free or by donation. The hours are Thursday and Saturday 10-4 and Sunday 1-4.

The beach here, and along St. Pete Beach, is quite lovely – a wide apron of clean sand with enticingly gentle seas. Parking is metered and closely monitored.

LOWER ISLAND ATTRACTIONS

Fort De Soto, ☎ 866-2484, is centerpiece of the park which it named, Fort De Soto County Park. Part of the fortifications are preserved: gun and ammunition rooms, 12-inch mortar cannons, and other features. Forty-five steps take you up to the fort's battery embankment, where the view of the now peaceful waterfront scene is the best part.

Egmont Key, less than two miles long and containing 398 acres, is a national wildlife preserve where you can explore history and nature. The ruins of Fort Dade occupy the northwest end of the island. Part of the ruins have eroded into the water to provide sea life and snorkelers with an artificial reef. Nature trails lead to gopher tortoise nests and a historic lighthouse.

Shell Key is a narrow strip of island with mostly sand, shells, and birds to see.

FISHING & BOATING

You won't lack for water-oriented activities in St. Pete Beach. Fishing and boating are a way of life here, and have been since human history was first recorded in these parts. You'll find deep-sea party fishing boats; they charge about $25 per person for a half-day, $40 for a full day, including license, bait, equipment, and cleaning. Private charters charge more – about $150-$200 plus tip for four to six persons a half-day, $250-$300 for a full day, and up to $400 for trips into deep waters.

A small sea-walled patch of park on Blind Pass at Sunset Way and Corey Avenue is designated **Fisherman's Park**. Restaurants are conveniently located at both ends.

Two exits off the Skyway Bridge take you to the north and south adjuncts of the **Skyway Fishing Pier,** ☎ 865-0668, created from the remains of an old bridge. There are picnic and rest areas at the same exits. To get on the piers, the state's only drive-on piers, you must pay $3 per car or $10 per RV plus $2 per person aged 13 and older, $1.50 for seniors, $1 for children aged 6-12. Both piers hold bait and tackle concessions and are open 24 hours daily.

In Pass-A-Grille, **Merry Pier** at Eighth Ave and Pass-A-Grille Way, ☎ 360-6606, is the focus of south-end water adventures. You can fish free from the pier, which also has restrooms, bait and tackle, and rod and reel rentals. It's also a good place to catch a fishing charter. The *Captain Kidd,* ☎ 360-6606, goes deep-sea fishing. Concessions are open daily 7-6.

The **Shell Key Shuttle,** ☎ 360-1348, departs from the pier three to four times daily for $10 adult fare, $5 children's fare, plus tax.

Across from the Don CeSar Resort, there's a boat ramp with limited metered parking at West Maritana & Casa Blanca. Launching facilities are also available at **Blind Pass Marina**, 9555 Blind Pass Rd, ☎ 360-4281.

Mid-island, **Dolphin Landings**, 4737 Gulf Blvd, behind Dolphin Village Shopping Center, ☎ 360-7411 or 367-4488, is a good place to look for charters, especially for trips to Shell and Egmont keys (see *Sights & Attractions*, above). Power and sail boat cruises typically are priced around $10-$30 per person for four hours to a full day. For the best sailing-snorkeling excursion to Egmont Key, contact **Capt. Randy**, ☎ 367-5122.

In Tierra Verde, you can launch your boat and do your other boat-related business at **Tierra Verde Marine Center**, 100 Pinellas Bayway, ☎ 867-0255.

Tierra Verde Boat Rentals, located at the marina, ☎ 867-0077, rents bowriders, center and duel consoles, and waverunners by the hour, half-day and full day. Hourly rate on all machines is $50; half-day rates, $150-$185; full day, $229-$245. Gas is included with waverunner rentals, but is extra for boats.

Sailing cruises from the marina to Shell Key and for dolphin watching with **Destiny Yacht Charters**, ☎ 430-SAIL, depart for half-days ($25 each) and sunset ($20 each). Discounts for kids under age 12.

Lady Anderson Cruises on the St. Pete Beach Causeway, 3400 Pasadena Ave S, ☎ 367-7804 or 800-533-2288, conducts dinner-dance, luncheon/dolphin, and gospel music/dinner cruises aboard a sleek triple-decker. Adult rates begin at $20; $18.50 and up for seniors; $13.50 and up for children. Tax and gratuities are included.

SNORKELING & SCUBA

The St. Petersburg Beach Artificial Reef and a deep-water wreck provide popular dive destinations in less than 30 feet of water.

Many charter boats to Egmont Key provide snorkeling equipment so you can explore the fort ruins and their coral formations. Visibility is about 30 to 50 feet.

HIKING & BIKING

The hike around **Fort De Soto** (see *Sights & Attractions*, above), and up and down its steps, provides solid exercise with your history lesson. A one-mile interpretative nature trail takes you through scrub and mangrove terrain at the **Arrowhead Picnic Area** near North Beach at Fort De Soto Park. Biking is popular along the park's 10 miles of wide paths and in the campground.

Paths, some of them still brick-paved from when the island was a thriving military settlement, cross **Egmont Key** (see *Sights & Attractions*, above). One leads from the fort to the lighthouse, others meander.

Totally Active Sports at 7116 Gulf Blvd, ☎ 367-7059, rents mountain bikes and beach cruisers for $10 a day, in-line skates for $12 a day. Hours are 9-7 Monday-Saturday and 10-5 Sunday.

WHERE TO EAT

St. Pete Beach is perfect for the hungry adventurer with a limited pocketbook. Seafood restaurants up and down the strip serve fresh seafood, often in old fish-house style, meaning breaded and fried, or simply broiled or steamed.

The Pelican Diner at 7501 Gulf Blvd, ☎ 363-9873, however, caters to the needs of comfort food-seekers. You can't miss its classic chrome-sided diner-car architecture. Inside, you can order homemade specialties from the counter or booths. It's open daily for breakfast ($2-$5), and Monday-Saturday for lunch ($2-$5) and dinner ($5-$11).

For something off the beaten path, casual, waterfront, and locally loved, head to **Woody's Waterfront Café & Beach Bar** at Corey Ave and Sunset Way, ☎ 360-9165. You sit in the open air, under a ceiling of hanging surfboards, or under umbrellas on the patio overlooking the pass between Treasure Island and Sand Key. The fare is burgers and seafood baskets for around $4-$6. By the way, the "beach" part of the name is misleading; the beach is long gone.

When you do get ready to spend a lot of cash for a culinary splurge, head to **The Maritana Grille** at the Don CeSar Resort, 3400 Gulf Blvd, ☎ 360-1881. Dishes such as red snapper with baby spinach, toasted coconut, and fruited curry butter are executed in fine new Florida style and are priced à la carte in the $21-$28 range. Booths and tables sit in an atmosphere of aquariums and refined tropicalia. Reservations recommended.

On the bayfront with docking, **Wharf Seafood Restaurant**, at 2001 Pass-A-Grille Way, ☎ 367-9469, is a local's kind of place serving unpretentiously prepared fish, shrimp, crab cakes, and crab claws for lunch and dinner daily for $4-$11.

Hurricane Restaurant at Ninth Ave and Gulf Way in Pass-A-Grille, ☎ 360-9558, is the island's best-known and most imposing restaurant. The three-story Victorian building overlooks the beach and historic district. I find the food and service somewhat overrated, but it's worth at least one visit. Grouper is the specialty on the comprehensive menu. It's open daily for breakfast, lunch, and dinner. Prices are $1.50-$14.

WHERE TO STAY

In St. Pete Beach, there are as many different kinds of lodging as there are different kinds of visitors. A lot of these places are beach-front and geared to activity in the waves.

Families will love **TradeWinds** at 5500 Gulf Blvd, ☎ 367-6461 or 800-237-0707, where there are free paddleboats to navigate the property's canals, a

TradeWinds.

Pizza Hut, a putting course, free tennis clinics, a kids program, pools of all sizes, and a game room named Videoville. Rates for rooms and suites in season range from $159 to $195, in summer/fall from $135 to $159.

The 50-year-old **Don CeSar Resort** at 3400 Gulf Blvd, ☎ 360-1881 or 282-1116, is the doyenne of local beach resorts. Palatial, yet playful, it houses amenities from dual swim pools and kids program, to watersports rentals and a spa. High-season rates for rooms and suites begin at $275; in off-season they begin in a range $175-$225.

The beach at Don CeSar Resort.

You can stay more inexpensively at the new **Don CeSar Beach House** at 3860 Gulf Blvd, ☎ 360-1881 or 800-282-1116, a sister property only a few blocks away, and still use the resort's great programs and facilities with free transportation provided. High-season rates start at $235, shoulder season rates at $180, and summer rates for one-bedroom suites begin at $130.

Inn on the Beach at 1401 Gulf Way in Pass-A-Grille, ☎ 360-8844, has 12 cozy, clean, comfortable, and nicely appointed rooms with a view of the beach. Rates are $60-$150 in season, $40-$125 in the off-season.

Tierra Verde Yacht & Tennis Resort at 200 Madonna Blvd in Tierra Verde, ☎ 867-8611 or 800-934-0549, is a seaworthy community gathered around a yacht basin. Its 66 apartments come in three sizes for two to six people, all with kitchenettes and private balconies. Other amenities include tennis, a huge swimming pool, a jacuzzi, restaurants, bars, and entertainment. Rates in season are $90-$130; in summer, $65-$110.

CAMPING

The region's best campground occupies St. Christopher Key in **Fort De Soto County Park**, ☎ 866-2662. The 235-site campground is spotless, surrounded by water, and perfect for fishermen, hikers, and bike riders. Rates are $17.75 per night, minimum two-night stay.

NIGHTLIFE

Party-down day and night at St. Pete Beach. You'll be in good company. Many party places are located within resorts. Watch local papers for what band is playing where and at what time.

Stormy's at the Hurricane at Ninth Ave and Gulf Way in Pass-A-Grille, ☎ 360-9558, creates a Caribbean atmosphere where you can enjoy live jazz and other styles nightly.

At **Harp and Thistle Pub**, 650 Corey Ave, ☎ 360-4104, you can listen to Celtic folk music while you sip an Irish beer.

St. Petersburg

Downtown St. Petersburg is an old city previously known for its aging population. Since the 1880s, when Peter Demens gave the city a railroad and the name of his Russian hometown, St. Petersburg has been associated with healthful climes and restorative waters. In its early days, retirees and convalescents flooded the peninsular town looking for rest and rejuvenation. This took its toll on St. Petersburg. For many years it looked like a worn-out rest home waiting room.

But new blood has been transfused into the city recently, making its waterfront district a happening place for lovers of the outdoors and other visitors. The rejuvenation is ongoing, turning St. Petersburg into a thriving metropolis with its own college, major sports arena, world-class museums, and fashionable shopping district. Sophisticated and savvy, it presents the flip side of the barrier islands' swimsuit-and-suntan-oil mood.

BASICS

Off of Interstate 275, take Interstate 175 or 375 to get to downtown. Numbered streets run north-south, numbered avenues run east-west. Second Street is closest to the waterfront. Beach Drive is where First Street logically would be, at bay's edge. Fourth Street North is Highway 92, which takes you to Tampa Bay bridges. Central Avenue is the dividing point between avenues north and avenues south. It also connects downtown to the beaches.

Tour downtown on the **Looper** trolley daily 11-5. Tour begins at The Pier (see *Sights & Attractions*, below), 800 Second Ave NE, ☎ 821-6164, and costs 50¢.

INFORMATION

St. Petersburg Area Chamber of Commerce is located at 100 Second Ave N, Ste. 150, ☎ 821-4715, open Monday-Friday 9-5. Or visit **The Pier Visitor Information Center** at 800 Second Ave NE, ☎ 821-6164, open 10-9 Monday-Thursday, 10-10 Friday-Saturday, 11-7 on Sunday, or the **Suncoast Welcome Center** at 2001 Ulmerton Rd, ☎ 573-1449. It's open daily 9-5.

Sunrise over Vinoy Basin, St. Petersburg.

SIGHTS & ATTRACTIONS

The Pier, 800 Second Ave NE, ☎ 821-6164, a futuristic structure in the shape of an upside-down pyramid at the end of a long wharf, is the core of downtown action. It's the place to shop, dine, party, fish, rent a boat, and catch a charter. It's open 10-9 Monday-Thursday, 10-10 Friday-Saturday, 11-7 on Sunday. Parking is $3, which includes trolley transportation from lots to the Pier.

On the second floor, you'll find the **Pier Aquarium**, filled with fish exhibits and huge tanks. Donations of $1 are requested. Hours are 10-8 Friday-Saturday, 12-6 Sunday.

The *HMS Bounty*, ☎ 896-5668, a re-creation of the ship used in MGM's 1962 film version of *Mutiny on the Bounty*, docks at The Pier from November to April. You can tour it for $5 adults, $4 seniors, $3 students, or sign up for a cruise.

Explore art through the ages at the **Museum of Fine Arts**, 255 Beach Drive NE, ☎ 896-2667. Gallery rooms and gardens display the works of major artists, including Georgia O'Keefe, Edgar Degas, and Paul Gauguin. Admission is $5 for adults, $3 for seniors, $2 for students older than 6. Sunday admission is free. Hours are 10-5 Tuesday-Saturday, 1-5 Sunday.

St. Petersburg Museum of History at 335 Second Ave NE, ☎ 894-1052, is not your normal, stuffy historical museum. Light and airy, it features a circa-1910 Benoist airboat hanging from the ceiling – the first recorded airplane to fly a commercial route by crossing from Tampa to St. Petersburg – and costumes you can "try on" by standing behind glass pull-out displays and looking in the mirror. Other vignettes realistically depict life throughout the history of St. Petersburg. Adult admission is $4, $3.50 for seniors, and $1.50 for children ages 4-17. Hours are Tuesday-Saturday 10-5 and Sunday 1-5.

One of downtown's most impressive treasures, the **Salvador Dali Museum** at 1000 Third Street S, ☎ 823-3767, houses the world's largest collection of original works by the renowned surrealist artist, with melting clocks, men hatching from eggs, and all. Some of his works reach floor to ceiling, others are small preliminary pencil sketches. Special exhibits complement permanent ones. Browse the museum store for something unusual. The museum is open Monday-Saturday 9:30-5:30 and Sunday 12-5:30. Cost for adults is $8; for seniors, $7; for students, $4; for children age 10 and under, free.

In the same neighborhood, adults enjoy **Great Explorations, The Hands On Museum** at 1120 Fourth Street S, ☎ 821-8992, as much as children do. It is divided into seven arenas, one devoted to pre-schoolers and others with names like Puppet Space, Touch Tunnel, Body Shop, and Safe Cracker. The newest, The Idea Factory, puts children's creativity to work in Einstein's Garage. The museum also hosts changing experimental exhibits. It is open Monday-Saturday 10-5 and Sunday 12-5. Adult admission is $6; seniors, $5.50, and children ages 4-17, $5.

One of St. Petersburg's oldest attractions, **Sunken Gardens** at 1825 Fourth Street N, ☎ 896-3186, provides cool, lush relief from the city. More than 5,000 varieties of plants thrive in the sinkhole garden. Visitors see hundreds of birds, a biblical wax museum, and bird and alligator shows. It's open daily 9:30-5. Admission is $14 for adults and $8 for children.

FISHING & BOATING

Since 1889, **The Pier** (see *Sights & Attractions*, above) at 800 Second Ave NE, ☎ 821-6164, in its various incarnations, has lured fishermen. A bait house on the south side takes care of tackle and bait needs. Fishing charters and rental boats depart from its docks. To rent boats, waverunners, paddle boats, and sailboats from The Pier, call Pierside **Waterworks**, ☎ 363-3000.

The Caribbean Queen, ☎ 895-BOAT, departs for one dolphin and three sightseeing tours daily. Adults pay $10 plus tax; seniors, $8; juniors ages 12-17, $8; and children ages 3-11, $5. Snacks and beverages are available for purchase.

Competitors line up in the annual Southern Ocean Racing Conference (S.O.R.C.) in the waters off St. Petersburg.

HIKING & BIKING

For a peaceful brush with nature and six miles of hiking and biking trails, head to **Boyd Hill Nature Center** at 1101 Country Club Way S, ☎ 893-7326. Beneath oak canopies you can picnic, play on the playground, visit caged birds, spot butterflies, visit the nature center, and stroll in quietude. Admission to trails is $1 for adults, 50¢ for children ages 3-17.

The 47-mile **Pinellas Trail**, ☎ 464-4751, begins in downtown St. Petersburg at 34th Street and Eighth Ave S, then heads north through city, town and country following an old railroad route. You can hike, bike, jog, or skate it.

You can rent bikes and in-line skates at the Pier. Call **Pierside Waterworks**, ☎ 363-3000.

OTHER ADVENTURES

At **Biplane Rides**, Albert Whitted Airport, ☎ 895-6266, your air taxi is a 1933 WACO UIC originally owned by William Randolph Hearst. Three passengers pay $55 per flight and up for short to extensive tours.

WHERE TO EAT

Downtown St. Petersburg has fine choices for dining out. Easiest for visitors are the many options at **The Pier** (see *Sights & Attractions,* above), 800 Second Ave NE, ☎ 821-6164. The food court provides a bakery, coffee and tea, pizza, steaks, burgers, and ice cream, all reasonably priced and above standard fast-food fare. Often you're entertained by minstrels.

Nick's on the Water at The Pier, ☎ 898-5800, has great Italian dishes and seafood. Try the seafood lasagna or rigatoni alla vodka. Open daily, lunches are $5-$9, dinners $8-$17. Reservations suggested for dinner.

On the fifth floor, **ChaCha Coconuts**, ☎ 822-6655, is a fun place to eat, sky-high, panoramic, and all done up in bright, Caribbean colors. It serves lunch and dinner daily at $5-$7 for sandwiches and $7-$10 for entrées. Try the lime garlic grouper.

Away from downtown, **Skyway Jacks** at 6701 34th Street S, ☎ 866-3217, is legendary. A colorful version of passé funk, it's popular with fishermen, businessmen, and all sorts. The food is homemade, Southern style, and plain cheap. Open daily, it prices its popular breakfasts at $3-$5, lunches $1.50-$4, and dinners $4-$7. Look for the big chicken out front.

WHERE TO STAY

Other than business travelers, most people head to the beaches to stay. Lodging downtown tends to be priced slightly higher than on the beaches, but is quieter and more sophisticated.

To luxuriate totally, do what the rich folk back in the '20s did: check into the Vinoy. The **Renaissance Vinoy Resort**, 501 Fifth Ave NE, ☎ 894-1000 or 800-HOTELS-1, is a renovated vision of roaring plenty with long, arched hallways, plush rooms (some with spas), pampered dining and pooling, and a convenient location on downtown's waterfront. The marina, tennis courts, and fitness center caters to outdoors activists. High and shoulder season rates range $190-$330; off-season, $130-$210. Ask about packages.

Downtown St. Petersburg has a number of bed-and-breakfast and small accommodations. **Bay Gables** at 136 Fourth Ave NE, ☎ 822-0044, is among the former, ensconced in a lovely 1910 Victorian house decorated with antiques. It is steps away from downtown's shopping

shopping district, and features a tea room and garden. Rooms and suites range from $85-$135 and include private bath.

Missed by the renovation-upgrade craze, **Beach Park Motel** at 300 Beach Drive NE, ☎ 898-6325, offers affordable, clean, and convenient lodging downtown. Rooms, efficiencies, and apartments are $50-$70 in season, $40-$60 off-season.

CAMPING

Close to the beaches, **St. Petersburg Resort KOA Kampground** at 5400 95th Street N, ☎ 392-2233 or 800-562-7714, gives you the option of tent, RV, or air-conditioned cabin camping on lovely, oak-shaded grounds. It's great for outdoors enthusiasts, providing bike and canoe rentals, boat slips, a fishing dock, a swimming pool, three hot tubs, bike trails, miniature golf, shuffleboard, volleyball, bocci ball, and children's playground. Rates for two adults in winter are $28-$43; in summer, $22-$33.

NIGHTLIFE

ChaCha Coconuts (see *Where to Eat,* above) at The Pier, ☎ 822-6655, and other Pier businesses sponsor indoor and outdoor events with live rock or reggae, and often with mobs of people.

Club Detroit/Jannus Landing at 16 Second Street N downtown, ☎ 896-1244, is another hot spot for live music. Cover charges vary.

Fans of big band dancing or the movie *Cocoon* should visit the classic **Coliseum Ballroom** at 535 Fourth Ave N, ☎ 892-5202 or 800-334-2223, ext. 5202, where part of the above-mentioned flick was filmed. It's open for afternoon and evening sessions; call for specific times. Cover charge is around $4-$12.

SHOPPING

In "The Quarter," as locals are beginning to call downtown's pier/waterfront area, you'll find great shopping, especially for art. **The Pier** (see *Sights & Attractions,* above) at 800 Second Ave NE, ☎ 821-6164, holds a gamut of specialty-souvenir shops, including one devoted entirely to hats and another to cartoon memorabilia.

Book-lovers should head to block-long **Haslam's Book Store**, 2025 Central Ave, ☎ 822-8616, Florida's largest book seller.

Chapter IV

Tampa

Area code: 813

Tampa is big city – skyscrapers, industry, traffic jams, the whole bit. Many of its guests are there on business. Tourists and adventurers are more likely to head to the islands of St. Petersburg/Clearwater.

Still, Tampa has its vacation appeal, and has since the 1880s, when Henry Plant brought his railroad to town and built an elaborate hotel designed after the Alhambra in Spain. With its deep port and easy water accesses, Tampa thrived. Cigars constituted one of its earliest big money-making industries. Cigars built an entire city named for industry magnate Don Vincente Martinez Ybor. Today Ybor City retains the essence of the Cuban cigar-makers and their immigrant work force and is the city's best cultural attraction. Teddy Roosevelt added to Ybor City's historic allure. Stationed with his Rough Riders in the vicinity during the Spanish-American War, he frequented a local club.

Busch Gardens is Tampa's major attraction. It, along with the new Florida Aquarium, a number of museums, professional sports, and parks, gives Tampa a lot to offer the sightseer. Outdoor enthusiasts fare less well. They will find a lot indoors that deals with nature. In the great wide open, Tampa Bay, Hillsborough Bay, and the Hillsborough River, which wends its way from civilization to sheer wilderness, do generate some excitement. Most adventure is sought on the water and away from city lights. This chapter generally covers Tampa and its outskirts as far north as Fletcher Avenue and as far east as Interstate 75.

The chapter is divided into three parts: Downtown, Ybor City, and Outlying Areas. The latter is further divided into Northwest Tampa (the area around the airport), Northeast Tampa, and South Hillsborough County, the region between Tampa and Bradenton (see Chapter V).

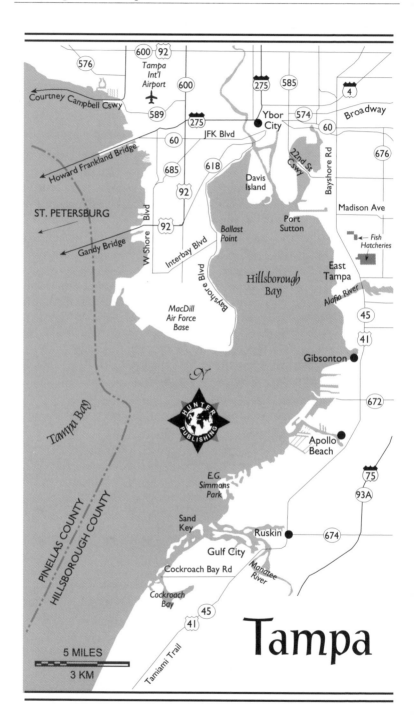

576
600 92
Tampa Int'l Airport
600
Courtney Campbell Cswy
589
275 585
4
Ybor City
574
Broadway
60
676
JFK Blvd
60
Howard Frankland Bridge
685
618
22nd St Cswy
Bayshore Rd
92
Davis Island
Madison Ave
ST. PETERSBURG
92
Ballast Point
Port Sutton
Fish Hatcheries
Gandy Bridge
W Shore Blvd
Interbay Blvd
Bayshore Blvd
Hillsborough Bay
East Tampa
Alafia River
MacDill Air Force Base
45
41
Gibsonton
N
672
HUNTER PUBLISHING
Apollo Beach
Tampa Bay
E.G. Simmons Park
75
93A
Sand Key
Ruskin
674
Gulf City
Cockroach Bay Rd
Manatee River
PINELLAS COUNTY
HILLSBOROUGH COUNTY
Cockroach Bay
45
41

Tampa

5 MILES

3 KM

Tamiami Trail

Transportation, Etc.

Tampa International Airport, ☎ 396-3690, is the West Coast's largest. Major domestic airlines include **American,** ☎ 800-433-7300, **Continental,** ☎ 874-7151 or 800-525-0280, **Delta,** ☎ 286-1800 or 800-221-1212, **Northwest,** ☎ 800-225-2525, **TWA,** ☎ 229-7961 or 800-221-2000, **United,** ☎ 800-241-6522, and **USAir,** ☎ 800-428-4322. **Air Canada,** ☎ 800-776-3000 and **British Airways,** ☎ 800-247-9297, are among international airlines that land in Tampa.

Rental cars are available at the airport and other locations throughout the area, including **Alamo,** ☎ 800-327-9633, **Avis,** ☎ 800-331-1212, **Hertz,** ☎ 800-654-3131, and **Budget,** ☎ 800-527-0700. For ground transportation to and from the airport, contact **United Cab,** ☎ 253-2424, **Yellow Cab,** ☎ 253-0121, and **The Limo Airport Connection,** 572-1111 or 800-282-6817. **HARTline** (Hillsborough Area Regional Transit), ☎ 254-HART, runs buses through the city. By permit, bike riders are allowed to transport bicycles on special bus bike racks. Fares are $1-$1.50, exact change is required.

Tampa lies at the crossroads of interstates 75, 275, and 4. Interstate 275 rushes east-west north of downtown, then north. It connects St. Petersburg to Interstate 75. Interstate 4 branches off of Interstate 275, crosses Interstate 75 farther south, then heads to Orlando. Interstate 75 forms an eastern border to the metropolitan area. Highway 41 pierces the city limits on the east side of town. The fastest route through town is Crosstown Expressway (Route 618), a toll road that runs north-south from Highway 92 to downtown, then squiggles east-west to Interstate 75, with limited exits. Three bridges cross Tampa Bay from St. Petersburg/Clearwater (Chapter III). North to south, they are Courtney Campbell Causeway (Route 60/Memorial Highway), Howard Frankland Bridge (Interstate 275), and Gandy Bridge (Hwy 92).

INFORMATION

For information on area attractions, contact **Tampa/Hillsborough Convention and Visitors Association,** 111 Madison Street, Suite 1010, Tampa, FL 33602-4706, ☎ 223-2752 or 800-44 TAMPA. The **Visitor Information Center** is located at Madison Street and Ashley Drive and is open Monday-Saturday 9-5. **Greater Tampa Chamber of Commerce** at 801 E Kennedy Blvd, Tampa, FL 33602, open Monday-Friday 9-5, is another source of local information.

Gasparilla Pirate Fest.

Events

Tampa's most celebrated event takes place in February – **Gasparilla Pirate Fest**, ☎ 273-6495, re-creating the legend of a local hero, the pirate Gasparilla. On Invasion Day hundreds of swashbuckling pirates raid the city aboard the three-masted *Jose Gasparilla* pirate ship and lead a boisterous parade along Bayshore Boulevard. Month-long festivities include street dances, foot races, and art shows.

Ybor City's **Fiesta Day**, ☎ 248-3712, street festival and illuminated night parade, runs concurrently with Gasparilla Days, as does the **Florida State Fair** at Florida Expo Park, ☎ 621-7821 or 800-345-FAIR (FL), admission $4-$7.

Ybor City's liveliest event happens in October. **Guavaween**, ☎ 248-3712, a Latin-flavored celebration, features a costumed street party and night parade. Admission is about $5.

Snow in Florida? Get it while it's cold at December's **Santafest**, ☎ 274-8615 or 274-8518. Events include snowball fights, ice-skating, a parade, kids games, and a visit from St. Nick.

First Night, ☎ 231-8507, rings in the New Year in downtown Tampa with hundreds of entertainers. Admission: $5 in advance, $10 at the door.

Downtown Tampa

Downtown Tampa, a hub of business activity, is restructuring to widen its appeal to tourists. Each year, a new attraction increases the area's tourism opportunities. Scored into segments by waterways and channels, Tampa's downtown is also the center of shipping activity. Much of the restoration takes place in the once-unsightly shipping zones of the Channel District, where a 16-story, 24-screen megatheater is being built.

Sights are basically divided between the neighborhoods of Hyde Park on the east side, downtown/Harbour Island in the center, and the under-renovation Channel District, on the east side.

BASICS

From Interstate 75, the Crosstown Expressway (Route 618, exit 50), a toll road, is the quickest way to downtown. From St. Petersburg, cross Gandy Bridge (Hwy 92) and hop on the expressway. Off of Interstate 4, take exit 1 and head south on 22nd Street.

In Hyde Park, Swann Avenue is the main through-street. Kennedy Boulevard, to the north, forms one border for the neighborhood, and leads into downtown. Bayshore Boulevard is Hyde Park's 7½-mile

Bayshore Boulevard, overlooking Hillsborough Bay.

show-off promenade, where visions of the deep blue intermingle with the grandeur of old homes.

Main downtown streets running north and south are Ashley, Tampa, and Florida streets. Platt and 13th streets take you into the Channel District. 22nd Street headed south crosses McKay Bay and hits Highway 41; headed north, it gets you to Ybor City.

TIP *The new, green **Tampa-Ybor Trolley**, ☎ 254-HART, shuttles you around the area's sights for 25¢ a passenger, running daily 7:30-5:30. You can take the **People Mover** from downtown to Harbour Island (see Shopping, below). Board at the Fort Brooke Parking Garage on Whiting Street and have exact change for the 50¢ toll (25¢ for seniors, children ages 4 and under free) each way. It runs continuously Monday-Friday 7:30-4 and Saturday-Sunday 7:30-5:30.*

SIGHTS & ATTRACTIONS

Tampa Jai-Alai at 5125 S Dale Mabry, ☎ 831-1411, gives you a taste of Florida's own exotic, fast-paced betting sport (the ball moves up to 180 mph) brought here by the Cuban population. Admission is $1; reserved seating, $1-$3; clubhouse restaurant seating, $3-$4. Parking is $1; $3 by valet. Performances are scheduled at noon and at 6:45 pm Monday, Wednesday, Friday, and Saturday. Spectators can also lay wagers on simulcast dog and horse racing.

To learn all about Tampa's history, visit the bizarre structure you can't help but notice. Built in the 1890s to lodge rich railroad arrivals, the **Henry B. Plant Museum** at 401 W Kennedy Blvd, ☎ 254-1891, with its onion domes and minarets, looks like a set for the *Arabian Nights*. Amid period-furnished rooms, the fate of the hotel and a portrait of the times are explored. Hours are Tuesday-Saturday 10-4 and Sunday noon-4. A $3 donation is suggested for adults, $1 for children ages 12 and under.

The **Tampa Bay Performing Arts Center** at 1010 N MacInnes Place, ☎ 222-1000 or 800-955-1045, is home to 12 performing arts groups and host to operas, ballets, Broadway musicals, and more. Call for schedule and ticket prices.

The newly opened **Tampa Bay History Center**, downtown in the Tampa Convention Center Annex at 333 S Franklin, ☎ 228-0097, has graphics, hands-on displays, and artifacts from 12,000 to 100 years ago. The displays are being developed for relocation in a permanent headquarters within the next few years. Admission is free; donations accepted. It's open Tuesday-Saturday 10-5 and Sunday 1-5.

Downtown also has its classic treasures, including the gothically embellished **Tampa Theatre** at 711 Franklin Street, ☎ 274-8981. Restored to its 1926 grandeur, it stages films, concerts, and other special events. Guided tours and open houses tell the theater's story, including tales of the resident ghost, a former projectionist. Call for tour times. Donations are requested.

In the mood for culture? Visit **Tampa Museum of Art** at 600 N Ashley Drive, ☎ 274-8130. Its seven galleries host five changing and three permanent exhibits of classic antiquities, 20th century American art, and Florida artists. A separate family gallery has hands-on items. Admission is $5 for adults, $4 for seniors and students, and $3 for children ages 6-18. Everyone enters free from 1-5 Sunday and 5-9 Wednesday. It's open 10-5 Monday-Saturday, 10-9 Wednesday, and 1-5 Sunday. Tours are available; call for times.

The **Florida Aquarium** at 701 Channelside Drive, ☎ 273-4020, is the jewel of downtown redevelopment, part of the Garrison Seaport Center in the so-called Channel District. Beneath a seashell-shaped glass dome, exhibit areas replicate the state's different aquarian environments: mangrove estuary, freshwater, beach, marine, and reef – the most popular with its sharks, angel fish, and other intriguing creatures of the deep. A new interaction adjunct allows children to dig for beach treasures and build a reef. Audio rentals are available. Admission for adults is $13.95; for youth 13-18, $12.55; for children 3-12, $6.95; and for seniors ages 60 and up, $12.55. Hours are 9-6, but are shortened in the fall.

Nearby, the **Tampa Bay Lightning** hockey team plays in the huge new **Ice Palace**, near the Florida Aquarium at 501 E Kennedy Blvd, ☎ 223-4919, October through April. Individual game tickets range $16-$57; ☎ 287-8844 to order, or 229-8800 ext. 1 for ticket packages.

Highly acclaimed, the **Museum of African American Art** at 1308 Marion Street, ☎ 272-2466, fills its eight galleries with a permanent collection of paintings, graphics, and sculpture from this and the last century. Admission is $3 for adults and $2 for seniors and students. It's open Tuesday-Friday 10-4:30 and Saturday 10-5.

FISHING & BOATING

You're never far from water in Tampa, even in the middle of downtown. Its variety of water bodies gives salt- and fresh-water fishermen their due. From downtown, it's easy to hook up with a charter headed for deep waters. For a fuller menu of fishing and boating opportunities, head to the beaches around St. Petersburg (see Chapter III). Outlying areas (see below) offer better access to canoeing and freshwater pursuits.

Ballast Point Pier at 5300 Interbay Blvd on the south end of Bayshore Blvd, ☎ 831-9585, extends 1,000 feet into Hillsborough Bay.

The **Tampa Town Ferry,** ☎ 223-1522, taxis you or your vehicle to Harbour Island and up the Hillsborough River to outlying attractions. Prices per person, $4-$16; cars, $3.

Captain Dave Markett, ☎ 962-1435, charges $300-$500 to take you and a boatload of fishermen out to the flats. Excursions last four to eight hours.

Starlite Cruises depart from Garrison Seaport Center at 651 Channelside Drive, ☎ 228-1200, with a variety of excursions. Eco-sightseeing tours cost $7 for adults and $4.65 for children. Longer tours range in price from $9 to $35 for adults. Dinner and dance cruises charge extra for meals.

You'll find boat ramps at these four locations: on the east side of the Gandy Bridge, on Bayshore Boulevard near Platt Street, at Marjorie Park on Davis Island's south end, and on the 22nd Street Causeway.

HIKING & BIKING

For a quiet nature walk in the city, head to **McKay Nature Park** at Crosstown Expressway and 34th Street, a 150-acre refuge for more than 180 species of birds and other wildlife. Trails head into uplands habitat.

Blades & Bikes Westshore at 201 West Platt Street, ☎ 251-0178, rents bikes for about $8 an hour. Prices go down with length of rental and number of renters. Safety gear included. It's open daily with varying hours.

OTHER LAND SPORTS

Bayshore Boulevard, billed as the world's longest continuous sidewalk (6.3 miles), is perfect for in-line skating and jogging. It runs between Hillsborough Bay and some of the town's loveliest old homes.

You can rent skates from **Blades & Bikes Westshore** at 201 W Platt Street, ☎ 251-0178, for about $6 an hour. It's open daily with varying hours.

The downtown Tampa skyline rises above shrimp boats docked at Port Tampa.

WHERE TO EAT

Tampa stays on the cutting edge of cuisine trends and has carved out a reputation for its fine and eclectic dining. Some of the classics still remain the favorites, however, in this town of old and new.

The place to go for burgers is **Jimmie Mac's** at 113 S Armenia Ave, ☎ 879-0591, in its circa-1920s digs. Decide from a long roster of burgers, including turkey, vegetable, buffalo, Cajun, and other varieties; also grouper sandwiches, steaks, and desserts. It's open daily for lunch and dinner, then turns into a singles hang-out after-hours. Prices, $4-$14.

For that special night out, there is no other choice than **Bern's Steak House** at 1208 S Howard Ave, ☎ 251-2421, where steaks are cut, aged, and prepared to perfection. The main menu diversifies into other meats and seafoods, as well. The wine selection is renowned, as is the upstairs dessert parlor, with cozy TV-equipped booths and some 40 dessert selections. Count on a slow, enjoyable evening of fine dining. Entree prices start at $18.50. It's open daily for dinner. Reservations are required.

The Colonnade at 3401 Bayshore Blvd, ☎ 839-7558, is also a Tampa institution, and has been for more than 60 years. Open daily for lunch and dinner, it specializes in seafood and steak, with prices in the $10-$26 range and a terrific bay view.

Selena's at 1623 Snow Ave, ☎ 251-2116, has made a solid name for itself in the unlikely realm of Cajun-Italian cuisine. Open daily for lunch, dinner, and Sunday brunch, it exudes the charm of Old Hyde Park Village. At lunch, po-boy sandwiches, quiches, and other specialties are $4-$9. Pasta, chicken, steak, and veal dishes on the dinner menu are $7-$16. Reservations recommended for dinner.

WHERE TO STAY

Tampa Bay area visitors with a yearning for adventure typically park themselves in Tampa's northern regions or out on St. Petersburg's beaches (see Chapter III). If you want to or must stay in the inner city, downtown has plenty of rooms in all price categories.

Top-of-the-line **Wyndham Harbour Island Hotel** at 725 S Harbour Island Blvd on Harbour Island, ☎ 229-5000 or 800-822-4200, is close enough to all the downtown attractions, yet aloofly removed. Sports enthusiasts will be happy about guest privileges at the Harbour Island Athletic Club (fees charged), with 20 tennis courts, five racquetball courts, and two squash courts. A pool, marina, dining, and entertainment complete the amenities. Rates change according to availability; call for current quotes.

Holiday Inn – Ashley Plaza at 111 W Fortune Street, ☎ 223-1351 or 800-ASK-VALU, is more reasonably priced at $100-$164 for a room or suite in season; in the off-season, prices change with availability. Many of the rooms have a view of the river, plus you're within walking distance of downtown sights, particularly the Performing Arts Center.

SHOPPING

Old Hyde Park Village at Swann and Dakota avenues, ☎ 251-3500, is hip, trendy, scenic, with lots going on besides the upscale, name stores that line old streets. Shops open Monday-Saturday 10-6, Thursday and Friday until 9, and Sunday 12-5.

Across the channel from downtown center, **Harbour Island** has elite allure with posh dining, shopping, and housing. The People Mover (see *Basics*, above), takes you there from downtown, or you can drive across the bridge.

Ybor City

Ybor City emerged out of a puff of smoke in the 1890s. Here, Cuban immigrants from Key West settled to make a name for Tampa in the burgeoning cigar industry. Germans, Italians, and other nationalities came to work the factories and give the neighborhood a boom-time aura and distinctive flavor. The district and its cobbled streets have been trying for a couple of decades to recover from a slump that eventually made Ybor City rundown. The emergence is slow, but sure. It's gradually growing into a trendy shopping, nightclub, and dining zone. The resurgence of cigar smoking is helping and Ybor City seems to be thriving these days. This spells news both good and bad: the down-at-the-heels aura is diminishing, but so are the inexpensive Cuban and Italian cafés for which the community was once hailed. Alas, on my last visit, my favorite, the Silver Ring, once proclaimed purveyor of Ybor's best Cuban sandwich, was being turned into still another slick eatery!

BASICS

Ybor City lies basically within a rectangle created by Columbus Drive, Nebraska Avenue, Seventh Avenue, and 22nd Street. Seventh is "main street." Nebraska or 22nd will take you between Ybor and downtown. Off of Interstate 4 west, exit at #1.

INFORMATION

Contact the **Ybor City Chamber of Commerce** at 1800 E Ninth Ave, ☎ 248-3712. It's open weekdays 9-4.

SIGHTS & ATTRACTIONS

Historic cigar factories and workers' homes, many of them reborn as shops, art galleries, and restaurants, fill the 110-block Ybor City district.

The **Ybor City State Museum** at 1818 E Ninth Ave, ☎ 247-6323, surveys the political, social, and cultural factors in Spain, Cuba, and the US that influenced the district's boom era. It occupies an old bakery building, where Cuban bread was once baked. Hours are Tuesday-Saturday 9-noon and 1-5.

La Casita House Museum, at 1804 E Ninth Ave, sits among a row of six "shotgun" cottages (named for their straight-through design), typical of those where cigar factory workers lived circa 1895. This one is furnished. You'll find it in **Preservation Park**, a period reconstructed streetscape. Museum hours are 10-noon and 1-3 Tuesday-Saturday. Combined admission/tour for the Ybor City State Museum and La Casita is $2.

Tour the **Ybor City Brewing Company** at 2205 N 20th Street, ☎ 242-9222, a new arrival on the tour circuit, manufacturer of Ybor Gold beer. It occupies an 1890s cigar factory. Admission is by $2 donation; hours are 11-3 Tuesday-Saturday.

HIKING & BIKING

Stop at the Chamber of Commerce (see *Basics*, above) if you're interested in taking a self-guided walking tour of the area.

A free guided walking tour is available January-April, at 10:30 pm on Tuesday, Thursday, and Saturday; May-December on Thursday and Saturday. The tour takes about 1½ hours and departs from the lower level of Ybor Square (see Shopping, below) at 1901 N 13th Street.

WHERE TO EAT

Once an enclave of inexpensive Cuban sandwiches, black bean soup, Cuban coffee, and other ethnic staples, Ybor City is watching its dining scene turn yuppy. But there are a few hold-outs where the past is still palpable.

Ybor's most renowned restaurant, The **Columbia**, survives in rare form at 2117 E Seventh Ave, ☎ 248-4961. You can't miss it: gaily tiled and Mediterranean in form, it takes up a full city block. Inside, the rooms go on and on, each with its specific character. The main dining room is high ceilinged, with balconies and fountains. The Columbia, founded here in 1905, has spun off into locations throughout Florida, but this is the flagship. Along with its authentic Spanish-Cuban cuisine, it serves up live flamenco dancers Monday-Saturday. The restaurant is open daily for lunch and dinner. Dishes such as *paella, boliche, ropa vieja,* Spanish-style seafood, and chicken with yellow rice are $10-$17.

Also a historic landmark, **Café Creole & Oyster Bar** at 1440 E Ninth Ave, ☎ 247-6283, gives second life to an elite turn-of-the-century club.

Elegant red-brick archways and casual formality recall its heyday, when Teddy Roosevelt was a regular. Open daily for lunch and dinner, it's especially known for its Wednesday night crawfish and shrimp boils and jazz. Specialties smack of Cajun influence: crab cakes, crawfish étoufée, and jambalaya. Lunch prices are $6-$10; dinner prices, $9-$16.

La Tropicana at 1822 E Seventh Ave, ☎ 247-4040, hangs on to old Ybor traditions, with Cuban sandwiches for $3, black beans and rice for $2, and Cuban coffee for $1 or less. It's open for breakfast and lunch every day but Sunday.

On a trendier note, **The Spaghetti Warehouse** at Ybor Square, ☎ 248-1720, looks antiquish, the way some upscale chains do. It purveys standard Italian-style sandwiches and specialties, including spaghetti a dozen or so ways. Open daily for lunch and dinner, its prices are $5-$9.

WHERE TO STAY

Don't plan on staying right in Ybor City or you'll be disappointed. There's no place to stay. For lodging, check the other sections of this chapter. Downtown hotels are closest.

NIGHTLIFE

From flamenco dancers to cool Southern jazz, you'll find the full extent of music in Ybor City's thriving clubs, the heart of Tampa's nightlife.

Café Creole & Oyster Bar (see *Where to Eat*, above) at 1440 E Ninth Ave, ☎ 247-6283, is jazz headquarters, along with **Jazz Cellar** at Ybor Square, 1916 E Seventh Ave, ☎ 248-1862, which is open Friday and Saturday nights only. **Club Irie** at 2015 E Seventh Ave, ☎ 242-4743, specializes in reggae, while **Blues Ship Club & Café** at 1910 E Seventh Ave, ☎ 248-6097, plays live rhythm and blues. **The Irish Pub** at 1721 E Seventh Ave, ☎ 248-2099, sings a Celtic tune and the **Columbia** restaurant (see *Where to Eat*, above) at 2117 E Seventh Ave, ☎ 248-4961, features authentic flamenco dancers Monday-Saturday. Most clubs charge a cover.

SHOPPING

For art, crafts, antiques, and cigars, you'll want to head to Ybor City. Wander the streets or visit **Ybor Square** at Eighth Ave and 13th Street,

☎ 247-4497 – cigar-factories turned into a shopperia, listed on the National Register of Historic Places. It's open daily 10-6, Sunday noon-5:30. It also contains several restaurants.

Outlying Areas

BASICS

Interstates 275 and 4 zip you across Tampa's northern reaches. Columbus Drive and Martin Luther King Jr. Blvd make for a slower drive from west to east.

The northwest quadrant, part of Westshore, is home to Tampa International Airport and professional sports teams. Dale Mabry Highway (Highway 92) is the major north-south artery. The northeast quadrant lies across Interstate 275 on its way north. Nebraska Avenue (Highway 41) parallels it to the east. Busch Boulevard, Fowler Avenue, and Fletcher Avenue are roads you'll no doubt be spending time on in this part of town. They travel east-west.

To reach the southern towns of Hillsborough County, take either Highway 41 or Interstate 75, exits 47 and 46.

INFORMATION

For specific information about Ruskin and environs, contact the Ruskin Chamber of Commerce at 315 Tamiami Trail, Ruskin, FL 33570, ☎ 645-3808.

NORTHWEST TAMPA SIGHTS & ATTRACTIONS

Sports fans head in this direction, to the intersection of Dale Mabry Hwy and Martin Luther King Jr. Blvd, near the airport. Here, the **Tampa Stadium** hosts the National Football League's **Tampa Bay Buccaneers**, ☎ 872-7977, in winter, major league soccer's **Tampa Bay Mutiny**, ☎ 961-GOAL, beginning in April, and major league farm team, the **Tampa Bay Cyclones**, ☎ 985-5050, in summer. Call individual team lines for ticket information.

Nearby, the Yanks play March's spring exhibition games at the new **Legends Field**, ☎ 879-224 or 800-96-YANKS, which replicates the team's home field. In the off-season, there's rookie and semi-professional baseball. Tickets cost $3-$5.

Tampa's one saltwater beach, **Ben T. Davis Municipal Beach**, lies on the Courtney Campbell Causeway, ☎ 274-8615. Lifeguards are on duty during busy times, plus there's picnicking and good swimming and fishing.

To the north on Old Tampa Bay, **Upper Tampa Bay Park** at 8001 Double Branch Rd, off of Rte. 580, ☎ 855-1765, offers nature-lovers a peek into many biological communities, from oyster bars to freshwater ponds and oak hammocks. Its nature center has a saltwater aquarium and exhibits on snakes and other indigenous critters. A boardwalk runs along a bay view. The park is open daily 8-sunset.

Kids and animal-lovers especially like Tampa's oldest attraction, **Lowry Park Zoological Garden**, located at 7530 North Blvd, ☎ 932-0245. Its 24 acres have manatees, Florida panthers, Sumatran tigers, an Indian rhinoceros, and other exotic and native animals in their natural habitat, plus a petting zoo and amusement park rides. A new discovery center contains a walk-in globe with a video kaleidoscope and puppet theater. The park is open daily 9:30-5. Admission is $7.50 for adults, $6.50 for seniors, and $4.95 for children ages 3-11 – not including rides.

Next door, the **Children's Museum of Tampa**, ☎ 935-8441, has hands-on exhibits and a miniature outdoor city. Admission is $3 for ages 2 and older. Hours are 9-4:30 Monday-Thursday, 9-3 Friday, 10-5 Saturday, and 1-5 Sunday.

NORTHEAST TAMPA SIGHTS & ATTRACTIONS

On the east side of Interstate 275 at the Bird Street exit, **Tampa Greyhound Track**, ☎ 932-4313, holds evening races daily except Tuesday and Sunday, and matinees on Monday, Wednesday, and Saturday. Admission is $1-$2.50. No live racing takes place from January-June, but it remains open for simulcast wagering.

Tampa's number one attraction, **Busch Gardens** at 3000 Busch Blvd, ☎ 987-5082, requires a whole day to experience all of its 300 acres and various African lands, such as Egypt, Morocco, and Timbuktu. Each land contains its own theme adventure rides, shops, shows, and restaurants. African animals wander freely; you swoop over them by skyride or monorail. The Myombe Reserve features a gorilla area with plexiglass where visitors can "rub noses" with the beasts. There's free beer in the beer gardens, to steel your nerves for such roller-coasting terrors as the Kumba and the new Montu – the tallest and longest of its kind. Some of the rides will get you soaked, so bring extra clothes and rent a locker. Opened in the summer of 1997, Edge of Africa allows visitors a close up and personal wildlife experience. Adult admission is $34.95; for children 3-9, $28.95 (plus tax). Parking costs $4. Normal operation times are 9:30-6 daily, but hours are extended during summer and other select times.

Next door's **Adventure Island** at 10001 Malcolm McKinley Drive, ☎ 987-5600, is owned by Busch. It's one of the best of the water parks, with a Key West theme and attractions like the Splash Attack maze, the Endless Surf pool, Caribbean Corkscrew, and Tampa Typhoon. It's open 10-5 or longer, and closes November-March. Admission is $29.95 for adults, $19.95 for children 3-9 (tax extra). Parking costs $2.

As for discovery attractions, the **Museum of Science & Industry (MOSI)** at 4801 E Fowler Ave, ☎ 987-6100 or (800) 998-MOSI, tops the list and claims to be the largest science center in the Southeast US. Here you can explore some 450 exhibits dealing with weather, health, flight, space, and Florida's environment and natural history. The planetarium features daily star gazing. A unique domed theater shows 180° views of volcanoes, the planets, the Amazon Rain Forest, and other filmed natural phenomena. On more than three miles of nature trails, you can explore local habitat. Admission is $11 for adults, $9 for seniors and college students, and $7 for kids aged 2-12. Admission to

The Serengeti Plain, with the Crown Colony House restaurant, Busch Gardens.

the theater costs $4-$6; combination tickets are available. The museum is open 9-4:30 Sunday-Thursday and 9-9 Friday and Saturday.

Lettuce Lake Park at 6920 Fletcher Ave, ☎ 987-6204, occupies 240 acres with a cypress swamp, alligators, birds, a wildlife boardwalk, an observation tower, a bike path, a playground, a fitness course, and picnic areas. Donation of $1 per car suggested.

As you travel farther from city center, opportunity for adventure in a natural setting increases. **Tampa Outdoor Adventures** is a group of businesses that work collectively to offer visitors a range of exciting activities, including hot-air ballooning, fishing, canoeing, and float plane excursions. They are listed separately below, under *Fishing & Boating* and *Other Adventures*. For information on all, ☎ 223-2752 or 800-44-TAMPA, option 6.

SOUTH HILLSBOROUGH SIGHTS & ATTRACTIONS

A few steps south of the big city, rural agricultural communities are evolving into winter retirement enclaves. Quiet towns such as Apollo Beach, Ruskin, and Sun City, away from the mobile home parks and tomato fields, are fine places to launch a canoe or cast a rod into Hillsborough Bay.

In Apollo Beach, you can see manatees as they migrate to warmer waters in winter at **Tampa Electric's Manatee Viewing Center**, Big Bend and Dickman roads, ☎ 228-4289. An observation platform, educational displays, and a video familiarize visitors with the behavior of Florida's "gentle giants." It's open daily 10-5, November 18-April 6. Admission is free.

You can find good access to adventure at **E.G. Simmons Park** on 19th Ave NE, two miles west of Hwy 41, ☎ 671-7655. It has picnic facilities, a boat ramp, a sandy beach in the bay with roped-off swimming area, a campground, and wildlife areas. It closes at 5 pm.

FISHING & BOATING

Light Tackle Fishing Expeditions, part of Tampa Outdoor Adventures, ☎ 963-1930 or 800-44-TAMPA, option 6, tailors its outings to your fishing fantasies, ranging from four to eight hours and starting at $75 for a half-day, including beverages, tackle, and bait.

Canoe Escape, part of Tampa Outdoor Adventures, ☎ 986-2067 or 800-44-TAMPA, option 6, takes you on excursions into the Hillsborough River, where wildlife abounds close to city limits. It provides outfitting and shuttle service for two-hour to full-day excursions, priced at $26-$32 per double canoe (extra person, $8). Canoe owners pay $12-$17 for shuttle. Hours are weekdays 9-5 and weekends 8-6.

To kayak the river, contact the **Agua Azul Kayaks, ☎** 530-7555. It rents equipment and leads tours from Riverfront Park on Fletcher Ave. Single rentals cost $12.50 per hour, $35 per day. Tandems also available. Four-hour tours cost $42 each, including food and beverages.

You can also try navigating the river by crew rowing. The **University of Tampa's rowing team, ☎** 253-6281, teaches informal lessons at open sessions on Thursdays at 6 pm and Sundays at 9 am. The first lesson is free, and subsequent lessons cost $25 each.

The scenic **Alafia River** runs along the northern edge of south Hillsborough and is suited mainly to small crafts and canoes. The waterway runs east-west from Hillsborough Bay at Gibsonton. **Alafia Marine** at 9810 Vaughn in Gibsonton has a boat ramp you can use for a fee.

The **Little Manatee River** south of Ruskin is a designated canoe trail with paved ramps off of Hwy 41, three miles east of Ruskin.

Canoe Outpost on Hwy 301 in Wimauma, ☎ 634-2228 or 800-229-1371, outfits canoeists and kayakers for two-hour to overnight camping excursions on the Little Manatee, priced at $20-$56 including rentals, $10-$20 for shuttle service only.

E.G. Simmons Park (see *Sights & Attractions*, above) on 19th Ave NE, two miles west of Hwy 41, ☎ 671-7655, has a boat ramp into Hillsborough Bay.

To launch your craft into the Hillsborough River, use the ramp at **Lowry Park** (see *Northwest Sights & Attractions*, above), 750 North Blvd, for a nominal fee. There are also areas for fishing and picnicking there.

HIKING & BIKING

Museum of Science & Industry (MOSI) (see *Sights & Attractions*, above) at 4801 E Fowler Ave, ☎ 987-6300 or (800) 998-MOSI, has three miles of Back Woods trails where you can hike and experience local habitat.

Walkers, runners, cyclists, and skaters all take to the 2.2-mile trail in 126-acre **Al Lopez Park** at 4810 N Himes Ave.

You can take a leisurely hike around the cypress swamp wildlife boardwalk at **Lettuce Lake Park** (see *Northeast Tampa Sights & Attrac-*

tions), 6920 Fletcher Ave, ☎ 987-6204. It also has a bike path and fitness course. $1 donation per car suggested.

Eureka Springs on Eureka Springs Rd, near the junction of Interstate 4 and Hwy 301, ☎ 744-5536, has trails and boardwalks to hike, as well as a lovely botanical garden, greenhouse, and picnic area.

OTHER ADVENTURES

Vertical Ventures, near the airport at 5402E Pioneer Park Blvd, ☎ 884-ROCK, offers the thrill of rock climbing at an indoor gym. It caters to all levels of learners, from beginners to experts. A pro shop rents and sells equipment, and visitors can watch from a viewing deck. The gym is open Tuesday-Friday 3-10 and Saturday and Sun 9-5.

Big Red Balloon at 16302 E Course Drive, part of Tampa Outdoor Adventures, ☎ 969-1518 or 800-44-TAMPA, option 6, lifts off at sunrise for a four-hour, 1,000-foot-high view of Tampa's outlying wildlife and skyline. Prices begin at $135 for children, $150 for adults. Sunrise flights include champagne brunch.

 Sea Wings Aviation is part of Tampa Outdoor Adventures, ☎ 963-1930 or 800-44-TAMPA, option 6. Its sky-high sightseeing excursions run $54-$150 for 20 minutes to an hour in a three-seat float plane.

WHERE TO EAT

For top-shelf dining, make your reservations at **Armani's** in the Hyatt Regency Westshore at 6200 Courtney Campbell Causeway, ☎ 281-9165. Exquisite views and superb northern Italian-style seafood and other specialties, including a large antipasto bar, are the draws. A jacket is required. It's open for dinner daily except Sunday. Entrées are $15-$27.

If your idea of atmosphere is junkyard chic, you'll love **Skipper's Smoke House** at Skipper Rd and Nebraska Ave, ☎ 971-0666. Particularly if you favor plain, ungarnished seafood. Slurp "sliders" in the oyster bar or relish Black Bean Gator Chili and other Florida and Cajun specialties, ranging in price from $5-$14. It's open for lunch and dinner daily except Monday.

Wieners are an artform at **Mel's Hot Dogs**, 4136 E Busch Blvd, ☎ 985-8000. Select from a classic Chicago-style dog, a bagel dog, bacon dog, corn dog, and others. Wash it down with a beer, wine, or soda. Prices run $3-$7.

WHERE TO STAY

Hotels cluster near the airport on Tampa Bay at Courtney Campbell Causeway and around Busch Gardens. Most are the chain variety, with everything from budget to luxury.

Near the airport, **Hampton Inn** at 4817 W Laurel Street, ☎ 287-0778 or 800-HAMPTON, is a good value, with complimentary continental breakfast, a heated swimming pool, and free local airport and local restaurant shuttle. Rates in season are $82-$90, and off-season $70-82.

Tampa Airport Hilton at Metrocenter, 2225 N Lois Ave, ☎ 877-6688 or 800-445-8667, offers more luxury at $89-$329 in season for a room or suite. It has a restaurant, bar, pool, hot tub, tennis, and airport shuttle.

Doubletree Guest Suites at 3050 N Rocky Point Drive W, ☎ 888-8800 or 800-222-TREE, gives you a water view for your money. It's located at the Courtney Campbell Causeway and charges $155 in season, with lower off-season rates. Amenities include airport shuttle, pool, whirlpool, sauna, exercise room, and business center. Its 203 suites are designed with separate bedroom and living areas.

To stay close to northeast-side attractions, try the **Holiday Inn-Busch Gardens** at 2701 E Fowler Ave, ☎ 971-4710 or 800-99-BUSCH. It and its pool are popular with families, which can make it somewhat noisy at times. Rates for a room or suite are $80-$260 in season, $60-$200 in the off-season.

Outside of Tampa to the north, **Saddlebrook Resort** at 5700 Saddlebrook Resort, Wesley Chapel, ☎ 973-1111 or 800-237-7519, is a destination in itself, especially for golfers and sports-lovers. It offers 36 holes of golf (with another course on the way), three swimming pools, 45 tennis courts, volleyball, basketball, lawn games, a fitness center, and a spa and sauna, along with a kids program and a variety of dining options. Rates in season range $215 for a room to $360 for a two-bedroom suite; off-season, $105-$325. Ask about packages.

CAMPING

E.G. Simmons Park (see *Sights & Attractions*, above) on 19th Ave NE, two miles west of Hwy 41, ☎ 671-7655, has an open campground with a view of the bay. Fees are $12 a night including electricity.

NIGHTLIFE

Skipper's Smoke House (see *Where to Eat*, above) at Skipper Rd and Nebraska Ave, ☎ 971-0666, has established itself as THE place for alternative music in the Tampa Bay area. Live reggae, zydeco, and blues bands play open-air in the backyard of the ramshackle restaurant, nightly except Sunday. Cover charge varies.

Chapter V

Bradenton/Sarasota

Area code: 941

Though distinctly individual in character, the metropolitan areas of Bradenton and Sarasota often get lumped together. The two do sort of melt into one another geographically, but anyone who has gotten to know the cities can feel immediately when they've crossed the boundaries. This is demonstrated most dramatically on Longboat Key, a 12-mile island split between Sarasota County and Bradenton's Manatee County. In Bradenton's northern half, you find an old fishing village with easygoing seafood restaurants and beach cottages. In the Sarasota portion, everything climbs several steps upscale and manicured landscaping exalts the island's prima donna status.

So while northern Bradenton and its islands of Anna Maria and Longboat Key exude something more casually old-Florida, Sarasota and its string of island pearls affect utter sophistication, save for Siesta Key, with its strains of beachy, subtropic island behavior.

Bradenton and Sarasota each trace their identity back to a male historic figure. In Bradenton, it's none other than Hernando De Soto, whom historians claim made his first New World landfall on local shores. As a result, Bradenton has a propensity for preserving history. Its Manatee River, Gulf front, and Intracoastal bays offer ample scope for watersports.

Sarasota owes its development and artistic reputation to, ironically, the circus, which wintered there beginning in the late 1800s. In contrast to circus raucousness, however, John Ringling was a man swayed by esthetics. The art he loved had a bit of three-ring showiness to it, nonetheless, as shown by the baroque Italianate palace he built himself in Sarasota. It comprises, along with his art museum complex, Sarasota's most renowned attraction. Ringling is also responsible for building bridges – with his circus elephants, it is told – to Sarasota's cherished islands, the West Coast's most exclusive. On Sarasota's islands, you'll find a world-class shopping arena, the coast's whitest beach, a premium marine laboratory, nature parks and beaches, and a love for the sea and its pleasures.

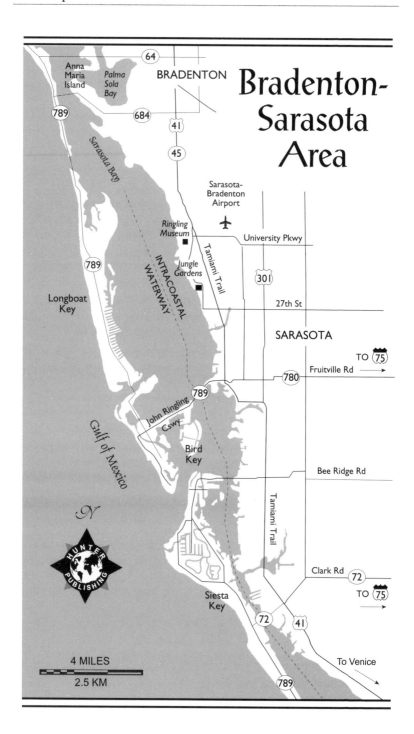

Bradenton-Sarasota Area

At the southern reaches of Sarasota County, Venice hides in the shadow of its neighbor. Along with nearby communities of Osprey, Casey Key, Nokomis, and Nokomis Beach, it has much to offer seafarers and adventurous landlubbers on its Myakka River and Gulf front, and in its unexploited parks and beaches.

TRANSPORTATION, ETC.

Sarasota-Bradenton International Airport (SRQ), ☎ 359-2770, is situated in Bradenton, three miles north of Sarasota. Major domestic airlines include **American Eagle,** ☎ 800-433-7300, **Continental,** ☎ 800-525-0280, **Delta,** ☎ 800-221-1212, **Northwest,** ☎ 800-225-2525, **TWA,** ☎ 800-221-2000; **United,** ☎ 800-241-6522, and **USAir,** ☎ 800-428-4322.

Rental cars are available at the airport and other locations throughout the area. They include **Alamo,** ☎ 359-5540 or 800-327-9633, **Avis,** ☎ 359-5240 (airport), 795-0014 (Bradenton), or 800-331-1212, **Hertz,** ☎ 335-8848 (airport) or 800-654-3131, and **Budget,** ☎ 359-5353 (airport) or 800-527-0700.

Taxi companies that provide transportation to and from the airport include **Airport Shuttle Service,** ☎ 355-9645, **Diplomat Taxi,** ☎ 355-5155, **West Coast Executive Sedans,** ☎ 359-8600, or **Longboat Limousine,** ☎ 383-1235 or 800-LB-LIMO-1.

Highway 41 (Tamiami Trail) cuts close to the coastline in Bradenton and Sarasota, and takes you straight into downtown Sarasota. Highway 301 parallels 41 to the east through Bradenton. The two converge in Sarasota. Interstate 75 swings wide from the coast here, to the east of Highway 41.

For information on the area, call or write the **Manatee County Convention & Visitors Bureau** at PO Box 1000, Bradenton, FL 34206, ☎ 729-9177 or 800-4 MANATEE. Its welcome center is located off Interstate 75, exit number 43, and is open daily 8:30-5:30. Or contact the **Sarasota Convention & Visitors Bureau** at 655 N Tamiami Trail, Sarasota, FL 34236, ☎ 957-1877 or 800-522-9799, open Monday-Friday from 9-5.

EVENTS

Cortez Commercial Fishing Festival on Rte. 684 in Cortez, ☎ 795-4637, takes place on one day in late February, and consists of food vendors, country music, arts and crafts with a nautical theme, net-mending demonstrations, and educational exhibits describing Cortez's 100-year-old fishing industry.

For four days in March, the Ringling Estate (see *Sarasota Sights & Attractions*, below) hosts the wildly popular and artistically done **Medieval Fair, ☎** 355-5101.

In April, Bradenton's entire Manatee County celebrates its past during **Florida Heritage Month, ☎** 747-1998. A reenactment of Hernando DeSoto's 1539 landing highlights the events.

April also brings **Siesta Key Sand Sculpture Contest, ☎** 316-1268.

Head to Sarasota's islands to watch **The Suncoast Offshore Grand Prix, ☎** 955-9009, a national attraction that draws powerboat racers from around the world for Fourth of July week.

In Venice, the big event every August is the **Sharks Tooth & Seafood Festival, ☎** 488-2236, which means music, seafood, shark tooth scavenges, and marine life displays.

Bradenton

After Spanish explorer Hernando De Soto left his mark here in 1539, then continued on his way to discover the Mississippi River, Bradenton remained wild and unsettled until the sugar plantations of the 1840s and the cattle industry of the 1880s established themselves.

Some find Bradenton too sleepy to be fun. If you're a history buff, you'll refute that. But if you're looking for action, you'll head to the beaches or Sarasota.

Bradenton's outlying towns, particularly Palmetto and Ellenton, are more suited to adventure than Bradenton itself. Both of the above-mentioned lie north of Bradenton, on the opposite bank of the Manatee River.

Cortez juts into bay waters southwest of town. Its peninsular location catalyzed its development as a fishing town with lots of flavor and local color.

BASICS

Interstate exit 43 takes you along the north side of the Manatee River via Highway 30. At exit 42, Route 64 travels straight into downtown and to Anna Maria Island. Exit 41 follows Route 70 through the south part of town. Highways 41 and Business 41 stab through town's center. Highways 301 and 41 merge in the north, then split south of town.

The Manatee Cat transit system, ☎ 749-7116, travels around Bradenton, Palmetto, Cortez, Anna Maria, and Longboat Key. Basic fare is $1 for adults, 50¢ for seniors and children.

INFORMATION

Call or write for more information: **Manatee Chamber of Commerce,** 222 10th Street W, Bradenton, FL 34205, ☎ 748-3411. It's open Monday-Friday 9-5.

BRADENTON SIGHTS & ATTRACTIONS

Bradenton bygones are preserved in a shady park setting at **Manatee Village Historical Park**, 15th Street E and Sixth Ave E, ☎ 749-7165. Buildings of local historical significance include a circa 1860 county courthouse, church, Cracker farmhouse, one-room schoolhouse, smokehouse, and general store. Staff don period dress. Admission is free; hours are weekdays 9-4:30 and Sundays 1-4. The park closes Saturdays and Sundays during July and August. This is a great place for a cool picnic in the past.

Downtown's devotion to history is evident in its rejuvenating streets and old buildings, and at the **South Florida Museum**, 201 10th Street W, ☎ 746-4131. Displays cover local history through the eras of native Americans, Spanish conquistadors, and space exploration. Kids like the resident manatee, aquarium, and hands-on activity center. The **Bishop Planetarium**, ☎ 746-4131, adjoins the facility and hosts laser shows and children's programs in its 50-foot hemispherical dome. The museum and planetarium open Monday-Saturday 10-5 in winter, Sunday 12-5, and close Mondays May-Dec. 26. Admission for adults is $6; for children ages 5-12, $3.50.

To honor Bradenton's trademark historical event, the **De Soto National Memorial Park** at 75th Street NW, ☎ 792-0458, recalls the life and times of explorer Hernando De Soto – who is said to have made first New World landfall here – through displays, a film, an audio-narrated mangrove trail, and living history guides (in season only). The park also offers a lovely, out-of-the-way view of Old Florida and the Manatee River. Admission is free; hours are 9-5 daily.

OUTLYING SIGHTS & ATTRACTIONS

East of Interstate 75, **Lake Manatee State Recreation Area** at 20007 Rte. 64, ☎ 741-3028, provides an opportunity for communing with nature in 556 acres of wildlife habitat. You can swim in the freshwater lake (but beware of alligators), launch or rent a boat, fish, and picnic on grounds with a play area. Admission is $2 per vehicle, $1 for pedestrians and bicyclists.

Take a yesteryear trip into Bradenton's wilderness aboard the **Florida Gulf Coast Railroad Museum**, stationed in the east-side town of Parrish, ☎ 377-4016. Trains run Saturday and Sunday. Trips of an hour and 15 minutes duration cost $8 for adults, $5 for children.

De Soto Speedway, eight miles east of the interstate on Rte. 64, ☎ 748-3171, hosts Saturday night stock car racing February through November on a paved oval track. Call for current schedule and ticket prices.

Gamble Mansion.

To explore Bradenton's sugar-coated past, visit a masterfully restored sugar manor at the **Gamble Plantation State Historical Site** on Rte. 301 west of the interstate, ☎ 723-4536. Besides its former life as home for a sugar lord and the town's social center, you'll hear how the Greek-revival mansion, built in 1840, sheltered the Confederate Secretary of State as he fled for his life after the Civil War. Visitors can see the home by tour only, 8-5 Thursday-Monday. Tour times are 9:30, 10:30, 1, 2, 3, and 4 pm. Admission is $3 for adults, $1.50 for children ages 6-12.

Baseball fans can watch a professional team in action in March when the Pittsburgh Pirates play their spring exhibition season at **McKechnie Field**, Ninth Street and 17th Ave W, ☎ 748-4610. While in town, they practice from 10-1:30 at **Pirate City**, 1701 27th Street E, ☎ 747-3031.

FISHING & BOATING

You can fish for free from the **Bradenton City Pier** on Bridge Street Otherwise, most fishing and boating activity takes place on the islands or on the mainland at a fishing village named Cortez. Land and wading fishermen favor **Palma Sola Causeway** at Palma Sola Bay and Rte. 64, which heads from the mainland to Anna Maria Island.

For freshwater fishing, try **Lake Manatee State Recreation Area** (see *Sights & Attractions*, above) at 20007 Rte. 64, ☎ 741-3028. Flat-bottom boats rent for $5 an hour, $20 a day. Huge Lake Manatee, a dammed portion of the Manatee River, yields bass, perch, catfish, and other freshwater species. It has a boat ramp and fishing dock. Boat motors are restricted to 20 horsepower or less.

Miss Cortez Fleet at 4330 127th Street W in Cortez, ☎ 794-1223, has a well-established reputation for its fishing and sightseeing charters, which last from four hours to a day. Four-hour deep-sea fishing trips cost $25 for adults, $22 for seniors, $12.50 for children under age 12. Their four-hour cruises to Egmont Key (see Chapter III), cost $14, $12, and $8.

Annie's Bait & Tackle, open daily at 4334 127th Street W in Cortez, ☎ 794-3580, supplies fishermen, rents tackle, and arranges fishing charters.

The Seafood Shack Showboat Dinner Cruise at 4110 127th Street W, ☎ 794-5048, takes a scenic tour enlivened by entertainment and a cocktail bar. For the 1½-hour cruise, adults pay $12, children ages 4-11 pay $5; for the three-hour cruise, rates are $16 and $6. Cruises depart from the Seafood Shack restaurant every afternoon except Saturday.

To launch your own boat, proceed to **Palma Sola Causeway** at Palma Sola Bay and Rte. 64, where you'll find plenty of watersports activity.

Cortez Watercraft Rentals at the Cortez bridge, ☎ 792-5263, rents 21-foot pontoon boats for $99 a half-day, $155 a full day. Jet ski rentals begin at $35. It's open daily 8:30-6.

Manatee Airboat Tours at Perico Harbour Marina on Manatee Ave, ☎ 730-1011, zips you into manatee and wildlife habitat. Rides cost $12 per adult, $10 per child.

Canoeing adventures can last a half-day, whole day, or overnight at **Ray's Canoe Hideaway**, 1247 Hagle Park Rd, ☎ 747-3909. Canoe rentals run $7-$14; passengers under age 12 are charged $2; boat launching costs $3. Expeditions follow the Upper Manatee River, rich with lore, fish, and birdlife. Fishing pole rental is available. The facility closes Tuesday and Wednesday.

OTHER WATERSPORTS

Palma Sola Causeway Beach, on Rte. 64 heading to Anna Maria Island, is popular with windsurfers and waverunner operators, who can launch from the causeway's boat ramp. There are also restrooms and a picnic area.

WHERE TO EAT

The locals' favorite downtown is **The Pier** at Memorial Pier, 1200 First Ave W, ☎ 748-8087, known especially for its lunch buffet and Sunday brunch. Situated on the town's historic pier, it features large windows looking onto the water, a saltwater aquarium, a sporty-historic atmosphere, and reasonable prices: $6-$12 for lunch, $10-$19 for dinner entrées. Menu selections range from downhome (pot roast) to continental (red snapper meunière). It's open daily for lunch and dinner.

Crab Trap II at 4815 Memphis Rd, ☎ 729-7777, dresses in rustically tropical guises and sells Florida specialties such as 'gator tail, perch, crab, and other seafood. It's open daily for lunch ($6-$11) and dinner ($10-35).

WHERE TO STAY

As for lodging on the mainland, Bradenton offers nothing spectacular. Near the airport, you'll find the usual business-chain array. If you want something close to downtown, try the 150-room **Quality Inn & Suites** at 2303 First Street E, ☎ 747-6465 or 800-447-6465. Comfortable, clean, and convenient, it has a bar, playground, and reasonable rates: $65-$90 for a room or efficiency in season; $45-$75 in the off-season.

Holiday Inn Riverfront at Hwy 41 and Manatee Ave, ☎ 747-3727 or 800-23-HOTEL, has more atmosphere: Mission-style architecture, a river view, a courtyard pool with gardens and waterfalls. It has a restaurant, bar, and whirlpool besides. Peak season rates are $99-$129 for a room or suite; in the off-season, rates go down but vary day by day according to demand. It's best to call for an exact quote.

CAMPING

Many of the area campgrounds are designed for retired winter residents and don't allow children except as visitors. If you have kids, call first and ask if they are welcome.

Lake Manatee State Recreation Area (see *Sights & Attractions*, above) at 20007 Rte. 64, ☎ 741-3028, has 60 scrubby campsites and does accept families. Campsites start at $8.

You'll find several campgrounds in and around Palmetto, including **Frog Creek Campground** at 8515 Bayshore Rd, ☎ 722-6154. You can fish the creek or play shuffleboard and horseshoes. Tent camping allowed. Year-round rate for RVs with full hook-up is $28 a day; for tents, $25. Weekly and monthly rates available.

Sarasota Bay Travel Trailer Park at 10777 44th Ave W, ☎ 794-1200 or 800-247-8361, is another retiree camp, located on the bay with full RV hook-ups, a boat ramp and dock, fishing, horseshoes, exercise room, recreation hall, and entertainment. Daily rates for full hook-up are $25-$28.

Anna Maria Island

The largest of the Bradenton-Sarasota islands, it has three distinct communities. Northernmost Anna Maria has a casual air about it, along with a great public fishing pier, and some fun fish houses and bars. Holmes Beach, to the south, is more upscale, while Bradenton Beach, with its beach shops, sometimes borders on tacky but has some historic feel to it as well. The best beaches are at Holmes Beach and Bradenton Beach.

BASICS

Route 64 (exit 42 off of Interstate 75) intersects with Highway 41 and heads across the island's north bridge to Holmes Beach. From the south, take interstate exit 41 and follow Route 70 to Highway 41. Turn north on Highway 41, then west on Route 684, which takes you across the south bridge. Both bridges connect to Gulf Drive (Route 789), the island's major thoroughfare.

In Anna Maria, follow Pine Avenue and Bay Boulevard to find the town's sights. In Holmes Beach, Marina Drive takes you away from commercial traffic and along the Gulf.

In Bradenton Beach, Bridge Street is the center of the town's historic district. South of it, Route 789 connects to Longboat Key.

INFORMATION

For local information, call, write, or visit the **Anna Marie Island Chamber of Commerce** P.O. Box 1892, Holmes Beach 34218, ☎ 778-1541. Hours are Monday-Friday 9-5.

SIGHTS & ATTRACTIONS

Bayfront Park on Bay Blvd at Anna Maria's north end, rounds the tip of the island Gulf to bay, and stays relatively uncrowded. It offers picnic facilities, a playground, recreational opportunities, and a magnificent view of St. Petersburg's Sunshine Skyway Bridge (see Chapter III).

Small and intimate, the **Anna Maria Island Historical Museum** at 402 Pine Ave, ☎ 778-0492, keeps photographs, maps, records, books, a shell collection, a turtle display, and vintage videos in an old ice house. Next to it, the old jail house is a colorful sight. Admission is free; donations are accepted. It's open 10-1 May-September, 10-4 the rest of the year. It closes Monday, Friday, and Sunday.

In Holmes Beach, **Manatee County Park** on Gulf Drive and Rte. 64 is fun and sunny, with a playground, picnicking, lifeguards, a snack bar, showers, and a fishing pier.

Equally popular **Coquina Beach** lies in Bradenton Beach at the south end of Gulf Drive, and wraps around Gulf and bay. Here, beachers enjoy picnic areas, concessions, boat ramps, good snorkeling, a playground, lifeguards, and lots of shady Australian pine trees.

FISHING & BOATING

Along with the coast's usual complement of fish, Gulf waters around Bradenton are known as Jewfish Country. The huge fish school in great numbers around area wrecks and ledges.

Anna Maria City Pier at the northeast end of **Bayfront Park** (see *Sights & Attractions*, above) on Bay Blvd extends 700 feet into Anna Maria Sound and has food and bait concessions.

Rod & Reel Pier at 875 North Shore Drive in Anna Maria, ☎ 778-1885, has a café and bait shop. Admission is $1.25 for adults, $1 for kids ages 8-12.

In Bradenton Beach, a former bridge forms the T-shaped **Bradenton Beach City Pier** on Bridge Street. It reaches into intracoastal waters and holds a restaurant and bait house. Fee for fishing is 50¢ each (kids ages 12 and under free). You can walk on the pier for free.

Fishermen also cast off the bridge between Bradenton Beach and Longboat Key.

On the bay side of **Coquina Beach** (see *Sights & Attractions*, above) on Gulf Drive in Bradenton Beach, you'll find boat ramps and other facilities.

Rent power and pontoon boats at **Bradenton Beach Marina** at 402 Church Ave, ☎ 778-2288. Half-day rates are $135; full day, $185. Gas and tax are extra.

Bradenton Beach Sailboat Rentals at 1325 Gulf Drive, ☎ 778-4969, gives free sailing lessons with its rentals, which are $25-$35 an hour for G Cats. It also rents three-seat waverunners from $60 an hour.

Spice Sailing Charters at Galati Yacht Basin in Anna Maria, ☎ 778-3240, whisks you off on a sea breeze to Egmont Key (see Chapter III) for a half-day ($25 each) or sunset ($20) cruise. Prices include complimentary soft drinks. Sailing lessons are offered aboard the 27-foot vessel.

Oceanbound Kayak Shop at 5501 Marina Drive at Captain's Marina in Holmes Beach, ☎ 778-5883, rents solo and tandem kayaks. Two- to six-hour rentals and custom tours are available. Single rates begin at $12 for one hour; $15 for tandems. Sunrise and sunset guided tours cost $30 per person.

SNORKELING & DIVING

A sunken sugar barge and a close-to-shore ledge provide fascinating beach dives at **Coquina Beach** (see *Sights & Attractions*, above) at the south end of Bradenton Beach. Other wrecks and ledges lie 10 to 19 miles from shore. Look for gigantic jewfish.

SeaTrek Divers at 105 Seventh Street N in Bradenton Beach, ☎ 779-1506, leads two-tank, offshore dives for $50 each. Snorkel trips to Egmont Key (see Chapter III) cost $30 each. The store, which is open Monday-Saturday 10-6 and Sunday 9-4, also rents diving and snorkeling gear, plus teaches certification courses.

OTHER WATER ADVENTURES

Longboat Pass Parasail at 4110-A 127th Street W in Cortez, ☎ 792-1900, offers thrilling rides up to 1,200 feet, towed from the beach by an offshore racing boat. Rates run $35-$45 for about a 10-minute glide.

WHERE TO EAT

You'll find a delightful array of beach restaurants, local eateries, fish houses, and dressy dining in the three Anna Maria Island communities.

A great place to go for lunch is **The Sandbar**, beachside at 100 Spring Ave in Anna Maria, ☎ 778-0444. Get a deck table and watch the water world go by while you munch lobster salad or a seafood sandwich. It's open daily and also serves dinner. Prices for lunch are $6-$10; for dinner, $6-$22.

For typical Florida fish-house ambiance and food, try **Rotten Ralph's**, near the pier at 902 S Bay Blvd in Anna Maria, ☎ 778-3953. It straddles a dock within a marina, and serves fried seafood, steamed seafood pots, meat pies, sandwiches, and salads. Entrée prices run $5-$16. It's open daily for lunch and dinner.

The **Bridge Street Café** at 200 Bridge Street, ☎ 779-1706, serves the best breakfast around and in the best venue. Humble but lovable, it straddles the historic city pier, with some seating inside but the most scenic is out on the pier under umbrellas. It is also open daily for lunch and dinner, specializing in burgers and fried seafood baskets. Standard breakfast items cost $2-$5, burgers $4-$6 and seafood dishes around $7. The ultimate combination seafood platter costs $15.

WHERE TO STAY

There's much to choose from for lodging on Anna Maria Island. You can rent a home or condo, sequester yourself in historic B&B charm, or stay in the midst of beachdom bustle.

Rod & Reel Motel at 677 N Shore Drive, ☎ 778-2780, is tailor-made for fishing folks. Its 10 efficiencies are set on the shores of Tampa Bay, where a nice, long pier accommodates. Rates in season run $69-$108; off-season, $49-$82.

The island's most charming option, **Harrington House B&B** at 5626 Gulf Drive in Holmes Beach, ☎ 778-5444, is one of Florida's few beachfront B&Bs. Added to that are its history and casual elegance. The one cottage and each of seven main-house rooms and four beach-house rooms has its own bath, fridge, TV, and antique pieces. A dramatic cut-stone fireplace dominates the sitting room. Guests have free use of kayaks and bicycles. Rates run $129-$189 in high season, on holidays, and on weekends; $99-$139 in low-demand periods.

In Bradenton Beach, **Duncan House B&B** at 1703 Gulf Drive, ☎ 778-6858, is also historic, situated in an 1800s home that was moved to the beach from downtown Bradenton. A tropical color scheme and carved flourishes give it a whimsical personality. Cheery guest rooms, some with separate entryways, have private baths. It sits across the road from the beach, but has deeded access. Rates are $70-$90.

For rental homes and condos, contact **Betsy Hills Real Estate** at 419 Pine Ave, Anna Maria, ☎ 778-2291. Monthly rates range from $1,000 to $4,500. Weeklies available on some properties.

Longboat Key

A lovely, well-heeled island, Longboat Key has little to offer in the way of sights. Its public beaches are unspectacular. It provides pretty passage between Anna Maria Island and the islands to the south. Its marinas supply water adventure and its bike path offers exercise for scenery-gazers. The superlatives are reserved for its dining. Die-hard shoppers might enjoy browsing the pricey boutiques, but shopping is not covered separately here because the choices in Sarasota and its islands are so much better.

BASICS

Not directly connected to the mainland, Longboat Key can be reached by bridges from its northern and southern neighbors along Route 789, which here takes the extended name Gulf of Mexico Drive.

INFORMATION

Information is available from **Longboat Key Chamber of Commerce** at 5360 Gulf of Mexico Drive, Ste. 107, Longboat Key, FL 34228, ☎ 383-2466. It's open 9-5 Monday-Friday.

SIGHTS & ATTRACTIONS

Be sure to turn east off the north end of Gulf of Mexico Drive onto Broadway Street and visit **The Village**, Longboat Key's original settlement, where you'll find old-island spirit, a couple of great seafood restaurants, and wild peacocks roaming the streets.

FISHING & BOATING

The bridge at Longboat Key's northern end, spanning Longboat Pass towards Anna Maria Island, is a popular fishing spot.

For captained charters, bareboat adventures, and party cruises, contact **Spindrift Yacht Services** at 410 Gulf of Mexico Drive, ☎ 383-7781. Half-day offshore fishing excursions run $275-$400, according to vessel capacity. Bay fishing charters cost $230. Six-passenger cruises cost $250 for a half-day. Sailing ventures for six cost $200-$250.

Cannons Marina at 6400 Gulf of Mexico Drive, ☎ 383-1311 or 800-437-8865, rents out top-quality fishing boats, skiffs, and deck boats. Half-day rates are $50-$220; full day, $65-$290. Gas and tax are extra. It also rents tackle and water skis, and sells bait, tackle, and other supplies.

HIKING & BIKING

Cyclists slice through the 12-mile-long island's center along the paved bike path on Gulf of Mexico Drive. It's a flat, easy, scenic drive, flowered and manicured.

Rent your ride at **Backyard Bike Shop**, 5610 Gulf of Mexico Drive, ☎ 383-5184. Its selection of mountain, hybrid, beach, tandem, and BMX bikes rent for $7-$10 for a day, $25-$35 for a week. Skate rentals cost $5 per hour, $10 per day, $40 per week.

WHERE TO EAT

Dining is an art on Longboat Key. Either you do it sleeves rolled-up with gusto, or with pinkies extended while relishing haute cuisine.

To do the former, visit The Village (see *Sights & Attractions*, above), which contains two unpretentious restaurants long loved by locals and those visitors who have discovered them. **Mar-Vista Dockside Restaurant & Pub** at 760 Broadway Street, ☎ 383-2391, occupies a cozily a-kilter little building one could almost call a shack. Sit at the bar and tell fishing lies with the locals. You can also sit outside open-air overlooking the boat dockage or inside at a mismatched assortment of tables. The fish is squeaky fresh and fixed in a variety of appealing ways. It's open for lunch ($4-$8) and dinner ($5-$15) daily.

Nearby, **Moore's Stone Crab Restaurant** at 800 Broadway Street, ☎ 383-1748, specializes in stone crabs, only in season mid-October to mid-May. Other times and other dishes reflect Southern influences and Florida catches. Main courses are $9-$20. It's open daily for lunch and dinner.

The list of fine restaurants could go on for pages. For the splurge of a vacation (maybe of a lifetime), do **Euphemia Haye** at 5540 Gulf of Mexico Drive, ☎ 383-3633, unique and charming. Local products are prepared in international style with stunning results. The setting is boutique and intimate. Dishes like Grecian lamb shank and sea scallops in black bean sauce begin at $20, à la carte. Upstairs in the Haye Loft, the selection of desserts and coffees dazzles the mind and blows the diet. It's open daily for dinner. Reservations are recommended.

The Colony Dining Room at Colony Beach and Tennis Resort, 1620 Gulf of Mexico Drive, ☎ 383-5558, also has an impeccable reputation for serving the finest daily, for lunch, dinner, and Sunday brunch. It gets special acclaim for its wine list. The beach reaches up to the walls and their generous windows. Dishes are based on continental classicism, with creative nuances, all executed exquisitely. For lunch you'll pay $9-$11 for salads, sandwiches, and entrées. A la carte dinner prices for dishes like plantain-wrapped mahi mahi and slow-roasted duckling range from $19 to $29. Dinner reservations are required.

WHERE TO STAY

From beach cottages to grand high-rise resorts, Longboat Key offers it all. Most of its lodging you'll find on the Gulf or the bay, with ready access to adventure.

For fun on the beach, check into the **Holiday Inn Holidome** at 4949 Gulf of Mexico Drive, ☎ 383-3771 or 800-465-4436. It has an outdoor swimming pool (and kiddie pool), and one indoors under the Holidome. Outdoor recreation includes a wide beach, sailboat rentals, four lighted tennis courts, and a beach bar. There's also an indoor rec center, sauna, bars, and restaurants. Rooms and suites are $165-$250 in high season; $118-210 in low, with shoulder season rates in between.

The Colony Beach & Tennis Resort at 1620 Gulf of Mexico Drive, ☎ 383-6464 or 800-237-9443, is perfect for beach-lovers, tennis-players, and dining aficionados. It boasts 21 soft and hard tennis courts, a nice stretch of beach, a small but complete spa, top-rated restaurants (see *Where to Eat*, above), and a complete kids program. Rates for suites in peak season are $300-$450; in low season, $180-$420. Shoulder season rates, packages, and other room options available.

Serious sportsfolk will find bliss at **The Resort at Longboat Key Club**, 301 Gulf of Mexico Drive, ☎ 383-8821, US 800-237-8821, or FL 800-282-0113. The list of activities is practically endless: one 18-hole and three nine-hole golf courses, two tennis centers with 38 Har-Tru courts, bicycles, rafts, sailboats, boogie boards, kayaks, snorkeling gear, an Olympic-size swimming pool, jogging and biking paths, an exercise track, a health club, and a kid's club. Rates in the 232 guest rooms, club suites and one- and two-bedroom suites range $205-$715 in peak season, $115-$615 the rest of the year. (All suites have fully equipped kitchens.)

To rent privately owned homes and condos on Longboat Key and neighboring islands, contact **The Longboat Connection** at 3720 Gulf of Mexico Drive, ☎ 387-9707 or 800-469-4852. Monthly rates in high season range $1,400-$4,600; in off-season, $600-$2,200; in pre-season (mid-November to mid-January), $1,000-$3,800. Some weekly rentals available.

Lido Key/St. Armands Key

BASICS

The northern approach to Lido Key passes through Anna Maria Island and Longboat Key along Route 789. On Lido Key, Route 789 is called John Ringling Parkway. At St. Armands Circle, John Ringling Boule-

Lido Key.

vard/Causeway forms the western and eastern spokes; Boulevard of the Presidents heads south, then jogs into Benjamin Franklin Drive.

From Sarasota's south side, you can get to St. Armands Key, which is tucked into Lido Key's bayside belly, by crossing the John Ringling Causeway (Route 780), which branches off of Highway 41 (Tamiami Trail) from the mainland. From Interstate 75, take exit 39 (Fruitville Rd) or exit 38 (Bee Ridge Rd) to Highway 41 and follow the signs across the Ringling Causeway.

SIGHTS & ATTRACTIONS

Just north and east of the bridge from Longboat Key on Ken Thompson Parkway, City Island holds several eco-attractions for nature enthusiasts. The first, **Sarasota Bay Walk** at 1550 Ken Thompson Pkwy, ☎ 361-6133, takes you on a self-guided tour of the bay, estuaries, lagoons, and uplands along boardwalks and shell paths. Admission is free.

Nearby, **Mote Marine Laboratory and Aquarium** at 1600 Ken Thompson Pkwy, ☎ 388-2451 or 800-691-MOTE, specializes in the research and rehabilitation of marine mammals. Its most touted attraction is a 135,000-gallon shark tank, stocked with sharks and other local fish. Twenty-two smaller aquariums, a touch tank, and a touchless tank hold more than 200 varieties of common and unusual species. Visitors can watch recovering whales, dolphins, manatees, or whatever happens to be the latest guest, in its 55,000-gallon marine mammal recovery tanks. Newest to the facility, Hugh and Buffett, two manatees born in captivity, charm with their docile demeanor. Admission is $8 for adults and $6 for children ages 4-17. It's open daily 10-5.

Next door at **Pelican Man's Bird Sanctuary**, 1708 Ken Thompson Pkwy, ☎ 388-4444, you can visit some 200 local birds recovering from injury or illness. Admission is free or by donation daily 10-5.

Sarasota Ski-A-Rees Show takes place at City Island, behind Mote Marine, every Sunday at 2 pm. There is limited bleacher seating. Performers are amateur. Admission is free.

Nicest and sportiest of the island's Gulf strip of beaches, 130-acre **South Lido Beach** at the south end of Benjamin Franklin Drive, features a wide, sugar-sand white beach that wraps around Gulf to bay, fitness trails, a bayou for canoeing, volleyball, ball fields, and a shady picnic area. Fishermen enjoy casting into the pass at the tip.

FISHING & BOATING

Both passes at Lido Key's polar ends make for a good day of rod-and-reeling. The **New Pass Bridge**, and **Ken Thompson Pier** and **New Pass Pier** on City Island provide vantage points into north-end New Pass. **New Pass Bait Shop** on Ken Thompson Pkwy, ☎ 388-3050, serves angling needs in that neighborhood.

For south-end fishing in Big Sarasota Pass, go to **South Lido Beach** (see *Sights & Attractions*, above) at the end of Benjamin Franklin Drive It also offers Brushy Bayou, a boon to canoeists.

Tony Saprito Fishing Pier at Ringling Causeway Park accommodates fishermen with a bait concession and other facilities.

Capt. Bob Smith at 2529 Temple Street, ☎ 366-2159 or 350-8583, takes small charters into deep-sea, bay, and backwaters for four to eight hours. Rates range from $124 to $475, depending upon trip length, time of year, and number of people in party (up to six). He picks up at New Pass Bait Shop on Ken Thompson Pkwy.

Boat-owners will find three public ramps at **City Island** into New Pass, on the east side of Lido Key's north end.

From Mote Marine Aquarium (see *Sights & Attractions*, above), **Sarasota Bay Explorers** at 1600 Ken Thompson Pkwy, ☎ 388-4200, explores the natural side of Sarasota, which isn't that easy to find these days. Highlights of the naturalist-narrated trip are a close-up view of Rookery Islands (binoculars are provided) and a peek at sea life netted off the grass flats. Rates are $24 for adults, $20 for children. You can also purchase combination Mote-cruise tickets. A Tropical Sunset Cruise costs $18 and $14. Both excursions last almost two hours. Custom tours also available.

HIKING & BIKING

At **South Lido Beach** (see *Sights & Attractions*, above), trails take you through woodsy parts into the swampland of Brushy Bayou.

The Longboat Key bike path crosses the New Pass Bridge and continues for a few miles through Lido Key's northern residential section.

OTHER ADVENTURES

Go to **Flamingo Coast Rollerblade** at 478 John Ringling Blvd, ☎ 388-1889, for in-line skates at $6 an hour, $15 a day. It's open 10-7 Monday-Saturday and 10-6 Sunday.

WHERE TO EAT

Dining is centered in St. Armands Circle, where everything is classy or trendy, or both. Catch a snack in a deli or ice cream shop, or sit down to a multi-course culinary celebration.

Florida's chain of Spanish-cuisine restaurants, **Columbia**, has a storefront at 411 St. Armands Circle, ☎ 388-3987. Open daily for lunch and dinner, it serves authentic Spanish-Cuban dishes, such as *paella, ropa vieja*, and grouper a la Rusa. Dinner plates are $14-$20; lunches run $3-$15. Reservations recommended for dinner.

Café L'Europe at 431 St. Armands Circle, ☎ 388-4415, sits on laurels of many decades, serving classic French and continental fare in a warm red-brick setting. It serves lunch ($7-$15) and dinner ($16-$26 à la carte) daily. Reservations recommended for dinner.

WHERE TO STAY

If you're looking for Lido Key's beachy action, check into the **Holiday Inn** at 233 Benjamin Franklin Drive, ☎ 388-5555 or 800-892-9174, center of activity. Its 140 freshly decorated rooms are set up for business and pleasure. Poolside is a popular meeting spot for beachers taking a break from the sun. Call for rates, which vary according to time of year and availability.

Something more serene? **Half Moon Beach Club** at 2050 Ben Franklin Drive, ☎ 388-3694 or 800-358-3245, is unusual, understated, and expensive. Two Art Deco buildings in the shape of a half moon hold 85 guest rooms, efficiencies and suites, all with refrigerators and coffee makers. It's a little bit Florida, a little bit Europe in style. Accent is on outdoors, with bike rentals, a beach sundeck, volleyball, shuffleboard, and great sunsets. Rates in prime season for rooms and suites are $115-$225; in low season, $85-$179. Ask about packages.

SHOPPING

Flip-flops and fur coats (yes, in Florida!) intermingle at the spinning wheel shopping district that ranks itself with Rodeo Drive. **St. Armands Circle, ☎** 388-1554, was built as John Ringling had envisioned it. The inner park displays some of the baroque art he loved, as well as plaques honoring circus illuminati. "The Circle," as locals call it, holds pricey boutiques, upscale chains, art galleries, restaurants, and clubs. Horse-drawn carriages give sunset rides. Parking is free (but sometimes scarce) on the street and in a nearby garage.

Have fun, no matter what your age, at **Big Kids Toys**, 24 S Blvd of Presidents, **☎** 388-3555, where juke boxes, unusual games, and an antique-looking gas pump comprise the eccentric stock.

Sarasota's reputation for art galleries extends to its islands. At the Circle, look for **Four Winds Gallery** at 17 Fillmore Drive, **☎** 388-2510, which sells Southwest Native American art; **Oehlschlaeger Galleries** at 28 S Blvd of the Arts, **☎** 388-3312, which specializes in meche dolls; and **Wyland Galleries at 465 John Ringling Blvd, ☎ 388-5331**, showroom of the well-known namesake's wildlife art.

NIGHTLIFE

In a town where nightlife glitters, St. Armands Circle contends for a great deal of the action. Its clubs and restaurants host live local rock bands and national artists in an intimate setting.

Two of the most popular clubs include **The Patio**, 411 St. Armands Circle at the Columbia, **☎** 388-3987, and **ChaCha Coconuts** at 417 St. Armands Circle, **☎** 388-3300. Cover charges vary.

Sarasota

BASICS

From Interstate 75, take exits 37 to 40 to get to Sarasota. From north to south, University Parkway, Fruitville Rd, Bee Ridge Rd, and Clark Rd (Route 72) are Sarasota's big east-west streets. Highway 41 (Tamiami Trail) heads through town close to the bay. It intersects with Main Street and Bayfront Drive downtown. Between Highway 41 and Interstate 75, Tuttle Avenue, Beneva Rd, McIntosh Rd, and Cattlemen

Rd run north to south. Highway 301 branches off Highway 41 downtown.

Sarasota County Area Transit (SCAT), ☎ 951-5851, provides public
transportation around town.

INFORMATION

The **Greater Sarasota County Chamber of Commerce** at 1819
Main Street, Ste. 240, Sarasota, FL 34236, ☎ 941-955-8187, has
specific information on Sarasota. You can also contact the
Downtown Association of Sarasota, 47 S Palm Ave, Sarasota,
FL 34326, ☎ 951-2656.

DOWNTOWN SIGHTS & ATTRACTIONS

Downtown Sarasota has been
perking up its waterfront and
Main Street. Its renowned restaurants, art galleries, clubs,
and theaters compose the
Theatre and Arts District.

Grand dame of the down-
town theater scene, **A.B. Edwards Theatre** at 61 N
Pineapple Ave, ☎ 366-8450,
hosts the Sarasota Opera (see   *Sarasota Bayfront and Marina.*
Nightlife, below) in a beauti-
fully restored historic mission-style building. You can tour the facility
by appointment (and see the chandelier from the set of *Gone With the
Wind*) for $2. In summer, the theater hosts **Clown College,** ☎ 800-755-
9637, which puts on regular performances. Call for schedule and ticket
prices.

Marie Selby Botanical Gardens at 811 S Palm Ave, ☎ 366-5730, has
planted 10 acres with palms, bamboo, hibiscus, tropical food plants,
herbs, and other exotic gardens. It is particularly known for its collection of 6,000 orchids, set in a lush rainforest environment. The gardens
are open daily 10-5. Admission is $7 for adults, $3 for children ages 6-11.

OUTLYING SIGHTS & ATTRACTIONS

Sarasota Jungle Gardens.

Sarasota Polo Club at 8201 Polo Club Ln., ☎ 359-0000, competes on Sundays at 1 pm from mid-November to mid-April. Adult tickets are $4; children under 12 are admitted free.

East of Highway 41, the Chicago White Sox train during March at **Ed Smith Stadium**, 2700 12th Street, ☎ 954-SOXX. Tickets cost $4 and $5, with Thursday night specials.

North of downtown, **Sarasota Jungle Gardens** at 3701 Bayshore Rd, ☎ 335-5305, is worth a few hours' time to stroll peaceful gardens, watch exotic bird and reptile shows, and look at monkeys, flamingos, swans, wallabies, and other animals. Hours are 9-5 daily. Admission is $9 for adults; $7 for seniors, and $5 for children ages 3-12.

At **Bellm Cars & Music of Yesterday** at 5500 N Tamiami Trail, ☎ 355-6228, you can see 175 antique and classic cars, 1,200 antique and mechanical musical instruments, a blacksmith shop, a vintage penny arcade, and a livery stable. Adult admission is $8, $4 for children ages 6-12. It's open daily 8:30-6.

The best of Sarasota's attractions spreads out its circus and arts heritage over 66 bayfront acres. The **Ringling Estate** at 5401 Bay Shore Rd, ☎ 359-5700, was left to the state by John Ringling upon his death. Its cornerstone is **The John and Mable Ringling Museum of Art**, whose 22 galleries specialize in late Medieval, Renaissance Italian, and Spanish baroque works, including five original Rubens tapestries.

You can also visit **Ca'd'Zan,** Ringling's Italianate palace, built in the 1920s at a cost of $1.5 million; the **Circus Museum**, filled with calliopes, costumes, oversized clown props, wagons, and other Big Top art and memorabilia; the **Asolo Theatre**, an 18th-century Italian royal theater; and estate rose gardens.

Admission fees for all Ringling attractions are $8.50 for adults and $7.50 for seniors. Florida students and teachers (with ID) and children ages 12 and under enter free. Admission is free for everyone on

Ca'd'Zan.

Saturday, by provision of Ringling's will. The complex is open daily 10-5:30 pm; November-June, Thursday hours are extended 10-10.

Asolo Center for the Performing Arts at 5555 N Tamiami Trail, ☎ 351-8000 (box office) or 351-9010, ext. 4806 (tours), incorporates elements of a circa-1900 Scottish opera house and hosts the professional Asolo Theatre Company. You can tour for free. Call for performance schedule and ticket prices.

Buy some dog food (you may even win money!) at **Sarasota Kennel Club** at 5400 Bradenton Rd, ☎ 355-7744, where greyhound racing happens at matinee and evening shows. The club also simulcasts greyhound and horse racing from around Florida and other locations Monday-Saturday. Admission is $1.

FISHING & BOATING

Flying Fish Fleet at Marina Jack's in Island Park, ☎ 366-3373, has deep-sea excursions: half-day and summer sunset ($15-$24 each, depending upon age), six-hour ($20-$30) and all-day ($25-$35).

Big Catch, ☎ 366-3373, works out of Marina Jack's also, as a charter service. Expect to pay $50 each or $295 for a party of up to six for four hours. Six- and eight-hour rates also available.

Call **Gypsy Guide Service**, ☎ 923-6095, for light tackle and fly fishing in the bays and backwaters, half-day ($250) or full day ($400) and packages. Rates cover lunch and up to two fly fishermen or three spin fishermen.

For dining afloat, **Marina Jack II** at Marina Jack's Restaurant, Island Park, ☎ 366-9255, is one name you'll want to know. Take a lunch ($13) or dinner ($21) cruise aboard a 100-foot stern-wheeler, with live entertainment. Tax and gratuity are extra. Closed September.

LeBarge Tropical Cruises at Marina Jack's, ☎ 366-6116, is oh-so islandy, with live entertainment, palm trees on board, an aquarium bar, and your favorite seafood nibbles and exotic cocktails. Daytime cruises include narration and a bit of nature orientation. Accent is on party for the sunset cruises. The charge for either is $12. Children get a discount on the daytime cruise only.

Enterprise Sailing Charters also depart from Marina Jack's, ☎ 951-1833, for half-day afternoon ($35 per person) and sunset ($20) sails on a 41-foot Morgan. Passengers are allowed to bring their own snacks and beverages.

To learn how to sail or to rent a sailboat anywhere from 19- to 32-feet-long, head to **O'Leary's Sarasota Sailing School** at Bayfront Park, ☎ 953-7505. Rates vary for half-days ($100-$200), full days ($150-$275), and weekly ($700-$1,700). Captained boats also available. It also does water ski pulls at $80 an hour for up to eight people and rent personal watercraft for $60-$65 an hour. Sailing instruction costs $25 per hour, minimum of three hours.

To launch your own vessel, use the free ramps on Sixth Street at Boulevard of the Arts.

HIKING & BIKING

Bicycle Center at 4084 Bee Ridge Rd, ☎ 377-4505, offers pick-up and delivery. Mountain bike and beach cruiser rentals run $15 by the day, $30 by the week. It's open daily.

OTHER ADVENTURES

Gulf Coast Biplanes takes off from Sarasota-Bradenton Airport, ☎ 359-2246 or 800-359-9226, for sky-high adventure in a reproduction 1935 Super Waco open cockpit plane. Fifteen minutes will cost you $90; 30 minutes, $160. Prices are based on two people per flight and include tax.

WHERE TO EAT

If you're culinarily adventuresome, plan to spend a lot of time relishing Sarasota's highly competitive dining scene. The prevailing style is cutting-edge creative, but you'll also find top-rate ethnic restaurants, downhome cooking, old-Florida oyster bars, and classic continental.

Downtown leads with fine dining establishments. **Carmichael's** at 1213 N Palm Ave, ☎ 951-1771, is my favorite for splurging. Ensconced in a 1920s' home, the dining rooms are small and set eclectically with antique china. The menu favors game meats and local seafood, exotically prepared, on an ever-changing menu. Dinner ($18-$25 à la carte) Monday-Saturday. Reservations are recommended.

Bright and stylish **Bijou Café** at 1287 First Street, ☎ 366-8111, is another favorite for shoppers and theater-goers (it's across the street from the opera house). Its often-changing menu features things like roast duckling and potato-encrusted salmon. Lunch, served Monday-Friday, ranges from $6-$14, and dinner, served daily and à la carte, runs $15-$22. Reservations are recommended.

Away from downtown, **Michael's on East** at 1212 East Ave, ☎ 366-0007, is a contender with its "inspired cuisine." Creations reflect global influence: yucca-crusted Chilean sea bass sandwich, or Mediterranean sampler, for example. Known also for its fine wines, Michael's ultra-modern, fern-bar decor attracts the beautiful and *au courant* of Sarasota. Michael's serves lunch ($4-$13) Monday-Friday and dinner ($13-$26 à la carte) Monday-Saturday.

For something less budget-busting, look for one of Sarasota's old-Florida-style oyster bars. The best in the genre is **Phillippi Creek Village Oyster Bar**, waterside at 5353 S Tamiami Trail, ☎ 925-4444. It's most famous for its combo seafood steamer pots, but the sandwiches and other seafood items are fresh and tasty, too. You can sit inside the old Southern-style fish house or creekside on the patio or floating dock. It's open daily for lunch and dinner. A wide array of dishes range from $6 to $16.

Long-established and known for its value, **The Original Oyster Bar** at 7250 S Tamiami Trail, ☎ 924-2829, serves seafood and steaks under $10 daily for lunch and dinner. Don't expect fancy, but the food is good.

Sarasota is also known for its Amish/Mennonite restaurants, operated by members of a local farming community. Homemade goodness prevails over atmosphere. And the price is right. **Sugar & Spice** at 1850 S Tamiami Trail, ☎ 953-3340, is one such. You're apt to find baked chicken and dressing, beef and noodles, Swiss steak, or turkey and dressing as a daily special. Leave room for pie. It serves lunch and dinner daily except Sunday; entrées are $3.50-$10.

WHERE TO STAY

Most of the area's best lodging is on the beaches. Business visitors find chain and mom & pop places along Highway 41 around the airport.

One of the former, **Hampton Inn** at 5000 N Tamiami Trail, ☎ 351-7734 or 800-336-9335, includes continental breakfast. Rates are low. Call and ask the exact rate for the time you'll be visiting. There's a pool and a workout facility, and rooms are pleasant and quiet.

Hyatt Sarasota at 1000 Blvd of the Arts, ☎ 953-1234 or 800-233-1234, is an option for folks who want to be on the mainland, yet on the water, and can pay more. The skyscraping hotel overlooks a marina. Its 297 rooms and 12 suites are tastefully decorated, as are its spacious lobby and waterfront restaurant. Other amenities include lighted tennis courts, a fitness center, swimming pool, and close proximity to the Sarasota Quay and downtown attractions. Rates throughout the year fall in the $150-$250 range.

For rental homes and condos at all prices by the day, week, or month in Sarasota and the islands, contact **Michael Saunders & Co.** at 100 S Washington Blvd, ☎ 951-6668 or 800-881-2222.

NIGHTLIFE

Contrary to what you may have heard about the dearth of nightlife and culture in Florida's resort areas, Sarasota pulsates with live music and professional theater. For up-to-date information on community events, call the 24-hour ArtsLine at ☎ 953-4636, ext. 6000.

Most of the action is centered in downtown's **Sarasota Theatre and Arts District**. **Sarasota Quay**, Fruitville Rd at Tamiami Trail, is another happening place for all ages, all echelons.

Sarasota Opera performs at A.B. Edwards Theatre (see Downtown *Sights & Attractions*, above), 61 N Pineapple Ave, ☎ 366-8450, February-March. The troupe, which has been performing for more than 30 years, stages Puccini, Verdi, Tchaikovsky, and other classics at night and Sunday matinee performances in February and March. Tickets are $15-$52, not including special student performances.

For something more avant-garde, check out **Florida Studio Theatre** at 1241 N Palm Ave downtown, ☎ 366-9796. It uses its main and cabaret stages as testing grounds for up-and-coming playwrights during the December-August season and a summertime New Plays Festival. The box office is open daily. No shows on Monday. Cost of tickets varies.

Van Wezel Performing Arts Hall at 777 N Tamiami Trail, ☎ 953-3366 or 800-826-9303, looks like a big purple clam shell on the outside. Inside, the 1,761-seat hall hosts Broadway shows, major classical orchestras, ethnic music, dance, choral music, a Saturday kids program, and the Florida West Coast Symphony.

Sarasota Quay at Fruitville Rd and Tamiami Trail has several options for jazz, top 40, whatever your pleasure. Cover charges vary. Disco dancers head to **Club Bandstand**, ☎ 954-7625. Live bands perform on occasion. **In Extremis** at the Quay, ☎ 954-2008, parties with laser, light, sound, and video shows. It's state-of-the-art nightlife.

Old Heidelberg Castle at Rte. 301 and Fruitville Rd, ☎ 366-3515, is a city landmark featuring German music shows every night but Monday.

SHOPPING

Downtown Sarasota has undergone a recent renovation which turned its historic district into a shopping mall, where shops, boutiques, and restaurants occupy vintage buildings. It is best-known for its art galleries, most of which line Palm Avenue.

Book lovers won't want to miss **Main Bookshop** at 1962 Main Street, ☎ 366-7653, where discounted books on every subject fill four floors.

For bargains, check out **Sarasota Outlet Center** at Interstate 75's exit 40 and University Pkwy, ☎ 359-2020.

Siesta Key

Technically part of Sarasota, Siesta Key has developed a separate, slightly renegade personality, even compared to the other islands. It breaks from the other islands both spiritually and physically – its two bridges connect with the mainland, but not with the islands to the north. Siesta Key's renown was built upon sand – the whitest, finest, softest sand south of Florida's Panhandle. Unlike other West Coast beaches, Siesta Key gets quartz sand. It drifts down from the Panhandle, where the beaches derive from Appalachian mountain run-off.

Siesta Key's claim to the world's whitest beach has naturally made the island beach-preoccupied. It is quite heavily developed, but still within the boundaries of good taste that Sarasota sets. At town center, an artist's community lends it depth of character. At its fringes, resorts are non-chain and the wealthy have built up exclusive communities.

Where does all this leave the visitor with a yearning for outdoor excitement? In good standing. Fishing, boating, kayaking, snorkeling, and sports of all sorts are a strong part of this stunningly white beach world.

BASICS

Siesta Key Beach.

From Interstate 75, take exit 37 or 38 to get to Siesta Key. Exit 38 takes you to Bee Ridge Rd. Turn north on Highway 41 and west on Siesta Drive, which leads to the north bridge. Off of exit 37, head west on Clark Rd (Route 72), which changes names to Stickney Point Rd and crosses the south bridge.

On the island's north end, Higel Avenue and Ocean Boulevard are the main roads into the shopping district. Beach Rd runs Gulf-side, and intersects with Midnight Pass Rd, which travels to the island's south end, intersecting Stickney Point Rd.

*You can get around the island aboard the narrated **Siesta Key Trolley**, ☎ 346-3115. Reboardings are free with an advertiser's receipt.*

INFORMATION

For specific information on the island, contact the **Siesta Key Chamber of Commerce** at 5100 Ocean Blvd, Unit B, Sarasota, FL 34242, ☎ 349-3800. Its hours are Monday-Friday 10-5.

SIGHTS & ATTRACTIONS

People cross to Siesta Key mainly for the beach. Shopping and dining are a sideline. Not all of its beaches are created equal, however. **Siesta**

Key County Beach on Midnight Pass Rd at Beach Way Drive is a half-mile long and luxuriously wide. Its porcelain-white sands are plush, and a dream-come-true for recreationists. The park contains volleyball nets, tennis courts, a fitness trail, ball fields, a soccer field, playgrounds, lifeguards, and rental and food concessions. For slightly more seclusion, park on the street, rather than at the huge parking lot, or walk to the public beach's outskirts. For privacy and great snorkeling and fishing, head to the beach's south end, **Point of Rocks**. Parking access there is just south of the intersection of Midnight Pass Rd and Stickney Point Rd. Watch for the #12 access sign near the Siesta Breakers resort.

FISHING & BOATING

Good land points for fishing include the **Siesta (north) Bridge** and **Bay Island**, **Stickney Point (south) Bridge** or seawall, **Point of Rocks** (see *Sights & Attractions*, above), south of Siesta Public Beach, and **Turtle Beach's** pier and seawall at the island's south end on Blind Pass Rd. Turtle Beach park also has boat ramps, picnic facilities, a playground, volleyball, horseshoes, and a beach. This beach does not share Siesta Key's soft, white sand, however.

Mr. CB's at 1249 Stickney Point Rd, ☎ 349-4400, has fishing charters in Sarasota Bay for up to six people. Rates are $200 for a half-day, $375 for a full day. It also rents runabouts, center console boats, pontoons, and deck boats for use in Intracoastal waters. Daily rates are $120-$160; half-day, $80-$110, plus tax and gas. Rod and reel rentals and fishing licenses are also available. It's open daily 7-6.

Sweetwater Kayaks at 5263 Ocean Blvd, ☎ 346-1179, is geared toward instruction. An introductory two-hour session in the Gulf costs $45. Students learn in single kayaks. Advanced lessons, rentals, and extended instructional trips and tours are also available.

SNORKELING & SCUBA

Point of Rocks (see *Sights & Attractions,* above), on the south end of Siesta Public Beach near Midnight Pass Rd and Stickney Point Rd is a favorite spot with snorkelers looking for coral, caves, and marine life.

Mr. CB's (see *Fishing & Boating,* above) at 1249 Stickney Point Rd, ☎ 349-4400, sells snorkel equipment.

OTHER WATER ADVENTURES

Siesta Key Parasail, located at Mr. CB's at 1249 Stickney Point Rd, ☎ 349-1900, gives 800-foot-high rides for $40 each.

HIKING & BIKING

Bikers and joggers use the path that runs for 12 miles from Siesta Key's north bridge to Turtle Beach. You can rent one-speed beach cruiser bikes from **Mr. CB's** (see *Fishing & Boating*, above) at 1249 Stickney Point Rd, ☎ 349-4400, for $12 a day.

WHERE TO EAT

Casual and seafood are the catchwords of the Siesta Key restaurant trade. People drive out to the island just to eat.

Right before you reach the island at the south crossing, **Coasters Seafood Bistro** at Sarasota Boatyard, 1500 Stickney Point Rd, ☎ 923-4848, flanks the Intracoastal Waterway and its scenic boat traffic. It blends old and new Florida styles with its architecture and menu – fish-house fare with an inventive flair. Try the fish cakes with remoulade sauce or mahi-mahi with pineapple glaze. It is set in a New England-style building with lots of outdoor seating and is open daily for lunch and dinner. Menu offerings range from $10 to $17. Reservations accepted.

English and American casual eats are served up at **The Old Salty Dog**, 5023 Ocean Blvd, ☎ 349-0158: fish & chips, custom-made burgers, and other seafood and sandwich favorites. You can sit indoors in a pub setting or outdoors amidst Siesta's "downtown" activity. It's open daily for lunch and dinner. Prices are $6-$13.50.

When the occasion calls for a touch of formality, indulge in the acclaimed "bring the outdoors in" surroundings of **Summerhouse**, 6101 Midnight Pass Rd, ☎ 941-349-1100. The dinner menu, served daily, is based on continental classics executed to perfection. Entrée prices are $10-$23. Lighter fare is available upstairs in the bar.

WHERE TO STAY

Resorts and condos are packed in tightly at Siesta's mid-section, so you won't have a problem finding a room except at the height of the season. Non-franchised, each place exudes its own sense of style. Some of those with the most are listed here:

The Wildflower Inn B&B at 5218 Ocean Blvd, ☎ 346-1566, offers four apartments set above a popular vegetarian restaurant in the village shopping area, not far from the beach. Rates include breakfast in the restaurant. Each unit has a full kitchen, bedroom, and living area, all recently refurbished. Rates are $75-$100.

One of the area's earliest bed-and-breakfasts, **Crescent House B&B** at 459 Beach Rd, ☎ 346-0857, occupies an unpretentious old home that lies across the road from a beach access. Baths are shared. Antiques and a fireplace add homey touches. In-season rates are $85-$115; off-season, $60-$90.

Away from the beach, **Banana Bay Club** at 8254 Midnight Pass Rd, ☎ 346-0113, is suited to nature lovers. Located on the brink of a quiet lagoon bird sanctuary, it accords guests free use of bikes, canoes, and pool. Its seven guest units are decorated with unusual tropical flair, and are equipped with full kitchens. Rates for accommodations ranging from a studio apartment to a two-bedroom house are $135-$220 in season, $90-$150 off-season.

For rental homes and condos, you are best off working through the Chamber of Commerce (see *Basics*, above). Homes begin at about $2,000 a month and there's a one-month minimum requirement. Condos can be rented for any length of time.

NIGHTLIFE

I find the nightlife of Siesta Key more relaxed and less showy than Sarasota's in other hot spots. Reflecting the island's mix of creativity and wealth, the after-hours scene has a rowdy cast at one end of the scale, refined at the other.

For youthful, get-down action, the **Beach Club** at 5151 Ocean Blvd in Siesta Village, ☎ 349-6311, rules. It's open nightly with live contemporary bands. Slightly more upscale, **Coasters** (see *Where to Eat*, above) at 1500 Stickney Point Rd on the mainland at the south bridge, ☎ 923-4848, jams Wednesday-Saturday with live music.

For jazz, check out **Fandango's** at 5148 Ocean Blvd in the Village, ☎ 346-1711, Thursday-Saturday; or **The Summerhouse** (see *Where to Eat*, above) at 6101 Midnight Pass Rd, ☎ 349-1100, Tuesday-Saturday.

Nokomis Area

Some may call it the in-between zone, situated as it is between Sarasota and Venice. It encompasses the communities of Osprey, Casey Key, Nokomis, and Nokomis Beach, with a state park and other attractions for the curious and adventuresome visitor.

BASICS

The communities of Osprey and Nokomis lie along Highway 41 (Tamiami Trail). To get to Casey Key, turn west on Blackburn Point Rd south of Osprey. To get to the south end at Nokomis Beach, turn west on Albee Rd south of the town of Laurel. Exits 36 (southbound traffic only) and 35A (northbound traffic only) are the Interstate 75 exits most convenient to the area.

Narrow, twisty Casey Key road winds through the island from end to end.

SIGHTS & ATTRACTIONS

A woman named Mrs. Potter Palmer exerted nearly as much influence on Sarasota's growth and development as John Ringling. Although she was a well-known name among Chicago socialites at the time, we hear much less about her. Except at **Historic Spanish Point** at 500 N Tamiami Trail in Osprey, ☎ 966-5214. Assembled on the 30-acre estate she once owned back in the dawning days of the 1900s, a collection of local historic structures includes prehistoric Indian shell mounds, a pioneer homestead, an old schoolhouse, Mrs. Palmer's restored gardens, a late Victorian home, a reconstructed chapel, and a citrus packing house among them. Local actors give living history performances Sundays from January to mid-April. Guided walking tours of about two hours' duration are available daily 9-5 Monday-Saturday and 12-5 Sunday. Tram tours are available by 48-hour advance reservation three days a week. Adult admission is $5; $3 for children age 6-12.

The natural history of old Sarasota can be experienced at **Oscar Scherer State Recreation Area** at 1843 S Tamiami Trail, ☎ 483-5956. If you camp there, your neighbors will include river otters, alligators, scrub jays, bob cats, and bald eagles. The nearly 1,400-acre park also offers picnicking, a playground, hiking, freshwater swimming, canoe rentals, ranger-led tours, and fishing. Admission fee per car of eight passengers or less is $3.25 per vehicle, $1 for pedestrians and cyclists.

Casey Key is a scenic bite of old-island temperament that is unfortunately becoming more and more like its showy neighbors. These things happen as original family properties – tastefully demure – get sold and developed. The north end provides a pleasant, winding drive around an exclusive residential neighborhood. At its southern end, bustling **Nokomis Beach** is resortier. **North Jetty Park** tips the island, where a small pass separates it from Venice Beach (see *Venice*, below). This is a good place to get out of the traffic, have a picnic, swim, and catch lots of fish. It has lifeguards and concessions.

From Nokomis, inland on Route 72, **Myakka River State Park**, ☎ 361-6511, further appeases adventure hunger with camping, canoeing, and 28,875 acres of forest and wetlands. Tour the park via tram (winter only, ☎ 365-0100), boat, guided walks, canoe, bicycle, or horse (must provide your own mount). Admission is $4 per car to enter for the day. The tram tour, which takes you to areas not accessible by car, costs $7 for adults, $3 for children ages 6-12, and free for younger children on laps. The park is open for day use from 8 to sunset.

Myakka River State Park.

FISHING & BOATING

Cast into bay waters from the **Osprey Fishing Pier** at the west end of Main Street.

Locals tell you the best fishing is from the **North Jetty** (see *Sights & Attractions,* above) at the south-end Casey Key Rd Beach, where picnic areas give other members of the party something to do.

Marinas at both of Casey Key's bridges provide fuel, docking and food for boaters along the Intracoastal. They are **Blackburn Point Marina**, ☎ 966-3735, and **Casey Key Marina**, ☎ 966-1730, at the north end, and **Gulf Harbor Marina**, ☎ 488-7734, at the south bridge.

Don & Mike's Boat Rental at Casey Key Marina, 520 Blackburn Point Rd, ☎ 966-4000 or 800-550-2007, rents a variety of boats and water-sports gear, including ski boats, pontoons, jet skis, waverunners, pontoons, sailboats, sailboards, and water skiing equipment. It also offers sailing instruction. Power boat rentals are $75-$100 for a half-day and longer; 19-foot sailboats, $60-$75.

You'll find **launch ramps** at Captain's Cove on Blackburn Point Rd.

Bay Lady at Osprey Marina on Blackburn Point Rd, ☎ 485-6366, conducts two-hour narrated nature cruises in Venice's bays, Intracoastal waters, and bird sanctuaries, costing $9.50 for adults, $8.50 for seniors, and $6.50 for children ages 4-12.

Take a one-hour narrated tour of **Myakka River State Park** (see *Sights & Attractions,* above) on Rte. 72, ☎ 365-0100, aboard the "world's largest enclosed airboat," *Gator Gal.* The boat departs from the park's boat basin three or four times daily. Fare is $7 for adults and $3 for children ages 6-12, young children seated on an adult's lap ride free. The park also rents canoes, ☎ 361-6511, for use in its waterways. Rates are $10 for two hours, $25 for a full day.

Oscar Scherer State Recreation Area (see *Sights & Attractions,* above) at 1843 S Tamiami Trail, ☎ 483-5956, also rents canoes ($3 an hour, $15 a day) and conducts ranger-led canoe trips.

OTHER WATER ADVENTURES

Don & Mike's Boat Rental (see *Fishing & Boating,* above) at Casey Key Marina, 520 Blackburn Point Rd, ☎ 966-4000 or 800-550-2007, rents jet skis, waverunners, and sailboards. Rental rate for sailboards is $30 for three hours; for personal watercraft, $45 for one hour. Water skiing instruction is available.

HIKING & BIKING

Oscar Scherer State Recreation Area (see *Sights & Attractions,* above) at 1843 S Tamiami Trail, ☎ 483-5956, has more than five miles of nature trails, plus bike paths, which allow you to witness nature and wildlife along with your exercise. A one mile-plus nature trail accommodates disabled persons and includes audio speakers and a butterfly observation area. During winter season, rangers lead bird walks.

Myakka River State Park (see *Sights & Attractions,* above) on Rte. 72, ☎ 361-6511, is treasured by both bikers and hikers. It offers extensive nature trails, a bird walk, and close to 40 miles of wilderness backpacking trail through prairies, hammocks, and pine flatwoods. Bobcats, bald eagles, sandhill cranes, deer, and turkeys inhabit the less traveled areas of the park not accessible to motorists. Seven miles of road wind through the park for cyclists, who often incorporate the scenic ride into longer treks along Route 72. Bike rental rates range from $4 for two hours to $18 for a full day.

WHERE TO EAT

Urbanek's, at 110 Circuit Rd in Nokomis, ☎ 488-2941, is your best bet for grabbing a bite in this part of the world. Located across the south bridge from Casey Key, on the Intracoastal, it feels quaintly ramshackle, with outdoor seating and no-frills cuisine. It is popular with boaters, who can dock there and is open daily for lunch and dinner with the same menu, priced at $5-$19.

WHERE TO STAY

Nokomis Beach has several small lodges geared toward fishing or beaching. **A Beach Retreat** at 106 Casey Key Rd, ☎ 484-0071, addresses the latter with units on the back bay as well as beach, boat docks, and proximity to North Jetty. Many of its units have kitchens. Rates are affordable; call for exact quotes.

CAMPING

Two state parks in the area give you the best deal and optimum closeness to nature. At **Oscar Scherer State Recreation Area** (see *Sights & Attractions,* above), 1843 S Tamiami Trail, ☎ 483-5956, campers feel secluded in a huge waterside campground, thanks to the palmettos, pines, oaks, and other native vegetation. Camping rates are seasonal: $15-$17 in winter, $11-$13 in summer.

Myakka River State Park, ☎ 361-6511, is also nice, but tends to feel more closed-in and crowded. Rates are same as at Oscar Scherer, above.

Venice

Venice is the small-town version of Sarasota. It has the same Mediterranean architecture, fun beaches, art galleries, boutique shopping, and seafood restaurants as its big sister, but on a smaller scale. This keeps it less known, more lightly visited, but still as appealing to adventure-driven vacationers. In its past, it has hosted the Kentucky Military

Institute, winter headquarters for Ringling Brothers, Barnum & Bailey Circus, and the Brotherhood of Locomotive Engineers' retirement village, which built a model Italian city there. Above all, Venice is recognized for its shark-teeth collecting. Snorkelers and beach-combers search for fossil specimens that wash up from an ancient shark graveyard offshore. Its shark teeth caches, in fact, have given Venice an identity all its own.

BASICS

Exit 35 or 34 off of I-75 will get you to Venice Avenue. Highway 41 splits when it gets to Venice. Take the business end of it to cross the Intracoastal Waterway onto the island, where you will find the town of Venice proper. Turn west on Venice Avenue to head downtown and to the beaches. The Esplanade delivers you to Venice's resort district and to Tarpon Center Drive, which goes to the island's north-ern end beach and jetties. Harbor Drive sightsees residential areas and leads to south-end beaches.

INFORMATION

The **Venice Area Chamber of Commerce** at 257 N Tamiami Trail, Venice, FL 34285, ☎ 488-2236, can give you information about the location and about shark's teeth. It's open 9-5 Monday-Friday. You can also contact **Venice Main Street** at P.O. Box 602, Venice, FL 34284, ☎ 484-6722.

SIGHTS & ATTRACTIONS

Venice's pebbly beaches each have their distinct qualities. Most heav-ily visited is **Brohard Park** on Harbor Drive, where shark-teeth collec-tors and fishermen converge. It has picnic facilities, a restaurant, and a fishing pier (see *Fishing & Boating*, below).

South of Brohard, **Casperson Beach** on S Harbor Drive has most of the same amenities – picnic areas and dune walkovers – but fewer shark's teeth and more seclusion. A stroll along this beach leads to Manasota Key (see Chapter VI).

Good shark's teeth collecting is also reported at **Venice Municipal Beach** at Tarpon Center Drive. You can even rent a shark's teeth sifter here. Facilities include a picnic area, showers, concessions, and life-guards.

South of Venice, spa-goers find their way to a little-known attraction called **Warm Mineral Springs** at 12200 San Servando Rd, Warm Mineral Springs, ☎ 426-1692. Some believe this was the Fountain of Youth that Ponce de León sought. Its 2½-acre lake holds a temperature of 87° and soothes bathers with a high mineral content. The facility shows its 50-some years of age, but believers are believers, and they find the waters healthful. To enhance the dunk experience, there are organic mud treatments, saunas, massages, and a wellness center. An old fashioned cyclorama relates the history of Ponce de León's exploits and the area. Admission is $6.50. Visitors can rent beachwear, chairs, and towels.

FISHING & BOATING

The premier spot for fishing would be the **Venice Fishing Pier**. Among the state's longest at 750 feet, it furnishes showers, beach, a bait house, and a restaurant. Admission to the pier is $1 for adults, 50¢ for children.

The **South Jetties** on Tarpon Center Drive project into the pass toward Casey Key and are equally popular with the casting crowd.

Crows Nest Marina, ☎ 484-9551, and **Fisherman's Wharf Marina** at 505 N Tamiami Trail, ☎ 484-9246, serve boaters in the back waters.

Blue Seas at Fisherman's Wharf, ☎ 484-5788, takes party fishing boats into deep water. Trips last a few hours to a few days. Half-day trips are $23; full day, $33.

Boat ramps are located at **Marina Boat Ramp Park**, 215 E Venice Ave, and at **Higel Park** on Tarpon Center Drive.

Snook Haven at 5000 E Venice Ave, ☎ 485-7221, is a water adventurer's paradise on the banks of the Myakka River. It rents canoes and motor boats and leads tours on the river. Rates for canoe rentals are $12 for an hour to $30 for a day; for 12- and 14-foot boats, $20-$26 for an hour and $65-$75 for a day. There's also a boat launch and picnic-table dining (see *Where to Eat*, below).

See **Intracoastal Kayaks** at 127 E Tampa Ave #8, ☎ 485-8598, for rentals, tours, sales, and instructions. Two-hour solo rentals cost $20; $28 for tandems.

SNORKELING & DIVING

Fossil-seekers search underwater for shark's teeth and other finds, but visibility is often low. The greatest caches are found in water around

18 feet deep. Offshore, ledges harbor marine life one to five miles from the jetties at the north end.

SHARK-TOOTHING

Equip yourself with a "Florida snow shovel," screen baskets on long poles, available at local hardware stores for less than $15. Head to Brohard Park or Venice Municipal Beach (see *Sights & Attractions,* above). At the latter you can even rent special colanders. Anything with a screen mesh will work. Next, sift at water's edge and pull teeth! It's the thing to do in Venice. If you're confused about what you're looking for, stop at the Chamber of Commerce (see *Basics,* above), and pick up some samples and a guide. People get very serious about this, so be prepared to be shown up. If you're having no luck, head for Sharky's bar (see *Where to Eat,* below), dig a couple out of the box of sand at the entry way, and have a beer instead.

WHERE TO EAT

Swashbuckling, boating types will enjoy **The Crow's Nest Marina Restaurant** at 1968 Tarpon Center Drive on the South Jetty, ☎ 484-9551. Overlooking a yacht marina through tall windows, it is tastefully nautical through and through. The lunch and dinner menus offer seafood prepared flavorfully. It serves a Sunday brunch buffet, but otherwise is open daily for lunch and dinner, with price ranges of $6-$10 and $9-$17 respectively.

Sharky's on the Venice Fishing Pier at Brohard Park, ☎ 488-1456, is popular, but the quality of food seems watered-down by the demands of its crowds. Catch sunset and a relatively inexpensive meal here. Sunday brunches are especially popular, made interesting by a make-your-own Bloody (or Virgin) Mary bar. It's open for lunch and dinner Monday through Saturday, brunch and dinner on Sunday. Lunch prices for sandwiches and seafood plates are $5-$12; dinner's offerings are extensive in a $12-$19 range.

Snook Haven (see *Fishing & Boating*) at 5000 E Venice Ave, ☎ 485-7221, is a country fun kind of place on the Myakka River, where you can paddle a canoe, have some chow, and party every Sunday afternoon to live music. It's open daily for lunch and dinner, with sandwiches and meals ranging from $5 to $12.

WHERE TO STAY

Venice has a small but pleasant selection of hotels, motels, and condominiums. Among its nicest resorts, **Inn at the Beach** at 101 The Esplanade, ☎ 484-8471 or 800-255-8471, has the beach advantage: Venice Municipal Beach (see *Sights & Attractions,* above) lies directly across the street. Clean, modern, and stylish, it offers a small pool and rooms or one- and two-bedroom suites, which run $135-$249 in season; $85-$159 off-season.

Banyan House B&B at 519 S Harbor Drive, ☎ 484-1385, is part of Venice's old Mediterranean-fashion neighborhood of the mid-1920s. Distinct elements include a swimming pool that served the community as its first, a Greek goddess fountain under a huge banyan tree, cheery blossoms, a treehouse sundeck, a breakfast solarium, and a hot tub. Each of the four rooms has a private bath and fridge; three of them are efficiencies. Rates are $85-$110 in season, $70-$85 in off-season. Weekly rental apartments are available in a separate structure.

Warm Mineral Springs (see *Sights & Attractions,* above) at 12200 San Servando Rd, Warm Mineral Springs, ☎ 426-1692, provides 200 rooms with kitchens or kitchenettes. High-season rentals (February through March) run from $200-$345 per week. Rates the rest of the year begin at $145-$185 and range up to $250-$320. Daily rates are available for some units.

CAMPING

Venice Campground at 4085 E Venice Ave, ☎ 488-0850, is set under age-old oak trees along the Myakka River.

SHOPPING

Venice's shopping, like the town itself, is quiet, tasteful, and architecturally pleasing. Turn off Highway 41 onto **West Venice Avenue**. A beautiful sign heralds your arrival on a date-palm-lined boulevard where shops evoke the Mediterranean and cars politely stop for crossing pedestrians. Shops, galleries, and restaurants sell the gaudy and the elegant along the avenue and its side streets.

A block over, **Venice Centre Mall** at 226 Tampa Ave, occupies the former winter quarters of the Kentucky Military Institute. The building is listed on the National Register of Historic Buildings. Specialty shops fall into formation in a spit-and-polish hall.

Chapter VI

Charlotte Harbor Area

Area code: 941

Wide, deep Charlotte Harbor is a place known for pirates and tarpon. The pirates are long since gone, leaving only their names and sense of adventure upon the islands where they supposedly once had their lairs. The tarpon are still there, most notably off Boca Grande, one of Charlotte Harbor's islands, which are far-removed from the hum of mainstream tourism.

The harbor and its feeders – the Peace and Myakka rivers – section off Charlotte County. In one section, Punta Gorda acts slightly metropolitan, having been a major commercial fishing port in an earlier heyday. Across the Peace, urban sprawl claims smaller communities along the Tamiami Trail. Subdivided by the Myakka and Charlotte Harbor, a wide peninsula inhabited by golfing developments buffers Gulf barrier islands here from the development seen on islands to the north and south.

Charlotte County in general is a hushed location bookended by its more highly touted neighbors. What little tourism you do find in its highly residential communities has to do mainly with the great outdoors. Sports opportunities abound on all the waterfronts, especially fishing. The distance of the region's beaches from main thoroughfares keeps the barrier islands lightly visited. In eastern regions, wildlands have been preserved for sportsmen and nature lovers.

Transportation, Etc.

Sarasota-Bradenton International Airport (SRQ), ☎ 359-2770, and **Southwest Florida International Airport** (SWR) in Fort Myers, ☎ 768-1000, both bring you close to the Charlotte Harbor area. Flights arrive at the two airports from all over the US, from Canada, and from limited international destinations. Major domestic airlines include **American/American Eagle,** ☎ 800-433-7300; **Continental,** ☎ 939-9524 or 800-525-0280; **Delta,** ☎ 800-221-1212; **Northwest,** ☎. **TWA,** ☎ 800-221-2000; **United,** ☎ 800-241-6522; and **USAir,** ☎ 800-428-4322.

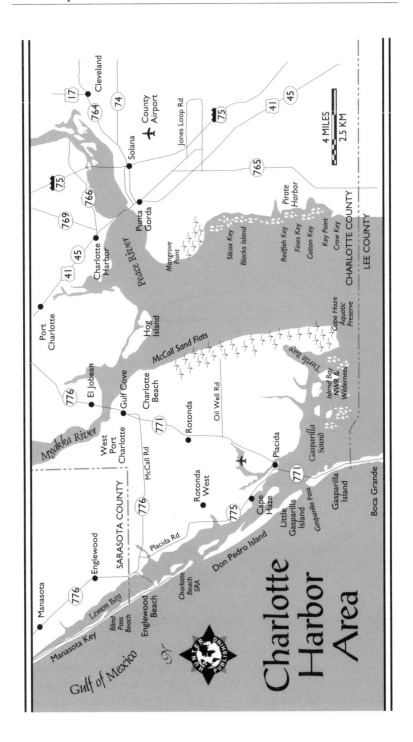

Rental cars are available at the airports and from locations within the immediate area, including **Avis**, ☎ 359-5240 (SRQ), 768-2121 (SWR), or 800-331-1212; **Hertz**, ☎ 335-8848 (SRQ), 768-3100 (SWR), or 800-654-3131; and **Budget**, ☎ 359-5353 (SRQ), 768-1500 (SWR), or 800-527-0700.

For transportation from SRQ, call **Airport Shuttle Service**, ☎ 355-9645, **Diplomat Taxi**, ☎ 355-5155, **West Coast Executive Sedans**, ☎ or 359-8600; from SWR, **Aaron Airport Transportation**, ☎ 277-7000, or **Airport Taxi**, ☎ 768-5400.

Highway 41 (Tamiami Trail) runs closest to the Charlotte Harbor coast line, north to south. Interstate 75 parallels it to the east. Main county roads – routes 771, 775, and 776 – take you into the area's hidden coastal regions, forming a rough triangle in the middle of Charlotte Harbor's peninsula. Route 31 runs north-south through the wilderness on the county's eastern extreme.

INFORMATION

For information on the overall area, contact the **Charlotte County Chamber of Commerce** at 2702 Tamiami Trail, Port Charlotte, FL 33952, ☎ 627-2222; or at 326 W Marion Ave, Punta Gorda, FL 33950, ☎ 639-2222. Hours for both offices are Monday-Friday 8-5.

Events

Boca Grande's celebrated tarpon season runs from April through July, culminating in July's **The World's Richest Tarpon Tournament**, ☎ 694-0568, with its hefty entry fee and up to $100,000 purse. Eight other tarpon tournaments also take place there, including **Millers Marina Tarpon Tide Tournaments**, ☎ 964-2232, the longest running, beginning in mid-May.

In October, the **Punta Gorda Waterfront Festival**, ☎ 639-3720, brings 'gator wrestling, water activities, music, food, and crafts to Gilchrist Park.

Manasota Key/Englewood

The island of Manasota Key is actually a continuation of Venice Beach (see Chapter V) to the north, but the only way to get from one to the other without leaving the island is by foot.

Although two communities lie on way-off-the-beaten-path Manasota Key, the quieter, more exclusive community to the north is actually known as Manasota Key, while the resortier one to the south is called Englewood Beach. In Manasota Key, homes – mostly upscale – greatly outnumber resorts and other commercial enterprises. Archaeological digs have unearthed a rich Amerindian past in Manasota Key. In the present, the entire community is a designated wildlife sanctuary. Its beaches are maintained in a more natural, less developed manner than those in Englewood Beach, a mecca for youthful and cost-conscious vacationers and day-trippers.

Across the bridge from Englewood Beach, the town of Englewood skirts the mainland. Mostly a destination for winter-long golfers and retirees, it's also where beach vacationers go for non-resort services.

The waters that lie between mainland and island – Lemon Bay and Stump Pass – belong to the 7,667-acre Cape Haze Aquatic Preserve, a haven for sportsfolk and nature lovers.

BASICS

Directions can get confusing here, so far from the main thoroughfares. That's what keeps it so blessedly undiscovered. In addition to the directions that follow, you may want to procure a map.

To approach the area from the north via Interstate 75, take exit 35 and follow River Rd to Route 776. From the south, take exit 32, head west on Route 776, and turn right (north) on Highway 41. From Highway 41, turn west on Route 776. Via Highway 41 north, turn onto Route 776 south of Venice.

Manasota Key has bridges at its north and south ends. From Route 776 at the north end, take Manasota Key Rd across the bridge. From the south end, turn west on Beach Rd (Route 776).

Manasota Key Rd is the north end's main route. Its name changes to Beach Rd in the south. Gulf Boulevard extends south of the bridge in Englewood Beach. Along it you'll find most of the town's resorts and a secluded beach.

Indiana Avenue (Route 776) comprises Englewood's "strip." To get into downtown, head west on Dearborn Avenue. East of Englewood's north end, Route 776 goes by the name McCall Rd.

Englewood Taxi, ☎ 475-1111, does airport pickups in Sarasota and Fort Myers.

INFORMATION

For information on Manasota Key's north end, contact the **Sarasota Convention & Visitors Bureau** at 655 N Tamiami Trail, Sarasota, FL 34236, ☎ 957-1877 or 800-522-9799, open Monday-Friday 9-5. To learn more about Englewood Beach and Englewood, contact **Englewood Area Chamber of Commerce**, 601 S Indiana Ave, Englewood 34223, ☎ 474-5511. Open Monday-Friday 9-5.

NORTH END SIGHTS & ATTRACTIONS

Manasota Key's two beaches are developed with services and facilities, but allow you to get away from it all and do some serious beach hiking. Fourteen-acre **Manasota Beach** at 8570 Manasota Key Rd draws crowds because it is conveniently located where the north bridge makes landfall on the island. Active beachers can hike up to Casperson Beach on the south end of connecting Venice Beach, or use the boat ramp facilities across the road on Lemon Bay.

Blind Pass Beach at 6725 Manasota Key Rd has 63 acres, and is the less used of the two. Both have picnic facilities, restrooms, and other conveniences.

ENGLEWOOD BEACH SIGHTS & ATTRACTIONS

Englewood Beach also has two distinct choices for beaches. If you like 'em secluded and natural, head for **Port Charlotte State Recreation Area** at the very south end. It has only a few parking spaces, which is a good-news, bad-news kind of thing. The good news is it limits traffic on the one-mile-long stretch of beach, which touches down in Stump Pass. Bad news: If you're not lodging on the beach, you'll have to bike or walk from the facilities at **Chadwick Park Beach**, ☎ 475-6606, located squarely where the south bridge meets the Gulf of Mexico. Because of its extensive picnic facilities and recreational options – volleyball and basketball courts, horseshoe pits, and other play areas – it draws crowds. It's also close to shops, restaurants, and watersports rentals. The park is open 6-11; parking costs $1 a day.

ENGLEWOOD SIGHTS & ATTRACTIONS

Indian Mound Park on Winson Ave in downtown Englewood (follow the signs from Dearborn Ave), ☎ 474-3570, preserves an ancient Indian midden mound more than 2,000 years old in a lovely bayside park. Take the short nature trail and have a picnic.

Pelican Pete's Playland at 3101 McCall Rd S, ☎ 475-2008, has miniature golf, go-carts, batting cages, a game room, and rides. It's open daily; hours change according to season. Fees are charged per activity.

FISHING & BOATING

The swift waters of Stump Pass flush out a wide variety of saltwater fish. Tarpon is king – the silver king, by name – but mackerel, snapper, grouper, and sheepshead also make worthy trophies. Try casting from the south end of **Port Charlotte State Recreation Area** (see Englewood *Sights & Attractions,* above) or from a boat in Lemon Bay. You'll find fishing piers along Beach Rd on the east side of the drawbridge.

For bait and gear, stop at **Island Court**, 1939 Beach Rd, ☎ 474-8236, open daily.

Boating, canoeing, and kayaking into Lemon Bay affords rich opportunities for wildlife spotting. Manatees, dolphin, ibises, egrets, herons, and a host of other birds hang out here.

Charter Boat Center, on Beach Rd, next to Barnacle Bill's, ☎ 475-9476, will take you deep sea fishing. So will **Silver Dollar Charters** at 1961 Beach Rd, ☎ 475-0512. Half-day rates amount to around $45 per person.

At Manasota Key's north end, the county maintains docks and a ramp on the Intracoastal Waterway, across the road from **Manasota Beach** (see North End *Sights & Attractions,* above). There are others at **Indian Mound Park** (see Englewood *Sights & Attractions,* above) on Winson Ave in downtown Englewood, ☎ 474-3570.

Weston's Resort (see *Where to Stay,* below) at 985 Gulf Blvd, ☎ 474-3431, rents boats and motors. Rates are $45-$60 (discounts for guests). **Bay Breeze Boat Rentals** at 1450 Beach Rd on the bridge, ☎ 475-0733, rents pontoon, fishing, and bowrider boats. It's open daily. Rates for a half-day rental are $65-$85; full day, $95-$135. Or try **Rocky's Recreational Rentals** at 1863 Gulf Blvd across from Chadwick Beach, ☎ 474-1022 or 800-314-4838, for 16- to 21-foot skiffs or pontoons, half- or full day, $50-$125.

Ko Ko Kai Charter Boat Service, 5040 N Beach Rd, ☎ 474-2141, at the small resort by the same name (located about mid-island) takes you island hopping to Gasparilla, Palm (see *Boca Grande*, below), Cayo Costa, Cabbage Key, Upper Captiva, and Captiva islands (see Chapter VII), and on fishing and shelling excursions. Half-day rates begin at $150 for up to six passengers.

Pontoon shuttles to Don Pedro Recreational Area (see Boca Grande *Sights & Attractions*, below) with **Capt'n Bob's Inshore Charters**, ☎ 475-6490, cost $6 per adult, $5 for children ages 1-10 for cruise only. For a burger lunch and cruise, fares are $15 for adults, $12 for children ages 3-10, $4 for children age 2 and under without meal.

SNORKELING & DIVING

Local waters, though sometimes low in visibility, hold a number of wrecks and reefs worth exploring at depths of 45 to 60 feet. A beach dive from the south end of Manasota Beach takes you to an area known as The Rocks. Snorkelers search for sharks teeth inshore.

Ko Ko Kai Charter Boat Service (see *Fishing & Boating*, above), 5040 N Beach Rd, ☎ 474-2141, does diving charters at a rate of $150 a half-day for up to six people.

To buy or rent equipment, go to **The Beach Place** at 1863 Gulf Blvd across from Chadwick Beach, ☎ 474-1022 or 800-314-4838, open daily.

OTHER WATER ADVENTURES

Bikes and Boards at 966 S McCall Rd, ☎ 474-2019, rents kayaks at $24.50-$28.50 for four hours. It also sells, and services surfboards, sailboards, skimboards, and bodyboards. It's open daily 10:30-6.

Grande Tours in Placida, ☎ 697-8825, rents kayaks for two hours at $20 a single, $25 a tandem. Half-day rates are $30 and $45; full days, $40 and $50. Canoes also available. Call for guided tour rates.

HIKING & BIKING

Take a hike on **Manasota Key Beach** (see North End *Sights & Attractions*, above). It's remote and connects to Venice's Casperson Beach, about 1½ miles to the north. Don't forget to take something to drink and to allow for the added difficulty of walking in sand.

Four miles of Beach Rd is shouldered with a bike lane, which starts in Englewood Beach and ends where the community of Manasota Key begins at the Sarasota County line.

Bikes and Boards, at 966 S McCall Rd, ☎ 474-2019, rents, sells, and services bikes for $6 a half-day. Its hours are daily 10:30-6.

WHERE TO STAY

Part summer camp, part classic resort, **Manasota Beach Club** at 7660 Manasota Key Rd, ☎ 474-2614, is a family-run 25-acre complex open only in season. You stay in a cabin-like room in wooded, beachy surroundings, and eat in the dining room. Somewhat exclusive (the club doesn't advertise), the focus is on nature, bird-watching, and resting – aside from the tennis courts, pool, bocci ball, shuffleboard, basketball, horseshoes, croquet, bicycling, sailing, windsurfing, and charter fishing available. The club is open only through the high season. Rates early January through early-April include three meals daily: $175-$185 per person. Pre- and post-season rates with no meals are $185 per cottage, and include the weeks between Thanksgiving and high season, and a couple of weeks after Easter.

Down at the south end, small condominium resorts and mom & pop motels rule. Outdoor types will find most of what they need at sprawling **Weston's Fish 'n Fun Resort**, 985 Gulf Blvd, ☎ 474-3431, which has apartments on the beach or back bay, tennis, pools, slips, a boat ramp, rentals, and a fishing pier. High-season rates are $50-$131 for fully furnished efficiencies and one- to three-bedroom apartments; $38-$115 in summer and fall.

Gasparilla Island & Out-Islands

The island Gasparilla got its name from a pirate of legend. Though pirate Gasparilla's actual existence has been disproved, his renegade spirit still lives on the island, which for decades remained aloof from development. The Gasparilla Inn set the tone back in the 1920s, when it was built to accommodate wealthy northern industrialists who arrived to exploit the deep harbor for phosphate shipping and cast for treasured tarpon in the island town of Boca Grande. Their influence kept the island exclusively wealthy for years, but in recent years, growth has visited Boca Grande and Gasparilla Island, as it has many of Florida's discovered treasures.

Tethered to the mainland by a long causeway, Gasparilla lies at the crossroads of island personalities. To its north, a string of islands, which through the years have become interconnected, resists the settling effect of attaching to the mainland. To its south begins a lily-pad trail of islands in various stages of naturalness and commercialism, islands that are covered in the next chapter (Chapter VII).

BASICS

From Highway 41, northwest of Port Charlotte, turn west on Route 776 (El Jobean Rd) and follow it Route 771, which leads you to the island. Toll is $3.20. If arriving by interstate, take exit 30 and head west on Route 776, then turn north on Highway 41 to get to Route 776, then proceed as above.

From Gasparilla Island and the Intracoastal towns of Placida and Cape Haze (on Route 775), you can find transport to the unbridged, interconnected out-islands of Little Gasparilla, Palm, and Don Pedro (see *Fishing & Boating*, below).

Boca Grande Taxi & Limo, ☎ 964-0455 or 800-771-7533, provides connections to all Florida airports. For more grandiose arrivals and departures, call **Boca Grande Seaplane,** ☎ 964-0234.

Gasparilla Island, Boca Grande.

INFORMATION

Contact the **Boca Grande Chamber of Commerce** at P.O. Box 704, Boca Grande, FL 33921, ☎ 964-0568. It is located in Courtyard Plaza at the island's north end; open Monday-Friday, 9-5. There's also **Visitor Information** on the second floor of the Theater Mall on Park Avenue, open daily 8-11.

SIGHTS & ATTRACTIONS

People daytrip to Boca Grande just to wander its one business street (Park Avenue) – where a historic depot and theater house small shopping malls – and to gawk at the mansions along the Gulf. These are in fact nearly impossible to see from the road, but the island's other historic buildings are readily accessible, including the **Gasparilla Inn** at Fifth and Palm streets (see *Where to Stay*, below), the historic churches downtown, the pretty-in-pink **Johann Fust Community Library** at 10th Street and Gasparilla Rd, Tarpon Avenue's historic fish-village shacks (known as **Whitewash Alley**), and the old dock worker cottages near the lighthouse.

Boca Grande Lighthouse.

Lighthouse Beach/Gasparilla Island State Recreation Area, south of Boca Grande on Gulf Blvd, ☎ 964-0375, fronts one defunct historic lighthouse and one in use. The plush beach encompasses 135 acres. Facilities include showers, restrooms, picnic tables, and grills. Swimming is treacherous because of the deep pass at the island's end, where in summer you can watch tarpon rolling. Parking is $2 per vehicle. The park is open daily until dusk.

The **Boca Grande Lighthouse** at Gasparilla Island State Recreation Area on Gulf Blvd, ☎ 964-0375, is 100 years old. Renovated to Old Florida style, it is open for tours the last Saturday of each month. Call ahead to make arrangements.

Take a shady, peaceful stroll or bike ride under the awesome tree canopy that lines **Banyan Street**, the area's most-photographed road.

Don Pedro Island State Recreation Area occupies 129 acres of un-bridged island north of Boca Grande. Access is by boat only. See the *Fishing & Boating* section below for details on how to get to Don Pedro for a day of isolated picnicking and beaching.

FISHING & BOATING

Fishing is practically synonymous with Boca Grande. Once winter's "social season" has ended, tarpon season brings a second influx of tourists, the rod-wielding type, from April through July. To learn the ropes about catching an in-your-dreams silver king, hook up with a pro through **The Boca Grande Fishing Guides Association,** ☎ 964-2266.

Capt. Fred Scott, ☎ 964-2333, is one experienced charter captain, whose rates for six passengers and less are $250 for a half-day of tarpon fishing and $500 for a full day; $160 for a half-day of other fishing. He also conducts island sightseeing, birding, shelling, and dinner trips, ranging from $60 to $135 for up to six persons.

An **old railroad bridge** that pokes into Gasparilla Sound is widely used as a public fishing pier. Enter it from the parking lot near Courtyard Plaza at the island's north end.

South Dock, the old phosphate shipping dock at the island's south end, provides another popular angling venue.

Tarpon fishing, Boca Grande Pass at the southern tip of Gasparillia Island.

For bait, tackle, and supplies, shop at **Millers Marina,** 222 Harbor Drive, underneath Lighthouse Hole restaurant, ☎ 964-2283.

Pass Marina at South Dock, ☎ 964-0607, has a ship's store with fishing gear and bait, plus a number of charter and ferry boats. From **Island Charters,** ☎ 964-1100, a ferry boat departs daily for Cayo Costa ($16 per person round-trip) and Cabbage Key ($20 per person round-trip). See Chapter VII for information on these destinations. Tax is not included in rates. Camper transportation to Cayo Costa and guest transportation to Useppa Island is also available. The **O.K. Bayou** ferry does one-hour sunset cruises at $9.50 per person, plus tax.

To rent a power boat, contact **Capt. Russ' Boat Rentals** at Whidden's Marina, First and Harbor streets, ☎ 964-0708. Boats 15-23 feet are available for half- or full days, $80-$200. Weekly rates also available.

Boaters can put in at the **Placida Public Boat Ramp** at the east end of the Boca Grande Causeway on Placida Rd (Rte. 771).

HIKING & BIKING

About a mile after Gasparilla Island's toll booth (only $1 fee for bike riders), the Boca Grande bike path begins. It follows an old train route along Railroad Avenue, through downtown, and seaside on Gulf Boulevard, for a total of seven miles.

Bike rentals are available at **Bike N' Beach**, 333 Park Ave, ☎ 964-0711) for $5 an hour, $9 for four hours. It's open daily; 9-5 on Sunday, 9-6 the rest of the week.

WHERE TO EAT

Boca Grande is a fun place to go for lunch or dinner in a novel setting. The experience is sure to teach your palate lessons on how seafood should really taste.

Water-lovers will enjoy the ambiance and fresh seafood at **Lighthouse Hole** on Harbor Drive, ☎ 964-0511. It overlooks a harbor filled with zillion-dollar yachts and marina activity. Indoors, you'll find an easy attitude, great grouper dishes, and a collection of baseball hats hanging from the ceiling. It's open daily for lunch and dinner. Lunch sandwiches, burgers, salads, and specials are $6-$9. Entrées are $14-$18 for dinner; reservations suggested.

For something slightly more formal, **Theater Restaurant** in Old Theatre Mall at Fourth and Park avenues, ☎ 964-0806, does linen and candlelight for dinner, and also serves lunch and Sunday brunch. The setting is unfinished wood and aquariums. Lunch will run you about $4.50-$9 for sandwiches, salads, and pasta dishes; dinner, in the vicinity of $15-$21 for crab cakes, key lime chicken, seafood pasta, and such. The food is flavorful, enhanced many evenings by live guitar music. The restaurant closes Sunday and August-September. Dinner reservations recommended.

If you're looking for a meal-time adventure, hop aboard the Palm Island Resort ferry at 7092 Placida Rd in Cape Haze and take the short, slow ride (fare $1 each) to **Rum Bay**, ☎ 697-0566. Tender baby-back ribs are a specialty; its daily lunch and dinner menus are complete with burgers, salads, chicken wings, fish, and steaks. Menu prices are $5-$7 for lunch, $10-$15 for dinner. The ferry departs hourly; reservations advised.

WHERE TO STAY

For the ultimate Boca Grande experience, book at the **Gasparilla Inn** on Palm Ave, ☎ 964-2201. That is, if you're of the right ilk or it's not "social season," December through April, when potential guests are often turned away even though rooms may be available – all to protect the interests of the duPonts, Vanderbilts, and other regular upper-echelon types who winter there. During tarpon season, April through June, the fishing buffs arrive. Amenities include an 18-hole golf course, a beach club with swimming pool, a restaurant, croquet, and afternoon tea. Rooms are rather simple in this historic, 1920s yellow wood palace. Cottages away from the main hotel prove less stuffy. Rates in social season, including three meals a day, are $179-$225; in tarpon season, including breakfast and dinner, $112-$148.

The **Innlet**, nearby at 11th Street and East Ave, ☎ 964-2294, belongs to the same operation as above, but this is more motel-like and adventure-oriented, perched on bayside banks. Accommodations are newly renovated, and guests have use of a pool, boat ramp, and dockage. All rooms have kitchens, and are $100-$125 in high season, $75-$85 in low.

A getaway to **Palm Island Resort**, ☎ 697-4800, US 800-824-5412, or FL 800-282-6142, will cure you of all reality-related blues. The Old-Florida-style villas, poised on a wide apron of sand, silky and soothing as baby powder, are a vision of fantasies unleashed. It's not for people who need lots of activity, although you can hook up with a number of different tours and charters, or swim and play tennis on the 200-acre property. Part of the resort sits around a harbor on the mainland, but the best part occupies Palm Island, where the main mode of transportation is golf cart. Rates for one-bedroom marina villas are $90-$135, depending on time of year. One- to three-bedroom island villas are $225-$380 in high season, and $150-$270 in off-season. Minimum two-night stay required.

Port Charlotte & Environs

Port Charlotte grew up on the Tamiami Trail as the area developed into a residential community tuned primarily for retirement. It consists of a strip of highway shopping centers, fast-food restaurants, and smaller branch communities, with no true downtown heart. It has a few attractions to offer sightseers, but not a lot in the way of adventure.

BASICS

Exits 30 and 31 take you into town from Interstate 75. Highway 41, aka Tamiami Trail, runs congestedly through its center. Kings Highway (Route 769) and Harbor View Rd are major streets to the east of Highway 41. Edgewater Drive is a main through-street to the west.

SIGHTS & ATTRACTIONS

In the offshoot town of Murdock you'll find the headquarters for **Texas Rangers Spring Training**, ☎ 817-273-5000, at **Charlotte County Stadium** on Route 776, off Hwy 41. The team plays its exhibition season during March; call for current ticket prices. In summer, the **Charlotte Rangers**, ☎ 624-2211, play; tickets are $3.50-$4.

The best bet for recreationists is the **Port Charlotte Beach** at the end of Harbor Blvd, ☎ 627-1628. The man-made beach is central to a variety of facilities and activities, including volleyball, basketball, tennis, horseshoes, a playground, boat ramps, a fishing pier, picnic facilities, and a swimming pool. Parking is 25¢ an hour or $2.25 a day. The park is open 6-9.

FISHING & BOATING

There is a fishing pier with bait and tackle concession at the **Port Charlotte Beach** recreational complex (see *Sights & Attractions*, above) on the southeast end of Harbor Blvd, ☎ 627-1628. It pokes into Alligator Bay off of Charlotte Harbor. The park also has a boat ramp.

Another boat ramp is located in **El Jobean Park** on El Jobean Rd.

Charlotte Harbor Pier juts into the mouth of the Peace River on Bayshore Rd in the community of Charlotte Harbor, which lies on the northern banks of the river.

For freshwater fishing, try the small lake at **Kiwanis Park** (see *Hiking & Biking*, below) on Donora Street at Victoria Ave.

Tarpon Hunter II in Port Charlotte, ☎ 743-6622, offers charters in Charlotte Harbor and backwaters. Specialties include fly and light tackle fishing. Rates are $180-$225 for a half-day; $275-$300 for a full day.

OTHER WATER ADVENTURES

Jacobs WaterSki Rides, ☎ 629-8855, gives lessons on skiing, wakeboarding, kneeboarding, barefooting, and trick skiing. Rates for lessons and towing range from $40 for a half-day, unlimited group size, to $245 for all day. All equipment is included.

HIKING & BIKING

Kiwanis Park on Donora Street at Victoria Ave, has a jogging/fitness trail, a self-guided nature trail, and a lakeside Audubon trail. Also picnic facilities. It's open daily, sunrise-9.

WHERE TO EAT

Highway 41 leaves a trail of fast-food and chain restaurants from one end of Port Charlotte to another. For something with more personality, head to Boca Grande or Punta Gorda.

Local places often change hands and names before you can make a return visit. One that gets current acclaim for its steaks is **Cap'n and the Cowboy**, 2200 Kings Hwy, ☎ 743-3969. It's open daily except Monday for lunch ($2-$10) and dinner ($11-$21).

Punta Gorda

Port Charlotte's neighbor across the river provides a historic counterpart to the newer town's lack of identity. Its history begins with Ponce de León, who is believed to have landed and suffered fatal Indian arrow wounds on the shores of Charlotte Harbor at Punta Gorda's western boundary. Within the shelter of the Peace River, a turn-of-the century community cropped up around a deep port and commercial fishing industry. Once a thriving city and resort, Punta Gorda today is a quiet, neighborly community where history is being revived and the wilderness beckons at the side door.

BASICS

Follow Highway 41 to reach Punta Gorda's heart. From Interstate 75, take the short drive off of Exit 29. Marion (westbound) and Olympia (eastbound) avenues are the main one-way streets downtown. Retta

Esplanade is a scenic riverside route to the north of and paralleling Marion Avenue.

DOWNTOWN SIGHTS & ATTRACTIONS

Explore Punta Gorda's past within its historic district, which hugs Tamiami Trail along Nesbit Street and Marion and Olympia avenues. Old commercial buildings have been spruced up for a second life. Take the drive along **Retta Esplanade** slowly. Absorb the riverfront scenery on one side, and the row of handsome historic homes on the other.

The exhibits at **Florida Adventure Museum of Charlotte County**, 260 W Retta Esplanade, ☎ 639-3777, deal with local natural history, ecology, and history. Changing exhibits deal with Native Americans, manatees, space travel, and other Florida-related subjects. Admission is $1. Hours are 8-5 Monday-Friday, 10-3 Saturday, closed Sunday.

To commemorate Juan Ponce de León's local landing in his quest for youth, **Ponce de León Historical Park**, on the west end of Marion Ave, holds an unpretentious monument, nature observation boardwalk into the mangroves, and lovely waterside picnic area with barbecue grills. Admission is free. It's open daily except Tuesday, dusk-dawn.

On the same grounds, **Peace River Wildlife Center** ☎ 637-3830, conducts tours among orphaned, injured, and recovering animals that are being rehabilitated for release. A donation is requested.

OUTLYING SIGHTS & ATTRACTIONS

East of town, the state has set aside 65,770 acres as one of its 62 designated hunting preserves at **Fred C. Babcock-Cecil M. Webb Wildlife Management Area**, off Route 31, ☎ 639-1531. Advance permission is required. There is a public shooting range on the property, accessible from Tucker Grade via Rifle Range Rd. The range is open daily during daylight hours, but closes the fourth Saturday of each month until 2 pm for hunter education training.

To slip into the bygones of Florida wilderness, enjoy the low-key attractions at **Babcock Wilderness Adventures** off Route 31, ☎ 489-3911 or 800-500-5583. A swamp buggy is your chariot through time and the pristine wetlands of 90,000-acre Telegraph Cypress Swamp.

The 90-minute tour shows you alligators, deer, relocated bison, turkeys, panthers, and a museum that chronicles the partial on-site filming of the movie *Just Cause*, starring Sean Connery. Admission is $17.95 for adults; $9.95 for kids 3-12. Advance reservations required.

Charlotte County Speedway at 8655 Piper Rd, ☎ 575-2422, runs a year-round schedule of weekend car-racing events. Cost of tickets varies; call for events and rates.

South of town, the **Charlotte Harbor Environmental Center** at 10941 Burnt Store Rd, ☎ 575-4800, conducts guided tours around four miles of nature trails, and displays educational exhibits about local wildlife. Admission is free. Hours are 8-3 on weekdays, 8-12 on Saturday, and 11-3 on Sunday.

FISHING & BOATING

Gilchrist Park (see *Hiking & Biking*, below) on Retta Esplanade, has a fishing pier that reaches into the wide mouth of the Peace River. For fishing needs, stop at **Bill's Tackle Shop** at 135 W Marion Ave, ☎ 639-1305.

Boat ramps in Punta Gorda are located at **Ponce de León Park** (see *Sights & Attractions*, above) on the west end of Marion Ave, at **Laishley Park** on Nesbit Street, at **Riverside Park** on Riverside Dr, on Washington Loop Rd, and on Darst Ave.

King Fisher Fleet at Fishermen's Village Marina, 1200 W Retta Esplanade, ☎ 639-0969, has been doing fishing, nature, and out-island boating excursions for many years. Rates for deep-sea fishing aboard a 35-footer are $450 per day for up to six persons; for back-bay fishing, $250 per day, $150 for a half-day for up to four. Sightseeing voyage fares begin at $5 for a sunset cruise. Day cruise fare is $18.95. Children board for half-fare. Tax is not included in prices.

The River Cat, ☎ 637-9222 or 800-308-7506, departs from Deep Creek Marina for a Peace River Lunch Cruise. Cost is $16.95. Other excursions include sunset, historic, and nature tours, $5-$12.95.

HIKING & BIKING

Gilchrist Park runs along the river on Retta Esplanade and has bike paths plus picnicking, a huge playground, basketball, and a tennis court.

The **Charlotte Harbor Environmental Center** (see *Outlying Sights & Attractions*, above) at 10941 Burnt Store Rd, ☎ 575-4800, has four miles of nature trails. Admission is free. Hours are 8-3 on weekdays, 8-12 on Saturday, and 11-3 on Sunday.

WHERE TO EAT

Many head to **Fishermen's Village**, a waterside shopping-dining complex at Maud and Marion avenues, to find a variety of meal-time options, from deli to sit-down.

The most formal at Fishermen's Village is **Smuggler's Captain's Table**, ☎ 637-1177. The setting is tastefully nautical, with lots of pewter, classic sailing ship models, and a great view of the river. Seafood and meat dishes with local island names are well-designed and tasty. **Harpoon Harry's Lounge** is more casual and also serves food. Both open daily for lunch and dinner. Luncheon sandwiches, salads, and entrées range from $5-$9, dinner entrées are $10-$22. Reservations are accepted for dinner.

Locals avoid that tourist scene, especially in season, and stick to downtown. One of the business community's best finds is **The Legal Café**, next to the courthouse at 210 Taylor Street, ☎ 637-0700. The menu comes on yellow legal paper clipped in a file folder with clever court-related descriptions. Staff is friendly and accommodating; the dining rooms are cheerful; the food unpretentiously good. Legal Café serves daily breakfast ($1.75-$4) and lunch ($4-$5).

WHERE TO STAY

Punta Gorda has its share of chain motels. To avoid them, try the local antithesis, **Gilchrist Bed & Breakfast Inn** at 115 Gilchrist Street, ☎ 575-4129. Tin-roofed and lattice-trimmed, the 1914 home holds guest rooms and two- and three-room suites priced at $85-$150 in winter, $65-$110 in summer. It is convenient to downtown's historic district and Gilchrist Park (see *Hiking & Biking*, above).

Sea Cove Motel at 25000 E Marion Ave, ☎ 639-0060, lies on the Peace River east of town, and offers fishing, swimming, and shuffleboard. Rates for rooms, efficiencies, and one- and two-bedroom apartments run $35-$58. Minimum stays required on efficiencies and apartments.

CAMPING

East of town, **Yogi Bear's Jellystone Park**, 9770 SW County Rd 769 (Kings Highway), ☎ 993-2111 or 800-795-9733, is newly opened. Overnight rates are $18-$29.50 for tents and RVs.

Chapter VII

Lee Island Coast

Area code: 941

"There is only one Fort Myers and 90 million people will find it out," declared Thomas Edison in the late 1880s. The genius inventor moved his winter quarters to town after northern chills threatened his health and he discovered a stand of bamboo on a Caloosahatchee riverside plot. The bamboo would come in handy for his experiments in creating a lightbulb. The area's balmy weather would extend his life another 46 years.

As Edison predicted, plenty have discovered Fort Myers, and it has grown into a major city, the hub of Lee County. The tourism bureau has adopted the name Lee Island Coast for this kingdom bordered by the Gulf of Mexico, mottled by islands, and stabbed through by the wide Caloosahatchee River. The moniker promotes what visitors these days favor about Fort Myers – its quiet, protected waters and proximity to wild and play-happy islands.

Lee County guards some of the West Coast's most precious historical and natural treasures. Edison's winter home and laboratory remain, along with the remnants of a peculiar turn-of-the-century religious cult at Koreshan State Historic Site. From more distant times, ancient wetlands survive untouched and protected, along with Calusa Amerindian mounds, wooded preserves, barrier islands, fruit farms, fishing communities, and wildlife estuaries. The Lee Island Coast offers endless possibilities for outdoor activity on land and sea.

Transportation, Etc.

Southwest Florida International Airport in Fort Myers, ☎ 768-1000, services this segment of coast, with flights from all parts of the country and to and from Canada, Germany, and limited other international destinations. Major domestic airlines include **American,** ☎ 800-433-7300; **Continental,** ☎ 939-9524 or 800-525-0280; **Delta,** ☎ 800-221-1212; **TWA,** ☎ 800-221-2000; **United,** ☎ 800-241-6522; and **USAir,** ☎ 800-428-4322.

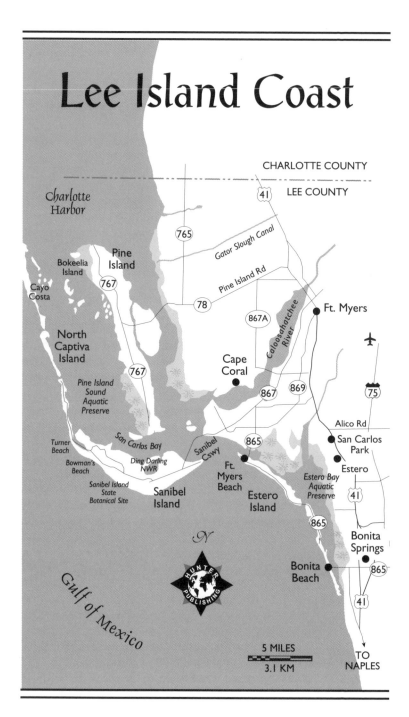

Lee Island Coast

CHARLOTTE COUNTY

LEE COUNTY

41

Charlotte
Harbor

765

Gator Slough Canal

Pine Island Rd

Pine
Island

Bokeelia
Island

767

Cayo
Costa

78

867A

Caloosahatchee River

Ft. Myers

North
Captiva
Island

767

Cape
Coral

Pine Island
Sound
Aquatic
Preserve

867   869

75

Alico Rd

San Carlos Bay

865

San Carlos
Park

Turner
Beach

Sanibel
Cswy

Estero

Bowman's
Beach

Ding Darling
NWR

Ft.
Myers
Beach

Estero Bay
Aquatic
Preserve

41

Sanibel Island
State
Botanical Site

Sanibel
Island

Estero
Island

865

Bonita
Springs

N

Bonita
Beach

865

Gulf of Mexico

41

TO
NAPLES

5 MILES

3.1 KM

Rental cars are available at the airport and other locations throughout the area, including **Avis,** ☎ 768-2121 (airport), 278-1294, or 800-331-1212; **Hertz,** ☎ 768-3100 (airport) or 800-654-3131; and **Budget,** ☎ 768-1500 (airport), 275-6886, or 800-527-0700.

Several taxi companies provide transportation to and from the airport, including **Aaron Airport Transportation,** ☎ 277-7000, and **Airport Taxi,** ☎ 768-5400.

Interstate 75 and Highway 41 (Tamiami Trail) are the major arteries, and they run parallel to each other north-south. Both connect to Tampa and Miami.

INFORMATION

Contact **Lee County Visitor & Convention Bureau**, P.O Box 2445, Fort Myers 33902-2445, ☎ 335-2631 or 800-237-6444.

Events

Like many things in Fort Myers, the town's grandest festival revolves around the memory of Thomas Edison. **The Edison Pageant of Light Festival** takes place in late January to early February and features a lighted night parade. ☎ 334-2550 for details.

Other popular events include the **Fort Myers Beach Shrimp Festival,** late February or early March, ☎ 463-0194; the **Caloosahatchee River Basin Festival,** ☎ 275-3435, held in March or April at the Calusa Nature Center in Fort Myers and featuring planetarium shows, guided tours, and folk demonstrations; Pine Island's **Mangomania** in July (admission), ☎ 283-7067; and Cape Coral's **Christmas Boat-a-Long**, a decorated boat parade with live entertainment, ☎ 574-0801.

The **Sanibel Shell Fair and Show,** ☎ 472-2155, kicks off the month of March, as it has for more than 50 years. Held at the Sanibel Community Center, it showcases sea life, specimen shells, and shell art. Other events that focus on the great outdoors include two hosted by 'Tween Waters Resort on Captiva Island: **Caloosa Catch & Release Fishing Tournament**, a four-day event in June, and the **Captiva Sea Kayak Classic**, taking place for three days in December and including a kayaking symposium and races (☎ 472-9484 or 800-223-5865, extension 318). The **Fort Myers Beach Sandsculpting Contest,** ☎ 454-7500, takes place early November at Outrigger Beach Resort and the Holiday Inn.

Cape Coral/North Fort Myers

North Fort Myers and Cape Coral lie on the north bank of the Caloosahatchee River, across from Fort Myers. They are two separate, relatively new communities. Cape Coral is the largest, a growing
residential town with interesting family attractions. It is gateway to
off-beat Pine Island and its complement of unbridged islands.

BASICS

Approaching from the north via Interstate 75 or Highway 41, you will
first reach North Fort Myers. To get to North Fort Myers and Cape
Coral off of Interstate 75, you must head west along Bayshore/Pine
Island Rd (Route 78, exit 26). Highway 41 takes you directly into North
Fort Myers. Again, head west on Route 78 to reach Cape Coral.

Del Prado Boulevard and Santa Barbara Boulevard are Cape Coral's
major east-west thoroughfares. Bridges cross to Fort Myers at Interstate 75, Highway 41, Business Highway 41 (Edison Bridge at Fowler
Street), Colonial Boulevard (Midpoint Memorial Bridge, under con-
struction), and Cape Coral Parkway/College Parkway.

Lee County Transit provides public transportation in Fort Myers. Full
fare is $1, 50¢ for seniors, and 15¢ transfers. For a schedule, call
275-8726.

INFORMATION

Contact the **North Fort Myers Chamber of Commerce**, at
13180 N Cleveland Ave, North Fort Myers 33903, ☎ 997-9111,
with questions. For information on Cape Coral, contact **Cape
Coral Chamber of Commerce**, P.O. 747, Cape Coral 33904,
☎ 549-6900 or 800-226-9609. A **Southwest Florida Chamber
of Commerce** visitor's information center is located at 1625 Cape
Coral Pkwy E, ☎ 542-3721, open Monday-Friday 9-5.

SIGHTS & ATTRACTIONS

Look for the overgrown conch shell on Highway 41 in North Fort
Myers, and you'll have found **The Shell Factory** at 2787 N Tamiami
Trail, ☎ 995-2141 or 800-282-5805. Admission and tours of the shell
processing facility are free. The main attraction is its bazaar for shells,

shell things, and other Florida souvenirs. It also offers a bumper boat ride, aquariums, and eats. Hours are 9-6 daily.

Many of Cape Coral's attractions are kid-oriented. A favorite for families on steamy summer days, **Sun Splash Family Waterpark** at 400 Santa Barbara Blvd, ☎ 574-0557, offers refreshment for all ages. The smallest can splash around shallow pools, climb on an alligator's back (not real, of course), or ride with mom and dad on an innertube. Taller ones will want to stand in line for the speed-demon slides. Lockers, snacks, and gifts are available. Coolers are not allowed in the park, but there is a picnic ground with play equipment outside the gate. Admission is by height: $8.50 for anyone 48 inches or taller; $6.50 for children under 48 inches and older than 2. From mid-March to the end of August, the park is open daily at 10 or 11. Closing hours vary between 5 and 9. After Labor Day, the park is open some weekends and holidays. Call ahead for current schedule.

The Children's Science Center, 2915 NE Pine Island Rd, ☎ 997-0012, is a five-acre, indoor-outdoor opportunity to learn about Florida ecology, electricity, computers, fossils, NASA satellites, and various scientific phenomena through games, puzzles, and other interactivity. It's open Monday-Friday 9:30-4:30, weekends 12-5. Admission for children ages 3-16 is $2; for adults, $4.

Batting cages, go-carts, bumper boats, miniature golf, and a video arcade make **Greenwell's Bat-A-Ball and Family Fun Park**, at 35 NE Pine Island Rd, ☎ 574-4386, a hit with the kids. It is named after Red Sox baseball player Mike Greenwell, a Cape Coral son. Hours are 10-10 weekdays and 10-12 midnight Friday and Saturday. Admission is per activity.

Learn more about the history of Cape Coral, a young river town created from a vast hunting preserve, at the **Cape Coral Historical Museum**, Cultural Park Blvd, ☎ 772-7037. Exhibits include one explaining the natural history of the burrowing owl, a local inhabitant and icon. Hours are 1-4 Wednesday, Thursday, and Sunday. Adults are asked to donate $1.

FISHING & BOATING

Headquarters for fishing types, boaters, and beachers, **Cape Coral Yacht Club**, 5819 Driftwood Pkwy, ☎ 574-0815, is a city facility set on the Caloosahatchee River. The public beach is enhanced by a barbecue area, shaded picnic tables, restrooms, outdoor shower, tennis, horseshoes, a heated pool ($1.50-$3.50 admission), adult and youth classes and programs, a 620-foot lighted fishing pier, and a free public boat ramp. A large beach pavilion is available for rental. The beach closes at dusk.

For bait, tackle, and fishing supplies, try **Tackle Haven**, at 4643 Coronado Pkwy, ☎ 542-2658. Hours are 8-4 weekdays, 6-6 weekends.

To rent a boat in North Fort Myers, see **Waterway Boat Rentals**, Marinatown Marina at 3446 Marinatown Lane, ☎ 997-0019. Half-day rates for pontoon boats are $80; for cabin cruisers, $100-$128.

HIKING & BIKING

Many of Cape Coral's city streets designate bike lanes. Bikers also branch out from town along rural roadways. One scenic, low-traffic route on the city outskirts, Burnt Store Marina Rd, connects to Pine Island Rd northwest of town.

OTHER LAND SPORTS

BMX Park, 1410 SW Sixth Place, has a Bicycle Moto-Cross track, as well as a picnic area, playground, and sand volleyball court.

WHERE TO EAT

Cape Coral is known for its Italian restaurants, growing Hispanic population, and annual Munich in Cape Coral festival in October. The following three dining recommendations reflect its multi-dimensional heritage.

At **Dario's Restaurant**, 1805 Del Prado Blvd in Coral Pointe Shopping Center, ☎ 574-7798, the menu is a mix-and-match Italian masterpiece. It combines veal, seafood, pasta, beef, and poultry with a variety of sauces and styles of preparation – oreganata, diavolo, marsala, pizzaiola, marinara, and francese, for example. The menu represents both northern and southern Italian gastronomy. It's open daily for dinner, Monday-Friday for lunch. Reservations are accepted. Main courses are $9-$24.

You can't miss **Iguana Mia**'s lizard-green exterior at 1027 Cape Coral Pkwy, ☎ 945-7755. The large dining room is casual, with plastic chairs and Mexican kitsch. One of the area's most popular Mexican restaurants (there is a spinoff in Fort Myers), it serves standard specialties with a few creative variations. Its chicken sampler plate is popular. It's open daily for lunch and dinner. Prices are $4-$17 for main dishes.

Restaurant Tannengarten, 3724 Del Prado Blvd, ☎ 549-1300, serves authentic German dishes in generous portions. Hearty meals begin with tangy sliced bread, soup, and a three-in-one salad containing greens, potato salad, and cabbage salad. The sauerbraten is excellent. Order spaetzle and red cabbage on the side if they're not included with your selection. Other offerings: wienerschnitzel, steak with sauteed onions, beef rolls, roast pork, liver dumplings. Under recent new ownership, the service tends to be slow. Open daily except Monday for dinner. Reservations recommended. Entree prices are $8-$17.

WHERE TO STAY

Not widely known for its tourism and resorts, Cape Coral offers mostly chain hotels. Visitors to the area tend to stay in Fort Myers or closer to the Gulf front.

For sports enthusiasts, **Cape Coral Golf and Tennis Resort**, at 4003 Palm Tree Blvd, ☎ 542-3191 or 800-648-1475, provides reasonably priced accommodations in a lovely golf course setting with newly renovated facilities. Rates in winter high season range from $108-$130; off-season, $99-$125. Golf and tennis packages available.

Pine Island & Out-Islands

You must be a specialty traveler to truly appreciate Pine Island. Only utterly devoted fisherfolk, history buffs, or exotic fruit and fresh seafood connoisseurs need apply.

Don't come here looking for beaches and yuppie bars. Go to neighboring Sanibel Island or Fort Myers Beach if that's the kind of traveler you are. Beaches do not really exist on Pine Island (there's one man-made beach in St. James City) and that is the very reason it has ducked tourism's inherent damage to island heritage and identity. Tucked between barrier islands and the Cape Coral mainland, Pine Island hides from hedonistic sun-seekers. Still today, as in centuries past, it is about Amerindian villages, farming, and fishing.

Pine Island's south-end Galt Island and its community of Pineland once held major Calusa Amerindian religious centers with elaborate canal systems and sizable shell midden mounds. In the Calusas' wake settled Cuban immigrants who set up fishing camps and began a way of life that continues to this day. A recent ban on net-fishing has changed life somewhat for Pine Islanders. Many have turned to related careers, such as crabbing and charter fishing guides.

BASICS

From Highway 41 or Interstate 75, take Route 78, aka Pine Island Rd (exit 26) heading west. The road shoots straight across the Pine Island Bridge to and through Matlacha (MATT-la-shay), one of the island's four communities, and into Island Center. At Route 767 (Stringfellow Rd), you turn left to reach St. James City, the biggest town, or right to go to Pineland and Bokeelia (Bo-KEEL-ee-ya).

Pine Island is the departure point for water taxis and charters to Useppa, Cayo Costa, Cabbage Key, and North Captiva islands (see *Boating*, below).

Light aircraft owners can use North Captiva's 2,300-foot grass airstrip. Few cars run on the island, but golf carts and bicycles can be rented there.

Cabbage Key operations are also based on Pine Island at Bokeelia. For reservations and information on transportation, ☎ 283-2278.

INFORMATION

Contact the **Greater Pine Island Chamber of Commerce**, P.O. Box 525, Pine Island 33909, ☎ 283-0888. An information center is located before the bridge to Matlacha on Pine Island Rd, open Monday-Saturday 10-4.

SIGHTS & ATTRACTIONS

At Phillips Park, **Museum of the Islands**, 5728 Sesame Drive, ☎ 283-1525, concentrates on the island's Calusa and fishing heritage with vignettes and a replica of an Amerindian midden mound, modeled after one excavated on the island. Hours are daily 1-4; closed Monday and Wednesday in the off-season. No admission; donations accepted.

Turn left on Pineland Rd for a scenic trip through time-stilled **Pineland**, a tiny town studded with historic Cracker shacks and Amerindian mounds. A plaque commemorates archaeological finds proving the island's importance as a Calusa cultural center.

To tour an important aspect of Pine Island livelihood, watch for signs on Stringfellow Rd for **Sunburst Tropical Fruit Company** at 7113 Howard Rd in Bokeelia; ☎ 283-1200. A fruit farm that grows mangoes and other exotic fruit, it conducts tours of the groves aboard a converted mango trailer. You can also sample and buy fresh (in summer) and processed fruits – chutneys, sauces, jams – year-round. Admission to the farm and nursery is free; tours cost $5 per adult and $2.50 for children 4-12. Call ahead for an appointment.

Lee Coast's unbridged islands may be its most tantalizing feature, especially for adventurers. Two barrier islands hold state parks with secluded beaches and other treasures.

North Captiva, also referred to as Upper Captiva, is a long, skinny island whose park lands contain primitive beachfront with no facilities. **North Captiva State Recreation Area**'s 500 acres at the island's southern end provide refuge for waterfowl, shore birds, and migrating species. Recreational boaters head here with their suntan lotion and picnics, or boat around to Safety Harbor on the northern lee side for lunch in one of four little restaurants. Home and condo rentals are available on the island (see *Where to Stay*, below).

Cayo Costa State Park, ☎ 964-0375, to the north, offers more formal beach facilities on its northern Gulf side. Rustic cabins and tent sites accommodate primitive campers (see *Camping*, below), and picnic tables, grills, pavilions, and showers serve the need of picnickers. **Johnson Shoals**, a sandbar to the north, is a popular stop for shellers. Off the beach, hikers can follow a trail to an old cemetery and other remnants of a bygone fishing community. Take lots of bug repellent. There's a dock on the Gulf side and sheltered moorings on the bay side, with a tram that runs between (50¢ round-trip for non-campers). There are also stretches to the south with no facilities, which are favored by lovers of isolation. Fee for admission to the park is $2 per family.

Cabbage Key.

Boaters know **Cabbage Key** principally as a lunch spot (see *Where to Eat*, below). There is also has a nature trail here (see *Hiking*, below).

FISHING & BOATING

Pine Island's lack of beaches keeps away throngs of wildlife-disturbing tourists. The even better news is that it attracts rich sealife to its mangrove inlets, canals, and mudflats – for example, the blue-eyed bay scallop, blue crab, and a wide variety of fish, from the tasty snook to the disdained catfish. Serious fisherfolk will find Pine Island, with its predilection for angling, pure heaven.

The bridge to Pine Island is known as the **World's Fishingest Bridge.** Get your supplies, bait, and licenses at **Seven C's Bait & Tackle Shop,** before the bridge in Matlacha, ☎ 283-1674.

Fishing charters run about $250 for a half-day, $350 for a full day. Contact **Captain Bill Cyzewski,** ☎ 283-0106, a long-time island guide.

Pine Island's backwaters are a great place for spotting manatees, dolphins, and rare birds. **Pine Island Sound Aquatic Preserve** encompasses 54,000 acres of protected submerged land and shoals. The **Pine Island National Wildlife Refuge,** offshore from the island's west side, can be seen only by boat. It consists of a number of keys, including **Big Bird Rookery,** the principal one.

Sea Kayaking on the Back Bay waters.

The best way to explore Pine Island's unplundered natural pleasures is with the **Gulf Coast Kayak Company** in Matlacha, ☎ 283-1125. It offers day trips into Matlacha Aquatic Preserve (part of the Pine Island Sound Preserve), overnight trips to Cayo Costa (see *Sights & Attractions,* above), and full moon and new moon astronomy ventures. Average cost for a four-hour nature tour is $35 per person. Call ahead to reserve.

From **Four Winds Marina** at 16501 Stringfellow Rd, Bokeelia, ☎ 283-0250, you can rent a 17- to 19-foot powerboat for $100-$135 a half-day, $150-$200 a full day. You can also board a daily water taxi to Cayo Costa and Cabbage Key, departing at 9:30 and returning at 4. Reserve through **Tropic Star Cruises,** ☎ 283-0015. Water taxi costs are $19 for adults, $12 for kids 2-11.

Island Charters, ☎ 283-1113, based at Pineland Marina, runs shuttle boats to North Captiva 9-5 daily for $15 one-way per person, $25 round-trip (discounts on groups of four and larger). It also does private charters to Cayo Costa and Cabbage Key, or for fishing, sightseeing, and shelling.

Boaters can use the public boat ramp at Matlacha Park for free.

On North Captiva, rentals are availabe from **North Captiva Island Club,** for Sunfish sailboats ($60/half-day), kayaks ($20-$30/two hours), and power boats ($140/half-day). Fishing and shelling charters can be arranged by calling ☎ 395-9303.

HIKING & BIKING

A short, sporadic bike path/route wends through Bokeelia and St. James City. Stringfellow Rd is lightly traveled and provides safe, easy, and extensive on-road biking. Plans are in the works for a continuous bike path connecting St. James City, Bokeelia, and Matlacha in a 40-mile loop.

Residents and guests of North Captiva most often get around via golf cart. The trails make for good hiking along paths covering several miles that lead to preserved state park land. You can also rent mountain, tandem, and beach bikes on the island. Cost is $10-$15 a day. Hourly and weekly rates also available.

On Cayo Costa, six trails cover five miles at the island's wooded north end. Cabbage Key provides a short, marked nature trail, perfect for walking off lunch in the Inn.

WHERE TO EAT

Mangoes and Pine Island are synonymous. The island hosts a mango festival (see *Events*, above) in the height of mango season. Exotic fruit farmers also grow guavas, longans, carambolas (star fruit), lychees, and other rare species. You can buy them fresh off the tree from stands along Stringfellow Rd.

With its fishy preoccupation, the island also has a reputation for fresh seafood. Matlacha's fish houses, where fresh oysters, shrimp, blue crab, grouper, snapper, pompano, and scallops are off-loaded for transshipment, are the place to buy. The island boasts a slew of small restaurants using local products, but with a Midwestern, comfort food approach.

A favorite of boaters and residents is situated on a canal in St. James City. The **Waterfront Restaurant** at 2131 Oleander Street, ☎ 283-0592, occupies a historic one-room schoolhouse and has indoor and outdoor seating. The menu ranges from grouper sandwiches to shrimp dinners, priced from $3 to $13. It is open daily except Wednesday for lunch and dinner.

One of the most delightful dining adventures the region has to offer involves island-hopping to somewhere with no cars and lots of character.

Cabbage Key Inn on Cabbage Key, ☎ 283-2278, is most popular among tour and recreational boaters. In a historic home built by novelist Mary Roberts Rinehart in the 1930s, diners tape autographed dollar bills to the wall and feast on cheeseburgers, stone crab, and grouper sandwiches. Open daily for lunch and dinner. Prices for lunch are $4-$9; for dinner, $16-$20.

Less known (but building a following) and harder to reach, **Barnacle Phil's** at 4401 Point House Trail in North Captiva's Safety Harbor, ☎ 472-6394, is known for its black beans 'n' rice – the rage among reclusive stars like Henry Winkler. It also serves burgers, fish sandwiches, and other casual fare, priced at $4-$6. Open daily for lunch and dinner.

WHERE TO STAY

Matlacha has lots of small fishing motels ensconced in its historic downtown section of knick-knack Cracker houses. St. James also has its fishing lodges, such as **Water's Edge** at Oleander & Sanibel Blvd, ☎ 283-0515. This place is on a canal and provides guests with boat slips and a ramp across the street. In-season rates range from $79-$93, off-season, $54-$85, for rooms and efficiencies.

Throughout the island, you can find rentals, from mobile homes to luxury condominiums. In season, monthly rental rates are $800-$2,300. For information call **Pine Island Realty**, ☎ 283-1028.

For the ultimate island getaway, escape to North Captiva. You'll find no cars, no pressure, and lots of peace. For home rentals, contact **North Captiva Island Club**, P.O. Box 1000, Pineland 33945, ☎ 395-1001 or 800-576-7343. Weekly rates are $800-$3,500 in season, $700-$2,500 otherwise. Bring groceries and supplies with you, or order them ahead when you reserve. Tennis courts, a fitness center, a pool, a game room, and children's activities are provided.

CAMPING

Fort Myers-Pine Island KOA in St. James City at 5120 Stringfellow Rd, ☎ 283-2415 or 800-992-7202, accommodates tent and RV-campers. Sites for campers with full-hookups run about $34 for two adults per night; tent sites with no hookups, $26. Weekly and monthly rates are available. The campground has three on-premises fishing lakes, a tennis court, shuffleboard, a pool and spa, saunas, horseshoes, laundry, activities, and its own tour/fishing boat.

At **Cayo Costa State Park,** you can reserve one of 12 rustic cabins or set up a tent on the Gulf. Bring your own drinking water. In season, huts are reserved a year in advance. Tent sites are less in demand. To reserve a cabin, ☎ 964-0375 Monday-Friday 8-5. Boaters can anchor bayside in a safe harbor.

Fort Myers

As the metropolitan hub of this slab of coast line, Fort Myers is home of Southwest Florida International Airport and a forthcoming university. It was settled back in the days when the Caloosahatchee River was the major thoroughfare, plied by steamboats. It got its "fort" designation during Civil and Seminole wars, which, in their wake, brought its first wave of settlers: soldiers who fell in love with the pleasant climate. Inventor Thomas Alva Edison moved his winter quarters here in the late 1880s, which brought other rich and famous types, including Henry Ford, his next door neighbor, and Harvey Goodyear.

In recent years, the focus of seasonal visitors has shifted to the Gulf front and Fort Myers struggles to keep its downtown alive.

BASICS

Highway 41 becomes Cleveland Avenue as it crosses the Caloosahatchee River from the north into Fort Myers. Exits off of Interstate 75 lead to the main east-west arteries: Palm Beach Blvd/Route 82 (exit 23), Colonial Boulevard/Route 884 (exit 22), and Daniels Parkway (exit 21). Traveling (roughly) north-south, historic and royal palm-lined McGregor Boulevard (Route 867) follows the river and its old homes. Summerlin Avenue (869), Cleveland Avenue, and Metro Parkway run parallel to the east.

INFORMATION

For information on Fort Myers, contact the **Greater Fort Myers Chamber of Commerce**, P.O. Box 9289, Fort Myers, FL 33902, ☎ 332-3624. A welcome center is located downtown at 2310 Edwards Drive It is open 9-4:30 Monday-Friday.

DOWNTOWN SIGHTS & ATTRACTIONS

Fort Myers' premier attraction remembers its most illustrious citizens. **The Thomas Edison Winter Home and Museum and Ford Estate** at

Edison Home, Fort Myers.

2350-2400 McGregor Blvd, ☎ 334-3614, conducts tours of the famous neighbors' river homes. See a lightbulb lit by its inventor – still glowing. Walk through Edison's botanical gardens whose rare plants he imported to use in experiments. The tour includes Edison's winter lab and a look at Ford's recently restored home. Afterwards, you are free to browse the museum, which displays many of Edison's 1,000 patented inventions. Admission for all attractions is $10 for adults and $5 for children ages 6-12. Guided tours are conducted every day, continuously from 9 to 3:30 Monday-Saturday and 12-3:30 pm Sunday.

Still developing, the **Imaginarium: Hands-On Museum and Aquarium**, at 2000 Cranford Ave, ☎ 337-3332, transformed the city's old waterworks into an interactive facility where you can feel a cloud, learn about the world of finance, touch a horseshoe crab, and see how a house is built. Be sure to check out the gift shop; it has a great collection of nature-oriented toys and books. Museum hours are 10-5 Monday-Saturday; 12-5 Sunday. Admission is $6 for anyone over 14 years old; $3 for children ages 3-12 when accompanied by an adult.

Nearby in a historic train depot, the **Fort Myers Historical Museum**, at 2300 Peck Street, ☎ 332-5955, displays prehistoric Calusa Amerindian models, graphic depictions, historical IQ games, rare glass and art collections, a circa-1930 private rail car, and changing exhibits. It's open Tuesday-Friday 9-4 and Saturday 10-4. Admission is $2.50 for adults; $1 for children under age 12.

The **Boston Red Sox** play their spring exhibition game season (March-April) at **City of Palms Park** on Edison Ave at Jackson Street, ☎ 334-4700. Tickets cost $9 and $10.

Broadway Palm Dinner Theatre, at 1380 Colonial Blvd, ☎ 278-4422, serves a lavish buffet with professionally performed comedies and musicals. Attend a matinee Wednesday, Thursday, Saturday, or Sunday for $28, or an evening show Tuesday through Saturday for $31-$34. Gratuities are extra. Children ages 12 and under pay $17 for any show.

OUTLYING SIGHTS & ATTRACTIONS

Small and homey, **Calusa Nature Center and Planetarium** at 3450 Ortiz Ave, ☎ 275-3435, offers a two-mile wildlife trail, a Seminole Amerindian village and a native bird aviary. Snakes, tarantulas, alligators, and bees are among the live animal exhibits. Staff demonstrate snake and alligator behaviors daily. The planetarium uses telescopes, laser lights, and astronomy lessons in its presentations. Museum and trails open 9-5 Monday through Saturday; 11-5 Sunday. Adult admission to the museum and trails is $4; children under age 12, $2.50. Call for astronomy and laser show times; admission is $2-$5.

Manatee Park, opened December 1996 at 10901 Rte. 80, opposite Florida Power and Light plant, ☎ 432-2004, features a manatee-viewing deck on the Orange River with special polarized filters, manatee exhibits, a canoe launch, and interpretive programs in season. It serves as a rescue and release site for rehabilitated injured manatees being returned to their native environment. The park is open daily 8-5 in winter, 8-8 in summer. Parking costs 75¢ an hour.

South of town, the **Lee County Sports Complex**, at 14100 Six Mile Cypress Rd, hosts **Minnesota Twins** spring league action. From April through August, the **Miracle Professional Baseball** team, member of the Florida State League, competes. For information on Miracles' games, ☎ 768-4210. For Twins tickets, ☎ 800-33TWINS. Twins tickets cost $7 and $10; Miracles tickets, $3 and $4.

Lakes Park at 7330 Gladiolus Drive in south Fort Myers, ☎ 432-2017, a 277-acre complex, has trails, playgrounds, picnic areas, a restaurant, paddle boats, canoes, and a model train you can ride. You can rent bikes (see *Hiking & Biking*, below), volleyballs, and horseshoes. The train runs every day except Monday. Parking costs 75¢ an hour or $3 a day. Train rides, ☎ 267-0052, cost $2 for persons over 4 years old. The park is open 8-6 daily.

FISHING & BOATING

Fishermen cast from the pier at **Centennial Park**, downtown on Edwards Drive near the Yacht Basin. It provides picnic and playground facilities. For freshwater fishing, try **Lakes Park** at 7330 Gladiolus Drive in south Fort Myers, ☎ 432-2017.

For deep-sea and backwater fishing charters or boat rentals, it's best to head out to the islands. One knowledgeable guide who operates out of south Fort Myers at Punta Rassa (just before the Sanibel Causeway) is **Capt. Dave Gibson**, ☎ 466-4680. He specializes in fly-casting (and offers instruction), backbay, and light tackle fishing, and charges $185 for up to three for a half-day, $350 for a full day.

In Fort Myers, you are more apt to find sightseeing tours – for instance, **J.C. Cruises**, which depart from the Fort Myers Yacht Basin, ☎ 334-7474 or 334-2743. Excursions aboard the 600-passenger, three-decker paddlewheeler *Capt. J.P.* last from three hours to a day and tour the Caloosahatchee River, the Gulf, and Lake Okeechobee. Some tours include dinner. Tickets cost $14-$74 plus tax (discount for children). Aboard an 80-passenger pontoon boat, its **Everglades Jungle Cruises** goes sightseeing and manatee spotting (November-April), costing $12 plus tax for adults, half-price for kids under age 12. Call for schedules.

On the east side of town, manatee-sighting cruises up the Orange River are the popular thing. Contact **Manatee & Eco Tours**, at Coastal Marine Mart, Rte. 80 at Interstate 75, exit 25, ☎ 693-1434. Adults pay $12, children under age 12, half-price. Tours begin at 10, 12, 2, and 4 daily and last two hours.

Boaters can launch their vessels from **Punta Rassa**, just before the Sanibel Causeway on Summerlin Rd.

For freshwater canoeing, you can rent at **Lakes Park**, 7330 Gladiolus Drive, ☎ 432-2017, for $7 an hour. Paddleboats and rowboats rent for the same rate; small electric motorboats, $12 an hour.

SNORKELING & DIVING

Fort Myers and vicinity has their share of dive operators. Because of the normal murkiness of local waters and lack of offshore reefs, dive trip leaders often take you out of the region for open-water dives.

To inquire about lessons and equipment, call **Underwater Explorers**, at 12600 McGregor Blvd, ☎ 432-0054.

HIKING & BIKING

Three miles of trails loop through the woods at **Calusa Nature Center**, 3450 Ortiz Ave, ☎ 275-3435. Admission to the trails is included in the price of museum admission (see *Sights & Attractions,* above.)

Centennial Park (see *Fishing,* above) has a short fitness trail, plus picnic pavilions, and a fishing pier. It's the site of open-air concerts and special festivals.

Lakes Park (see *Sights & Attractions,* above) at 7330 Gladiolus Drive in south Fort Myers, ☎ 432-2017, has extensive bike trails and a fitness trail, along with its other facilities. Bike rentals are $5 an hour. Parking costs 75¢ an hour or $3 a day. The park is open 8-6 daily.

Boardwalks meander one mile through wetlands ecology at 2,000-acre **Six Mile Cypress Slough Preserve**, Six Mile Cypress Pkwy at Penzance Crossing, ☎ 338-3300. It's open daily during daylight hours. Call ahead about interpretive tours. Admission is free; parking costs $3 per car.

A stretch of bike path along Daniels Boulevard reaches from Summerlin Avenue to the airport. Another path follows Linear Park, a length of recreational area fronting a canal parallel to Metro Parkway, between Colonial Boulevard and Six Mile Cypress Parkway.

The Summerlin path leads to the Sanibel causeway, which you can cross to connect with island paths (see *Sanibel & Captiva Islands*, below).

OTHER ADVENTURES

Get an aerial view of the coast's profile with **Classic Flight's Biplane Rides Scenic Tours**, at Fort Myers' Page Field, ☎ 939-7411 or 800-824-9464. Cruise open-air at 120 miles per hour in a new Waco Classic, made for two passengers. Rates start at $70 per trip for a half-hour. An extended flightseeing tour costs $150 for one or two passengers.

See it by balloon through **Balloon Odyssey**, ☎ 458-5750. Sunrise floats include a picnic champagne brunch for $150 each.

WHERE TO EAT

Downtown Fort Myers has an excellent selection of restaurants whose reputation is based on fine cuisine or waterfront location. Local seafood typically dominates the menu.

At **The Veranda**, a downtown landmark at 2122 Second Street, ☎ 332-2065, seafood comes accented Southern-style. In a historic Victorian-decorated home and its garden courtyard, diners enjoy fresh corn muffins with pepper jelly and creative entrées such as marinated grilled prawns with fresh tomatoes, basil, garlic, and parmesan served over linguine; or medallions of filet in smoky sourmash whiskey sauce. Leave room for the peanut butter pie. A la carte entrées are $14-$27. Lunchtime brings in the local business community for sandwiches, salads, and entrées in the $4.50-$9 range. It's open Monday-Saturday for dinner; Monday-Friday for lunch. Reservations recommended.

Shooters Water Front Café USA, at 2220 W First Street, behind the Holiday Inn Sunspree, ☎ 334-2727, is a fun, casual place on the river. Omelettes, pasta dishes, sandwiches, and other specialties are $7-$20. Evenings bring music to the outdoor bar, and a party boat that departs from its dock.

For a can't-miss good meal at a reasonable price, fall in line at **Outback Steakhouse**, at 12995 S Cleveland Ave in south Fort Myers, ☎ 936-1021. The steaks are the best value and best tasting. The menu also offers barbecued shrimp, baby-back ribs, and other meat specialties in a range of prices from $8-$18. It's open Monday-Saturday at 3, Sunday at noon.

At **Romano's Macaroni Grill**, 13721 S Cleveland Ave, ☎ 433-7786, the unusual atmosphere is part of the enjoyment: airy and loud, with paper tablecloths you can draw on, and Italian lessons aired in the restrooms. The well-executed pasta, veal, seafood, and grilled chicken dishes add to the restaurant's enjoyability. Lunch entrées run $5-$14; dinner, $8-$17. Open daily for lunch and dinner. At dinner, call ahead for preferred seating and to avoid a wait.

WHERE TO STAY

For the most part, hotels in Fort Myers are geared toward business and are chains. Prices below do not include the 9% room tax.

One of the swankiest, **Sheraton Harbor Place**, at 2500 Edwards Drive, ☎ 337-0300 or 800-833-1620, towers over the city yacht basin and is convenient to downtown's attractions. Its 417 rooms and suites are

Sanibel Harbour Resort & Spa.

modern and attractively decorated. Amenities include a restaurant, swimming pool, tennis courts, and exercise room. Rates begin at $79 out of season and are $120-$184 in high season.

To locate closer to the beaches, consider one of the two following options:

Radisson Inn Sanibel Gateway, at 20091 Summerlin Rd, ☎ 466-3797 or 800-333-3333, exudes Spanish mission style with fountains, tiling, and archways. The 156 units are small suites with mini-refrigerators and a second fold-out bed. Guests may use its swimming pool, fitness facilities, restaurant, and bar. Bicycle rentals are available. Rates range from a low of $59 off-season to a high of $149 in season.

More upscale and fitness-conscious, **Sanibel Harbour Resort & Spa,** ☎ 466-4000 or 800-767-7777, boasts first-class spa and exercise programs and facilities. Tennis buffs will be thrilled by the resort's 24 top-notch courts (12 lighted). Full service, the resort offers a couple of dining options (with or without spa cuisine), bars, swimming pool, excellent kids program, boating tours, watersports rentals, a bayside beach, and fishing pier. Rooms and suites, more than 360 in all, come in various sizes and prices: $250-$315 at season's height; $120-$225 in the off-season. Packages available.

Sanibel & Captiva Islands

Alluring names with an exotic ring, the sister islands of Sanibel and Captiva sound like adventure. Legend has it they were named by a Spanish pirate named Gasparilla. Whether or not the old legend holds water, the water holds plenty of opportunity for outdoor recreation, from voracious shelling to tarpon-fishing and 'gator-spotting. As much nature preserves as resort islands, Sanibel and Captiva provide prime wildlife experiences.

BASICS

From Southwest Florida International Airport or exit 21 off Interstate 75, head west on Daniels Parkway for about 10 miles. Turn left on Summerlin Rd (Route 869) and continue for about 10 miles to cross the Sanibel Causeway ($3 toll for most vehicles without stickers).

Turn right at the four-way stop sign at Periwinkle Way to get to Captiva Island. Turn right four miles later onto Tarpon Bay Rd and left on Sanibel-Captiva Rd. Drive about eight miles and cross the Blind Pass bridge.

Sanibel Island has two main roads that more or less parallel each other. Periwinkle Way is the main business route. Gulf Drive roves along the resorts, beaches, and homes at water's edge. It is segmented into East, West, and Middle Gulf Drive. Sanibel-Captiva Rd, known as San-Cap, connects the two islands at the Blind Pass bridge. On Captiva, the road becomes Captiva Drive, a lovely tunnel of jungle growth.

A trolley provides public transportation and sightseeing tours on Sanibel and Captiva. An island tour costs $10 for adults, $5 for kids under age 10; tax is extra. ☎ 472-6374 for a schedule.

INFORMATION

Contact the **Sanibel-Captiva Islands Chamber of Commerce** for more information: P.O. Box 166, Sanibel 33957, ☎ 472-1080. You'll find its information center on the left side shortly after the causeway ends; open Monday-Saturday 9-7, Sunday 10-5.

SANIBEL SIGHTS & ATTRACTIONS

Great blue heron, Sanibel Island beach.

Sanibel's prime nature attractions lie on Sanibel-Captiva Rd. The most prominent is **J.N. "Ding" Darling National Wildlife Refuge**, ☎ 472-1100. It takes up about half of the island with its 5,000 acres of wetlands and other habitat. Denizens of the haunting Everglades-like refuge include American alligators, manatees, pelicans, roseate spoonbills, Louisiana herons, ospreys, river otters, and bobcats. A five-mile drive takes you around the area, and you can climb the observatory tower for an osprey's-eye view, but it's best to follow the short trails into the mangroves or see the refuge by canoe or kayak (see *Fishing & Boating*, below). You can catch an interpretative tram from **Tarpon Bay Recreation**, at 900 Tarpon Bay Rd, ☎ 472-8900, for $7, adults, or $3.50, children ages 12 and under. Call for a schedule. Otherwise, admission to the refuge is $5 per car or $1 per cyclist or walk-in. It's open daily except Friday from sunrise to sunset. Admission to the refuge's visitor's center is free daily except Friday 9-5 (9-4 November-April).

Nearby, you can take a longer nature hike and learn more about native critters and ecology at the **Sanibel-Captiva Conservation Foundation Center** at 3333 Sanibel-Captiva Rd, ☎ 472-2329. Interactive teaching tools include a touch tank, a pliable lifesized manatee that children can climb, an alligator's jawbone, and wildlife blocks. The center hosts guided walking and boat tours (see sections on *Hiking & Boating*, below). Mid-November into April, the center is open every day except Sunday, 8:30-4. In the off-season, it closes at 3 and usually on Saturday. Admission is $2 for visitors 12 and older.

Bailey-Matthews Shell Museum, at 3075 Sanibel-Captiva Rd, ☎ 395-2233, is the only one of its kind in the US. It underlines Sanibel's reputation as a top shell-collecting destination. Opened in 1996, it employs nature vignettes, games, and artistically arranged displays to demonstrate the role of shells in ecology, history, art, economics, medicine, religion, and other fields. One of the most popular displays is the collection donated by the late actor Raymond Burr, who helped establish the museum. Kids can play games and win stickers. Hours are Tuesday-Sunday 10-4. Admission is $5 for ages 17 and older; $3 for children 8-17.

C.R.O.W. (Care and Rehabilitation of Wildlife), at 3833 Sanibel-Captiva Rd, ☎ 472-3644, replicates natural habitat to make comfortable its special patients – birds, bobcats, raccoons, rabbits, and other critters brought from near and far to mend and be reintroduced. Visit by appointment or regularly scheduled tours in season at 11 Monday-Friday and 1 on Sunday. Adults are asked to make a $3 donation.

Bowman's Beach, to the north on Bowman's Beach Rd, is the island's most secluded and arguably best shelling beach. It has picnic tables, restrooms, and shady trees. Parking is 75¢ per hour. Like all of Sanibel's beaches, it is maintained in its natural state, which means the sand is ungroomed (great for beachcombing) and facilities are basic.

Nearer to Sanibel's shopping and restaurant district, the **Sanibel Historic Village**, at 850 Dunlop Rd, ☎ 472-4648, has been a catch-all for the island's vintage homes and buildings, beginning with a pioneer

Cracker house that serves as a historic museum. Additions include a 1920s post office, historic general store, tea house, and turn-of-the-century island home that is being restored to house a French-cut Sanibel Lighthouse lens from the 1880s, along with maritime artifacts. The village is open 10-4 Wednesday through Saturday, mid-Octo-

Sanibel Island Lighthouse.

ber to mid-August. December through April, the village also is open on Sundays, 1-4 pm. Admission is by donation ($1 per adult suggested).

You'll find the circa-1884 **Sanibel Lighthouse** at the island's eastern tip, surrounded by a popular beach that bends from Gulf to bay side. Facilities include restrooms, a fishing T-dock, nature trail, and an interpretative station. Currents make it dangerous to swim at the island's southern tip.

CAPTIVA SIGHTS & ATTRACTIONS

Captiva shines more for its watersports opportunities than its tourist attractions. It's a lovely island, worth driving around and stopping for lunch, if you do nothing else. While exploring, peek in at **Chapel-By-the-Sea**, at 11580 Chapin Street, a charming country-style church close to the beach. Next to it, early settlers rest in a small cemetery. Stop and look for free anytime during the day.

For a brief history of the tiny island, visit the **Captiva History House**, ☎ 472-5111, at the entrance to South Seas Plantation Resort. Housed in a cottage once occupied by farm hands – back when the resort was really a plantation that grew key limes and coconuts – the small museum explores bygones with photos, artifacts, and the memories of a living reincarnation of the plantation's founder, C.W Chadwick.

FISHING & BOATING

The Sanibel Lighthouse Beach T-Dock, Sanibel Causeway, and bridge between Sanibel and Captiva attract fishermen praying for snook, tarpon, sheepshead, and snapper to grab their hook.

For bait, tackle, and fishing licenses, stop at the **Bait Box**, 1041 Periwinkle Way, ☎ 472-1618, open 7-6 daily.

Sanibel Light Tackle Outfitters, at Forever Green Center, 2025 Periwinkle Way, ☎ 472-2002, offers fishing outfitter and guide service, instruction, and equipment sales. It's open 8:30-6:30 daily (extended hours during season and some holidays).

Mangrove Fishing Adventures, ☎ 395-9647, leads three-hour sessions from Captiva on the fine art of fly casting. Cost is $50 per person.

For your charter and boat rental needs on Sanibel, go to **Sanibel Marina**, 634 North Yachtsman Drive, ☎ 472-2723. **The Boat House**, ☎ 472-2531, rents powerboats from there for use in Intracoastal waters only. Rates for 19- and 21-foot vessels are $90-$100 for a half-day, $165-$175 for a full day.

Several competent and knowledgeable fishing guides are headquartered at the marina. Rates for up to four people are $200 for a half-day, $400 for a full day. Guides are available for sightseeing charters to the upper islands as well.

Marina at 'Tween Waters.

On Captiva, **'Tween Waters Inn Marina** on Captiva Drive, ☎ 472-5161, rents and charters boats. To captain your own vessel, contact **Sweet Water Boat Rentals**, ☎ 472-6336. It rents 18½-foot center-console boats holding up to six passengers for $125 a half-day, $200 a full day. Tax and fuel are additional. **Captain Mike Fuery**, ☎ 472-1015, also stationed at 'Tween Waters, has a good reputation for finding fish or shells on boat charter tours.

Operators on Sanibel and Captiva conduct group tours to local places of interest on the high seas. Some are nature-oriented, others head to beaches and upper islands to fish or picnic. These provide a less expensive option for getting out on the water. **Adventures in Paradise**, ☎ 472-8443, uses its pontoon boat for backwater fishing, sealife encounters, and sunset cruises. Costs are $18-$35 for adults, $10-$25 for children older than 3. Trolley transportation to the cruise departure point across the causeway is provided from several resorts.

The **Sanibel-Captiva Conservation Foundation** (see *Sights & Attractions,* above) at 3333 Sanibel-Captiva Rd, ☎ 472-2329, does interpretative nature tours to the out-islands, cooperating with **Captiva Cruises**, ☎ 472-5300. They depart from South Seas Plantation Resort Marina. The 150-passenger *Lady Chadwick* runs nature and luncheon tours to the upper islands, including **Useppa Island**, a private club on an island where Zane Grey, Hedy LaMarr, and other stars of the 1920s came to fish for tarpon. With up to 40-foot shell mounds, it claims some of the highest elevation on the coast. Excursion fees are $17.50-$27.50 for adults, $10-$15 for children.

For an adventure under sail, **New Moon**, at 'Tween Waters Inn Marina, ☎ 395-1782, conducts excursions and teaches classes. Reserve in advance. Half-day cruises begin at $35 per person.

Offshore Sailing School, at South Seas Plantation Marina, ☎ 454-1700 or 800-221-4326, was founded by Olympic and America's Cup sailor Steve Colgate. It is internationally known for its sailing course and club. Weekend learn-to-sail courses cost $750 for adults, $395 for children ages 8-12. Week-long courses are $795-$895 for adults, $395 for children.

The islands offer various canoeing and kayaking adventures. **Tarpon Bay Recreation**, at 900 Tarpon Bay Rd, ☎ 472-8900, rents canoes and kayaks for exploring the backwaters of J.N. "Ding" Darling Wildlife Refuge (see *Sights & Attractions*, above), where you can spot alligators, manatees, roseate spoonbills, ibises, and other birds. Avoid going at low tide or you may have to portage. It also conducts guided ecology canoe tours of the refuge. Tarpon Bay Recreation is open daily 8-5. Canoe rentals cost $20 for two hours, $5 each additional hour. Guided tours cost $20 for adults, $10 for children age 12 and under for two hours and free paddle time.

For guided nature canoe tours along the Sanibel River by paddle, contact **Canoe Adventures**, ☎ 472-5218. You can rent canoes for $5 an hour, $10 for four hours, at **Castaways Marina**, 6460 Sanibel-Captiva Rd on Sanibel at the bridge to Captiva, ☎ 472-1112.

For guided sea kayaking, contact **Sanibel Sea Kayak Wildlife Tours**, ☎ 472-9484.

SNORKELING & SCUBA

Because of low visibility, island waters don't attract snorkelers and divers in great numbers, except for one specific sort: the sheller. By snorkeling off the sandbar that fronts island beaches, collectors find the great variety and numbers of shells for which Sanibel especially is famous (see *Shelling*, below). To collect live shells, you must, by law, be more than a half-mile from the mean high tide mark.

HIKING & BIKING

The best hiking trail on the islands takes you along four miles of natural habitat at **Sanibel-Captiva Conservation Foundation** (see *Sights & Attractions*, above) at 3333 Sanibel-Captiva Rd, ☎ 472-2329.

Sanibel's 23-mile **bike path** takes you around the island's main streets and back woods. Joggers and in-line skaters also use the paved trail. You can rent bikes and in-line skates from **Finnimore's Cycle Shop**, at 2353 Periwinkle Way, ☎ 472-5577, open daily 9-5. Bikes rent for $5-$10 (plus tax) a day; skates for $10, pads included.

SHELLING

Sanibel Island ranks among the world's best shelling destinations. Because, unlike the other Gulf coast barrier islands, Sanibel takes an east-west heading, it better intercepts the diverse shells that arrive from the Caribbean Sea. For generations, serious and casual collectors have gathered on Sanibel shores to do the so-called Sanibel Stoop as they look for shells. Shelling is equally good on all beaches, best after a storm and in winter. **Bowman's Beach** (see *Sights & Attractions*, above) is more secluded, so its shells are less picked-over.

Florida recently passed a law prohibiting the collection of live shells on Sanibel Island. This includes sand dollars and starfish. Captiva and the rest of Lee County limits collection of live shells to two per person per day.

Many charter boat operators conduct shelling excursions to the upper islands, particularly to **Johnson Shoals** off of Cayo Costa (see *Sights & Attractions*, above).

WHERE TO EAT

Seafood is the main course at Sanibel restaurants. Many feature a new Florida style that incorporates elements from New Orleans, the Caribbean, the Deep South, and the Pacific Rim.

The best in this genre is **The Greenhouse Grill** at 2407 Periwinkle Way in the Islander Center, ☎ 472-6882. Breakfast may be Texan frittata with black bean chili; for lunch, try a cilantro-grilled chicken club made with jalapeño cheese and apple-smoked bacon; for dinner choose from a changing selection of creative masterpieces such as green Thai curried vegetable stew or seafood étouffée. The intimate eatery is open daily for breakfast ($5-$8), lunch ($5-$13), and dinner (à la carte entrées $8-$28). Call for specific hours. Dinner reservations are recommended.

McT's Shrimp House & Tavern, at 1523 Periwinkle Way, ☎ 472-3161, is a perennial favorite that serves shrimp in every guise imaginable, including steamed in the shell all-you-can-eat. The atmosphere is casual, with old island charm. It's open daily for dinner. Entrées are $13-$18.

Lazy Flamingo, 6520 Pine Ave, ☎ 472-5353, acts like a neighborhood hang-out. The menu concentrates on seafood and finger foods. The grilled grouper sandwich is a sure bet. There are two restaurants bearing the name. The original one at Blind Pass, where Sanibel ends, is favored by locals. The newer one at 1036 Periwinkle Way, ☎ 472-6939, occupies a building shaped like a ship's bow. Both are can't-miss-'em pink. They open daily for lunch and dinner. Items are priced at $5-$15.

On Captiva, the **Mucky Duck**, on Andy Rosse Lane, ☎ 472-3434, is a must-do. Go early, put your name in, and spend the hour-or-so wait on the beach right outside the door. Sunsets here are spectacular. The menu covers seafood in sandwiches and fine dishes, plus a smattering of English specialties. The restaurant is open daily except Sunday for lunch and dinner. Lunches are $4-10; dinners $12-$17.

Also on Captiva, **Chadwick's**, at South Seas Plantation Resort, ☎ 472-5111, is the place to go for great all-you-can-eat buffets. Besides daily lunch ($9.25) and Sunday brunch ($16.95) spreads, it hosts theme nights, such as Caribbean and seafood ($19.50-$23.50). In summer, there's a once-a-week kids buffet. On the regular menu, seafood with an island flair dominates. Prices are $15-$20 for entrées. Open daily for breakfast, lunch, and dinner. Reservations for brunch and dinner recommended.

WHERE TO STAY

From simple beach cottages to big-name destination resorts, the islands have practically infinite possibilities. Prices in general are somewhat steep, but most resort units are equipped with kitchens, which saves on dining costs. They do not include the 9% room tax.

Sanibel's largest, most full-service resort, **Sundial Beach Resort**, 863 E Gulf Drive, ☎ 472-4151 or 800-237-4184, specializes in families, with kitchen-equipped suite units and a top-notch kid's recreation program. Amenities include restaurants, 13 tennis courts, on-site eco-center with touch tank, beach, watersports and bicycle rentals, five heated swimming pools, and 10 Jacuzzis. Winter rates for a one-bedroom condo are $284-$399; off-season, $151-$391. Two-bedroom condos also available. Ask about packages.

For something smaller and more laid-back on Sanibel, **Seaside Inn**, at 541 E Gulf Drive, ☎ 472-1200 or 800-831-7384, is a newly renovated old-island property on the beach with a swimming pool and modern studios, suites, and cottages. Each has some kitchen facilities. Continental breakfast is included in the rates: $239-$289 for single or double in high season, $124-$220 at other times. Guests are welcome to use facilities at Sundial Beach Resort, above.

The Castaways, 6460 Sanibel-Captiva Rd, ☎ 472-1252, spreads from Gulf to bay at Sanibel's north end. With its full-service marina and beach-cottage style, it provides equal doses of beach relaxation and adventure opportunity. It also has a swimming pool. Cottages are old but well-kept, with one to three bedrooms. Rates in season are $105 for efficiencies to $280 for three-bedroom cottage; $135-$265 off-season.

Also bay to Gulf on Captiva, **'Tween Waters Inn** on Captiva Drive, ☎ 472-5161, US 800-223-5865, or FL 800-282-7560, has rooms, efficiencies, apartments, and cottages, plus restaurants, a lively bar, a swimming pool, and a full-service marina (see *Fishing & Boating*, above). Rates in high season begin at $215 for a room and run up to $275 for a two-bedroom cottage. The range off-season is $135-$205. Packages available.

About a fourth of Captiva Island is occupied by **South Seas Plantation**, ☎ 472-5111, US 800-237-3102, or FL 800-282-3402, a spacious beach resort perfect for families. Pick whatever type of lodging best suits your requirements: hotel room, suite, villa, cottage, or home. Recreational opportunities are virtually endless, including an excellent kids program, two marinas with rentals and guides, a fishing dock, a nine-hole golf course, a fitness center, 18 swimming pools, 21 tennis courts, watersports rentals and lessons, excursion cruises, and 2½ miles of well-maintained beach. Plus there are several restaurants and lounges all within security gates. A free resort trolley transports you around the 330-acre property. High-season rates begin at $260 for a room and go up from there. Off-season rates are discounted.

Furnished homes, most of them on a beach or golf course, are available to rent throughout Sanibel (one-month minimum) and Captiva (one-week minimum). Range of rates: Sanibel, $2,000 to $5,000/month; Captiva, $1,500 to $8,000/week. Agencies offer condominiums at lower prices and with only a one-week minimum required on Sanibel. Contact **Sanibel Realty** at 1630 Periwinkle Way, ☎ 472-6565 or 800-572-6423.

SHOPPING

Not known as a great shopping mecca, Sanibel and Captiva are recognized for their art galleries – many of them dealing in wildlife renderings – and shell shops.

For shells, try **Showcase Shells** at Heart of the Islands Center, 1614 Periwinkle Way, ☎ 472-1971; or **Neptune's Treasures** in Treetops Center, 1101 Periwinkle Way, ☎ 472-3132, both on Sanibel, open daily.

Among the islands' many fine galleries are **Matsumoto Gallery** at 751 Tarpon Bay Rd on Sanibel, ☎ 472-6686, featuring the wildlife graphics of local artists; and **Jungle Drums** at 11532 Andy Rosse Lane on Captiva Island, ☎ 395-2266, which shows the wildlife work of local and national artists.

Fort Myers Beach

This resort town on Estero Island has a reputation for fun. It attracts a value-conscious clientele, including families and college students on spring break. Shrimping is a major industry, which brings seafood-lovers to its reasonably priced restaurants. Watersports enthusiasts also find plenty of reasons to visit.

BASICS

From Fort Myers' Southwest Florida International Airport or exit 21 on Interstate 75, follow Daniels Parkway west 10 miles to Summerlin Rd (Route 869). Turn left and follow Summerlin until you reach San Carlos Boulevard (about seven miles) and turn left. Continue to the island's Matanzas Pass High Bridge. After the bridge, you'll reach "Times Square," a busy intersection at the core of Beach activity. A right turn takes you to the quieter north end. Turning left leads you through the island's commercial district and southward to Lover's Key and Bonita Beach before reconnecting to the mainland.

 Fort Myers has a trolley that shuttles people to the mainland and to the beaches. Fare is 25¢ per passenger. ☎ 275-TRAM.

INFORMATION

For specific information on Fort Myers Beach, contact or stop in at **The Fort Myers Beach Chamber of Commerce** at 17200 San Carlos Blvd, Fort Myers Beach, FL 33931, ☎ 454-7500. Open weekdays 8:30-6, Saturday 10-6, and Sunday 11-5.

SIGHTS & ATTRACTIONS

Fort Myers Beach's biggest draw is its beaches. The main one, **Lynn Hall Memorial Park** on Estero Blvd in the commercial district, ☎ 338-3300, features a free fishing pier, a small playground, picnic tables, grills, restrooms, and a bathhouse. Hours are 7-10. Parking is limited and metered. Restaurants, bars, and shops line the beach. Several public beach access points lie to the south along Estero Blvd Park (only in marked areas). Cars are frequently towed for illegal parking.

Bowditch Point Regional Park, at the north end of Estero Blvd, ☎ 339-3300, is quieter, but has no parking. You must catch a trolley from the Park and Ride lot just north of the high bridge. Facilities include showers, restrooms, changing rooms, picnic tables, grills, a small playground, and hiking paths. The trolley charges 25¢ each and runs from 8:30 to sunset.

For wildlife and fewer crowds, head south and cross over the bridge to Lover's Key. **Lover's Key State Recreation Area**, ☎ 597-6196, and **Carl Johnson County Park**, ☎ 432-2000, soon to be combined into one upgraded state facility, are a lovely getaway with a totally natural beach lying on the other side of a wildlife-rich estuary. Admission to the county park is $3 per car and includes a round-trip mini-tram ride from the parking lot to the beach. Admission at the state park is $2 per car; you must walk to the beach across an estuary bridge. Facilities include free boat ramp, outdoor showers, restrooms, picnic tables, and grills. Hours are 8-5.

FISHING & BOATING

Fish for free from the pier at **Lynn Hall Memorial Park** (see *Sights & Attractions*, above) at the center of activity in Fort Myers Beach. You'll find bait and snack shops. Or cast off the bridge that connects the island's south end to Lover's Key.

Fort Myers Beach's fishing party boats provide a less expensive option than private charters and rentals. At **Getaway Deep Sea Fishing**, Getaway Marina at 18400 San Carlos Blvd, ☎ 466-3600, a 90-foot boat takes you to deep water for grouper, mackerel, snapper, and other offshore catches. All-day rates are $40 for adults, $25 for kids age 12 and under; reservations requested. For half-day trips from 9-2, rates are $25 and $20; no reservations necessary.

Boaters can use the free boat ramps at **Carl Johnson Park** (see *Sights & Attractions*, above).

Rent a boat at **Fish-Tale Marina**, 7225 Estero Blvd, ☎ 463-4448. Models include 15-foot Boston Whalers ($75 half-day, $130 full-day), 19-foot Grady Whites ($150, $225), 24-foot pontoons ($90, $150), and others. Refueling, collision insurance, and tax are extra. Open daily 8-4:30.

Island Water Tours depart aboard the *Pelican Queen* from Best Western Pink Shell Resort, (see *Where to Stay*, below) at 275 Estero Blvd, ☎ 765-4354, and offer pontoon cruises for bay fishing, Sanibel Island shelling, and nature observing. Cost is $18.50-$24.50 for adults. An archaeology tour of Mound Key (see Bonita Springs *Sights & Attractions*, below), led by a leading historian, takes place Saturdays 9-1, costing $32 for adults, $30 for seniors, and $15 for children. Reservations required.

Island Tall Ship Cruises.

For a little romance on the high seas, take a sunset cruise on the red-sailed, multi-masted *Island Rover* with **Island Tall Ship Cruises**, ☎ 765-7447, setting sail from Snug Harbor restaurant (see *Where to Eat*, below). Sunset tours depart daily except Monday and cost $25 per passenger. Two-hour day trips cost $15-$20 for adults, with a discount for children under age 12.

The ultimate water excursion takes you out to sea for dining, dancing, and gambling. **Europa SeaKruz**, ☎ 463-5000 or 800-688-PLAY, also departs from Snug Harbor restaurant (see *Where to Eat*, below) and takes daytime brunch buffet and evening sit-down dinner cruises daily. Cost is $27-$32 for adults, $12 for children under age 18.

OTHER WATERSPORTS

You can book a jet ski tour to see dolphins, or head skyward by parasail with Holiday Water Sports, located at **Best Western Pink Shell Resort** (see *Where to Stay*, below), 250 Estero Blvd, ☎ 765-4FUN, and **Best Western Beach Resort**, 684 Estero Blvd, ☎ 463-6778. Sun Cat, kayak, aquacycle, and waverunner rentals available, with lessons. Dolphin waverunner tours last 1½ hours and cost $70 per double.

HIKING & BIKING

Bowditch Point Regional Park (see *Sights & Attractions,* above), at the north end of Estero Blvd, ☎ 339-3300, and **Carl Johnson County Park** (see *Sights & Attractions,* above), ☎ 432-2000, sponsor Full Moon Madness night hikes along their nature trails.

You can rent bikes starting at $3 for one hour at **Scooters, Inc.**, at 1698 Estero Blvd, ☎ 463-1007. It's open daily 9-5.

OTHER ADVENTURES

Skim the skies in an ultralight aircraft on floats. Learn to fly one yourself. Contact **Fly & Sea,** ☎ 463-3970. Rate for a full island tour is $60, for a 15-minute flight, $35. Minimum age is 14.

WHERE TO EAT

Head to Fort Myers Beach for fresh seafood at good prices with great water views.

One of the island's oldest, **Gulf Shore Restaurant**, at 1270 Estero Blvd, ☎ 463-9551, serves a great breakfast. It is open for lunch and dinner also, daily. The lunch menu lists sandwiches and such in the vicinity of $6. Dinners, $10-$15, are basic seafood or meat dishes such as fried shrimp and BBQ baby-back ribs. Its bank of windows overlooks the Gulf. The Cottage, an adjunct, serves casual eats to the casually (swimsuits) dressed.

An old favorite recently redone in stylish Florida decor, **Snug Harbor Waterfront Restaurant & Café**, at 645 San Carlos Blvd, ☎ 463-4343, operates a fish market and sells only the freshest seafood in sandwiches, salads, pasta dishes, and other specialties. Its two indoor dining rooms and one outdoor dining area are situated on a dock hanging over the Intracoastal Waterway, which provides lots of waterfront scenery and action. It's open daily for lunch and dinner. Prices are $3-$13 for sandwiches and entrées.

Anthony's on the Gulf, at 3040 Estero Blvd, ☎ 463-2600, specializes in Italian dishes served in a modern, breezy, indoor-outdoor setting. Sandwiches, salads, and pasta dishes comprise the lunch menu, priced at $5-$9. Veal, seafood, and chicken entrées are $8-$14 on the dinner menu. It serves lunch and dinner daily.

WHERE TO STAY

Hotels, resorts, and condominiums line the beach for the entire nine mile length of Fort Myers Beach. Prices below do not include the 9% room tax.

The only true resort that is a destination in itself, **Best Western Pink Shell**, 275 Estero Blvd, at the island's quieter north end, ☎ 463-6181 or 800-237-5786, spreads Gulf to bay with an assortment of accommodation options, from classic stilted cottages to modern upscale condos, all with kitchen facilities. A restaurant, boat tours, a kids activity program, watersports rentals, swimming pools, and tennis courts complete the amenities. Daily rates in high season begin at $160 for an efficiency and go up to $370 for a two-bedroom beach villa; off-season, rates range from $99 to $275.

To be close to the action on Fort Myers Beach, try **Ramada Inn Beachfront**, at 1160 Estero Blvd, ☎ 463-6158 or 800-544-4592. It's crowded in among shops, restaurants, and hotels near the fishing pier, but has a nice patch of beach front, a small pool, a beach bar, and beach concessions. Rates range from a low of $78 for a room in the off-season to a high of $278 for a deluxe beachfront suite (with kitchen) in season.

At the island's south end, activity quiets down to an easy pace of beaching and playing in the water. **The Outrigger Beach Resort**, at 6200 Estero Blvd, ☎ 463-3131 or 800-749-3131, is casual and unstructured, with an on-site café, a pool, a sundeck, a tiki bar, and watersports concessions. Rooms and efficiencies are $105-$180 in season; $75-$125 in summer, with special package offerings available.

NIGHTLIFE

Fort Myers Beach parties day and night. Hot spots include **The Bridge**, at 708 Fisherman's Wharf, ☎ 765-0050; **Lani Kai Island Resort**, at 1400 Estero Blvd, ☎ 463-3111; and **The Reef**, at 2601 Estero Blvd, ☎ 463-4181.

San Carlos Park/Estero

Ground has been broken for Florida Gulf Coast University in the area of South Fort Myers/San Carlos Park, an already blossoming area. At its southern fringe lies Estero, an old, quiet community offering opportunities for outdoor activity.

BASICS

The communities of San Carlos Park and Estero straddle Highway 41 south of Fort Myers proper.

SIGHTS & ATTRACTIONS

Koreshan State Historic Site, on Tamiami Trail, ☎ 992-0311, puts Estero on the map. Contained within a park, the site has restored a commune established in 1893 by a religious cult that settled on the banks of the Estero River. Under the tutorship of Dr. Cyrus Teed (who adopted the Biblical name Koresh), members of Koreshan Unity believed the earth lined the inside of a hollow globe that looked down into the solar system. Teed and his followers envisioned an academic and natural "New Jerusalem." They planted exotic crops and vegetation and built a theater, one of several reconstructed buildings on the site. Besides exploring bygones, you can picnic, camp, walk the short nature trail, boat, fish, and canoe in the park. Day-use hours are 8-sunset. Admission is $3.25 per vehicle of eight passengers or less, $1 for extra passengers, pedestrians, and cyclists.

FISHING & BOATING

Koreshan State Historic Site (see *Sights & Attractions,* above), on Tamiami Trail, ☎ 992-0311, rents aluminum canoes for the four-mile trip into the park's wildlife asylum for $3 plus tax per hour, $15 plus tax per day. There is also a boat ramp in the park.

Across the street from the park, you can rent vessels at **Estero River Tackle and Canoe Outfitters**, 20991 S Tamiami Trail, ☎ 992-4050. Half-day rentals cost $17.50 to $22.50 for canoes, $12.50 per person for kayaks. $17.50 for single or double sea kayaks. There is a boat ramp on the river and it also sells bait and tackle. Open every day at 7.

WHERE TO EAT

Mel's Diner, at 19050 S Tamiami Trail, ☎ 267-2468, is a popular dining spot in these parts, famous for its down-home eats. Enjoy a meatloaf dinner, pork chops, and the like for around $6. It's open daily for breakfast ($3-$4), lunch (sandwiches and burgers, $2-$4.50), and dinner. Its homemade pies are the best.

CAMPING

Koreshan State Historic Site, on Tamiami Trail, ☎ 992-0311 (see *Sights & Attractions*, above), has 60 tent and RV sites with or without electricity that rent for $16 per night, plus tax and electricity, for up to eight people.

Bonita Springs/Bonita Beach

Once a fertile tomato-growing and fishing community, Bonita Springs is trading in farm land for grand residential communities these days. Tourism does not figure as importantly here as it does in neighboring towns, which keeps it a bit more low-key and natural. Fishing and boating possibilities abound, mainly from Big and Little Hickory islands, home of Bonita Beach. Other small, uninhabited islands attract wildlife and those seeking to spy upon them.

BASICS

Bonita Springs bills itself as Gateway to the Gulf, chiefly because its exit off of Interstate 75 (#18) comes closest to the beach. Just follow Bonita Beach Rd to its end, for about eight miles, to find the sands.

Highway 41, or Tamiami Trail, runs along the western edge of town. Old Highway 41 penetrates town center.

To reach Bonita Beach from Bonita Springs, turn west off of Highway 41 onto Bonita Beach Rd and follow it to the bend at the public beach, where it becomes Hickory Boulevard. This is the town's main thoroughfare.

You can also get to Bonita Beach by a more scenic route from Fort Myers Beach (however in winter, traffic moves very slowly during peak morning and afternoon rush hours): Follow Fort Myers Beach's Estero Boulevard south to Lover's Key along Route 865. Continue about three miles over another bridge to Bonita Beach's Hickory Boulevard. Resort services lie at the north and south end of the approximately three-mile-long island.

 A trolley shuttles people to the mainland and to the beaches. Fare is $1 for adults, 50¢ for children under age 12, unlimited boarding. ☎ 275-TRAM.

INFORMATION

You can get more information on Bonita Springs and Bonita Beach through **Bonita Springs Area Chamber of Commerce,** Box 1240 Bonita Springs 33959, ☎ 992-2943 or 800-226-2943. Its welcome center is open weekdays 9-5.

SIGHTS & ATTRACTIONS

Offshore **Mound Key** is an unexploited island of special interest to archaeologists and bird-watchers. Believed to have once been an important ancient native American site, digs now probe it for secrets of the past, many preserved within 30-foot-high shell mounds. A segment of the island is designated **Mound Key State Archaeological Site,** an arm of Koreshan State Historic Site (see Estero *Sights & Attractions,* above). Charter tours in the area take you there to do your own exploring, but artifact collecting is strongly discouraged.

Attend matinees or night races for $2 each (children under age 18 admitted free) at **Naples-Fort Myers Greyhound Track,** 10601 Bonita Beach Rd SE, ☎ 992-2411. Trackside dining is available. Call for current live racing times.

Ride the **Seminole Gulf Railway** from the platform in downtown Bonita Springs, just west of Old Highway 41, into the past and nature's hidden spots (☎ 275-8487 or 800-SEM-GULF). Round-trip excursions to Fort Myers cost $11 for adults, $6 for children ages 3-12, and depart Tuesday-Sunday. Special dinner, holiday, and themed excursions are scheduled throughout the year.

Bonita Beach has great recreational beaches. At **Bonita Public Beach,** on Hickory Blvd at Bonita Beach Rd, ☎, 338-3300, you'll find sheltered picnic tables, a new bathhouse and boardwalks, handicap access, lifeguards, a food stand, a Hobie Cat sailboat concession, and other watersports rentals and restaurants nearby. Parking costs 75¢ per hour; the lot fills early at busy times. North of the main beach, along Hickory Boulevard, 10 access points offer limited facilities and free parking.

The turnoff to **Barefoot Beach Preserve,** ☎ 353-0404, lies near main beach parking on Bonita Beach Rd. The preserve holds 342 acres that contain a coastal hammock, 8,200 feet of beach, and low dunes. Facilities include changing rooms, showers, restrooms, nature interpretation stations, and snack bar. Hours are 8-sunset. Parking is free.

FISHING & BOATING

Estero Bay Boat Tours at Weeks Fish Camp on Coconut Rd, north of Bonita Springs, ☎ 992-2200, can take you to where the fish are biting. Its sightseeing tours of Mound Key's Amerindian history and Big Hickory Island's wildlife are conducted by a local native and his staff, who know these islands and waters like family. Half-day backbay fishing charters cost $150 for up to four people; offshore costs $350. Two-hour sightseeing/shelling cruises cost $12 for adults, $8 for children under age 12.

Big Hickory Fishing Nook, at 26107 Hickory Blvd, ☎ 992-3945, can take care of all your fishing needs: bait, tackle, fuel, equipment repair, fishing charters, and rental boats. It's open daily. Pontoon and boat rentals cost between $35 and $120 for half-days; $60-$200 for full days (tax and gas extra on most rentals). Fishing charters with *Puddlejumper II* range from $270 for six people and four hours to $540 full day. Take a two-hour sightseeing trip for $40 per hour, two-hour minimum.

Bonita Beach Resort Motel (see *Where to Stay,* below), at 26395 Hickory Blvd, ☎ 992-2137, rents 20-22-foot pontoon boats for $50-$55 half-days, $85-$95 full days (fuel and tax not included). It sells live bait and tackle and rents rods for $4-$6. To rent pontoons, canoes, and kayaks, look for **G.R. Boating**, near the public beach at 4892 Bonita Beach Rd, ☎ 947-4889. Half-day rates for canoes and kayaks are $20-$40; for pontoons, $50-60 (fuel and tax extra.)

For fishing, sightseeing, cocktail, and picnic cruises, contact **Sheila-Marie & Manta Ray** charter boats at Bonita Bay Marina, Highway 41 and Bonita Bay Blvd, ☎ 566-6510.

HIKING & BIKING

A bike path runs the length of Bonita Beach, nearly three miles long, and connects to another at its south end, which leads to Vanderbilt Beach (see Chapter VIII). **Bonita Beach Bike,** at 4892 Bonita Beach Rd, Bonita Harbor Plaza, ☎ 947-6377, rents in-line skates and bikes, and does bike repair. Rates run $8 a day for kids' bikes to $12 for six-speed mountain bikes. In-line skate rentals are $8 for two hours, $16 for 24 hours, including knee, wrist, and elbow pads. Other specialty rentals also available. It's open Monday-Saturday, 9-5.

WHERE TO EAT

Seafarers will feel right at home aboard **The Ship Restaurant**, at 24080 N Tamiami Trail, ☎ 947-3333, shaped like a double-master but anchored on dry land. The hull holds its own bakery, coffee shop, butcher shop, and fish market. In a heavily nautical setting you can lunch on salads, sandwiches, and entrées ($5-$9); or choose from an extensive dinner menu offering fine steaks, fresh fish selections, pasta, pork chops, and chicken ($14-$17). Open daily for lunch and dinner.

Especially popular for its Sunday brunch, **The Rooftop Restaurant**, at 25999 Hickory Blvd in Bonita Beach, ☎ 992-0033, towers over Gulf and bay waters near the island's north bridge. Its seafood strudel and Derby pie (chocolate chip spiked with brandy) are signatures. It's open Tuesday-Friday for lunch; Tuesday-Sunday for dinner, and Sunday for brunch. Lunch prices are $6-$10; dinner entrées are $16-$18, Sunday brunch buffet costs $15.

Across Hickory Blvd, **Big Hickory Fishing Nook Restaurant**, at 26107 Hickory Blvd SW, ☎ 992-0991, is a classic old Florida fish house serving sandwiches, salads, fresh fish, raw bar items, and a wide variety of entrées. Dine in or out and watch the fish jump in the bay. It's open daily for breakfast, lunch, and dinner in season; hours vary off-season. Prices for lunch are $4.50-$9; for dinner, $10-$18.

WHERE TO STAY

Prices do not include the 9% room tax.

Hard-core fishing enthusiasts will want to drop anchor at **Bonita Beach Resort Motel**, 26395 Hickory Blvd, ☎ 992-2137, where there's an on-property marina complete with docking, a boat ramp, and boat rentals. It has Gulf access across the street and rooms, apartments and cottages, some with bay views. Rates run $68-$98 in high season; $44-$84 the rest of the year. Resort guests receive a discount on pontoon boat rentals or free boat dockage.

For a healthy retreat, **Shangri-La Historic Inn Resort & Spa**, at 27580 Old Hwy 41 Rd, ☎ 992-3811 or 800-279-3811, offers an unusual experience. Recently renovated with artsy, elegant appointments, the 1920s health retreat prepares vegetarian and macrobiotic cuisine, even offering an all-juice diet. The lovely, shaded grounds induce relaxation, as do its programs of yoga, meditation, beach-walking (via shuttle), and massage. Some of its anti-cellulite, anti-aging procedures are groundbreaking. Rates for rooms and cottages are $125-$245 and include a healthy buffet breakfast. Spa packages available.

Chapter VIII

South Coast & Everglades

Area code: 941

Collier County puts the "wild" in Florida's "West." Here was the stage for gun-slinging outlaws, plucky mosquito-slapping pioneers, and prosperous adventure-seekers. The former took cover in the Everglades' impenetrable, wet wilderness. Pioneers and visitors settled in around Naples, Marco Island, and the larger of the Ten Thousand Islands. Here, they tried to eke a living from bountiful sealife, year-round crops, and often a shady deal here or there. They invented swamp buggies – plodding, big-wheeled vehicles – so they could travel the Everglades' outback. They poled flatboats across the River of Grass and between the mangrove-clotted Ten Thousand Islands. They created a new way of life in these parts, a new life that thrived on adventure.

Naples eventually rose above the crudeness of pioneer settlement to make a stance in the ultra-civilized world. As an outpost for people of means looking to get away – completely away – from it all, it developed along exclusive lines etched in wetlands muck. Contrast defined Naples and its surroundings: pearlescent beaches and alligator-infested swamps, dapper neighborhoods and thatched Amerindian villages, Mercedes and swamp buggies.

The contrasts remain in this land at the end of Florida's West Coast. The wild juxtaposes with the refined at Naples' doorstep. Adventure still lures, especially in the past decade as Naples resorts, once considered snooty, urge their privileged guests into the rich life-giving muck of the Everglades, where life thrives at its rawest and most basic.

Transportation, Etc.

The closest major airport is **Southwest Florida International Airport** in Fort Myers (see Chapter VII). Taxi services will transport you to Naples in under an hour and to Marco Island in just over an hour.

Small commercial flights come into **Naples Municipal Airport**, ☎ 643-0733, usually shuttles and commuter flights from other Florida

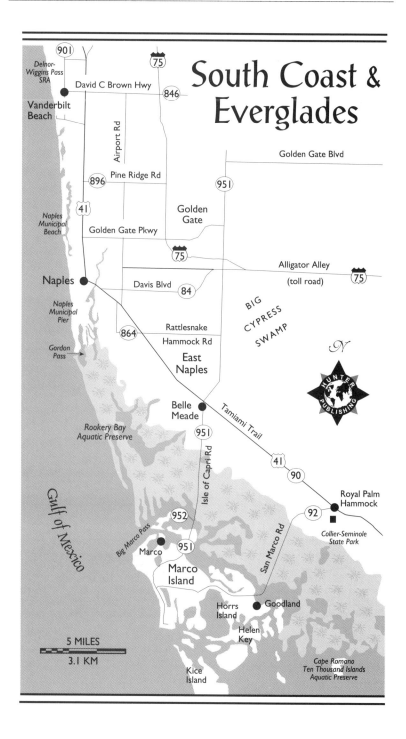

South Coast & Everglades

901

Delnor-
Wiggins Pass
SRA

David C Brown Hwy   846

Vanderbilt
Beach

Airport Rd

75

896   Pine Ridge Rd

41

Golden Gate Blvd

951

Naples
Municipal
Beach

Golden Gate Pkwy

Golden
Gate

75

Naples

Davis Blvd   84

Alligator Alley
(toll road)

75

Naples
Municipal
Pier

Gordon
Pass

864   Rattlesnake
Hammock Rd

BIG
CYPRESS
SWAMP

East
Naples

N

Belle
Meade

951

Tamiami Trail

Rookery Bay
Aquatic Preserve

Isle of Capri Rd

41
90

Gulf of Mexico

952

951

Big Marco Pass

Marco

Royal Palm
Hammock

92

San Marco Rd

Collier-Seminole
State Park

Marco
Island

Horrs
Island

Goodland

Helen
Key

5 MILES

3.1 KM

Kice
Island

Cape Romano
Ten Thousand Islands
Aquatic Preserve

ports, including **American Eagle, ☎** 800-433-7300; **Comm-Air Delta, ☎** 800-221-1212; and **USAir, ☎** 800-428-4322. From the airport you can rent a car through **Avis, ☎** 643-0900 or 800-331-1212; **Budget, ☎** 643-2212 or 800-527-0700; and other agencies.

For local taxi service, contact **Naples Shuttle, ☎** 262-8982, **Naples Taxi, ☎** 643-2148 or 775-0505, or for Marco Island, **Classic Taxi, ☎** 394-1888.

Highway 41, also known as Tamiami Trail, runs through the center of Naples, then heads south to the Everglades. Interstate 75 runs parallel to the east and south of Naples, connecting with Alligator Alley, which requires a toll of 75¢.

For information on the area, refer to specific bureaus listed under *Basics*, below.

EVENTS

The **Great Dock Canoe Race** takes place in May. Headquarters is The Dock at Crayton Cove restaurant, **☎** 263-9940.

Three times yearly (October, March, and May) the nationally televised **Swamp Buggy Races, ☎** 774-2701 or 800-897-2701, take place at Florida Sports Park on Rte. 951. Swamp buggies are vehicles adapted to the Everglades' marshy terrain; these are speedy, souped-up versions that add the thrill of race-car action to the event.

The **Goodland Mullet Festival, ☎** 394-3041, is a hometown event that draws a small crowd in January to eat fish and Indian fry bread, and to dance the Buzzard Lope, a goofy, high-energy step invented by event promoters.

In Everglades City, the **Everglades Seafood Festival, ☎** 695-4100, stars on the year's calendar in February, featuring music, an artisan fair, and lots of seafood.

Naples

"Walter, this is the most beautiful place in America. Let's build a town here," said Senator John Williams to publisher Walter Haldeman from the deck of their chartered schooner. With a toddy of Kentucky bourbon, they toasted their decision to move their families from Louisville to the wilderness that was then Naples. The year was 1885.

Perched on plush sands at the edge of Florida's primeval Everglades, meticulously manicured Naples today transcends its wild setting like a diamond in the rough. In fact, the only rough many visitors to this cultural oasis ever see is the one that sets them back two strokes on the seventh fairway. For along with Naples' reputation for outland poshness comes its claim for most golf holes per capita of any city in the US.

But it wasn't always that way. Naples' high-brow, high-rent status came about primarily in the past decade, after The Ritz-Carlton came to town. Not long ago, it was Florida's roughest neighborhood, roughest in the sense of unsettled and adventure-conducive. As gateway to the Ten Thousand Islands and the Everglades, it attracted wealthy sportsfolk along with unsavory characters taking cover in the land of great erasure. Naples still holds some of that undiscovered mystique, along with its polished image of glamour resorts, pricey shopping, an active arts scene, and groomed golf courses.

BASICS

Highway 41, or the Tamiami Trail, is Naples' main thoroughfare, known also as Ninth Street in town. From Interstate 75, take exits 17 and 16 and head west to reach North Naples; exit 15 gets you downtown and to south Naples.

Other main roads that run parallel to Highway 41 to the east are (east to west from the interstate) Goodlette-Frank Rd (Route 851) and Airport-Pulling Rd (Route 31). East-west trunks are Naples-Immokalee Highway (846) at the north edge of town; Pine Ridge Rd (896), Golden Gate Parkway (886), Radio Rd (856), and Davis Boulevard (84) in town; and Rattlesnake Hammock Rd (864) at the southern extreme.

 Naples Trolley Tours, ☎ 262-7300, transports you around town for a two-hour narrated lesson on 100 points of interest, with free re-boarding. It runs daily beginning at 8:30 am. Cost: $10 for adults, $5 for children.

INFORMATION

For information, visit or contact **Visit Naples**, 895 Fifth Ave S, Naples, FL 34102-6605, ☎ 941-598-3202 or 800-262-6141.

DOWNTOWN SIGHTS & ATTRACTIONS

Unlike most Florida cities these days, Naples has kept its heart and soul contained in its downtown section. Historic neighborhoods have been remade into fashionable shopping centers in Olde Naples (see *Shopping*, below).

The Naples Fishing Pier.

The district's most distinguished landmark, **The Naples Fishing Pier**, ☎ 434-4696, extends 1,000 feet into the Gulf (more under *Fishing & Boating*, below). It is the longest free pier in the state, and makes for a nice sunset stroll and a great place from which to cast. It juts out from the public beach on Gulf Shore Blvd at 12th Ave S and is open from 7:30 to 6. Parking is metered. More beach access points with parking lie to the north and south.

Nearby, **Palm Cottage** at 137 12th Ave S, ☎ 261-8164, demonstrates pioneer building methods and lifestyles. Made from Florida mahogany and tabby mortar, a sort of cement made from seashells, it has housed visiting celebrities such as Hedy Lamarr and Gary Cooper. Today it houses the **Collier County Historical Society**. It is closed weekends and late summer to early fall, otherwise open 2-4 daily or by appointment. Admission is free.

The city's most popular beach, **Lowdermilk Park**, is located along Gulf Shore Blvd at Banyan Blvd, ☎ 434-4698. The play-full park has 1,000 feet of sandy beach, outdoor showers, volleyball, a playground, two gazebos, a shaded pavilion, picnic tables, and a concession stand. Disabled users are accommodated by a special beach access, accessible restrooms, and free use of special wheeled surf chairs. Park hours are 11-3.

Part botanical garden, part animal attraction, **Jungle Larry's Zoological Park at Caribbean Gardens**, 1590 Goodlette Rd, ☎ 262-5409, lets you tour its 52 acres by foot, tram, or boat. Alligators, tigers, birds, elephants, snakes, and other animals take the stage for regularly scheduled wildlife demonstrations set in a simulated jungle. Adults pay $12.95; kids 4-15, $7.95. Elephant rides cost $2.50 each. The park is open daily 9:30-5:30. (Ticket office closes at 4:30.)

The Conservancy of Southwest Florida, Merrihue Drive at 14th Ave N, ☎ 262-0304, occupies 13 acres of mangrove and hammock habitat where you can tour a Nature Discovery Center with interactive and other displays and programs, a serpentarium, a wildlife rehabilitation facility, and nature trails. Free boat tours of the mangrove waterway are available (see *Fishing & Boating*, below). The facility also offers off-site nature hiking, canoe, and boat tours in conjunction with Briggs Nature Center (see *Marco Island*, below). Canoe and kayak rentals are available for use in the Gordon River, which runs through the property. Rental rates start at $13 for two hours. The facility is open 9-4:30 daily except Sunday, when it is open 1-5 January-March only. Nature Center admission is $5 for adults and $1 for children ages 5-17 (good for same-day admission to Briggs). Admission to nature trails is free.

OUTLYING SIGHTS & ATTRACTIONS

Corkscrew Swamp Sanctuary.

In Naples' outlying areas, the wilds encroach. To the north, one of the nation's most important birding and wildlife sites hides off the beaten path, 21 miles east of Hwy 41 off Immokalee Rd. **Corkscrew Swamp Sanctuary**, ☎ 657-3771, operated by the National Audubon Society, comprises 11,000 pristine acres, two miles of boardwalk that cross wetlands inhabited by rich plant and marine life, alligators, deer, otters, and wild hogs. The sanctuary is most famous for its 700-acre stand of bald cypress trees – the largest pure, unmixed forest of the specimen found anywhere in the world. More than 500 years old, the trees grow up to 130 feet tall, forming a natural, moss-hung cathedral ceiling. They are the habitat of choice for the endangered wood storks that favor the sanctuary as their nesting ground. The sanctuary is open daily: May-November, 8-5; December-April, 7-5. Admission is $6.50 for adults, $5 for college students, and $3 for children age 6-18.

For a beachfront away from mid-town's bustle, relax, fish, and hike at **Delnor-Wiggins State Recreation Area**, at Rte. 846 and Gulf Shore Drive N, ☎ 597-6196. An observation tower gives you a treetop view of the park's two waterfronts: the Gulf of Mexico and Vanderbilt

Channel, the latter of which separates the island from the mainland and affords boating opportunities. Fishing is great in the swift pass waters; but don't swim there. Besides a boat ramp and fish-cleaning station, you'll find picnic facilities, bathhouses, lifeguards, and lots of natural vegetation and beach. The park is open daily 8-sundown and costs $4 per vehicle with 2-8 passengers, $2 for a single occupant in a vehicle; $1 for pedestrians and bikers.

Families find fun away from the beach at **King Richard's Amusement Park**, 6780 N Airport Rd, ☎ 598-1666. Rides and activities include water bumper boats, batting cages, video and other electronic games, go-carts, a kiddie train, and two 18-hole miniature golf courses. Admission is per attraction. In season, it is open at 12-9 Monday-Thursday, 12-10 Friday-Saturday. In off-season, hours are shortened.

One of the area's most unusual attractions, **Teddy Bear Museum of Naples**, at 2511 Pine Ridge Rd, ☎ 598-2711, is stuffed with bears of all sizes and ages. Some are collectors items, such as a signed first edition copy of A.A. Milne's *Winnie the Pooh*, others are posed in vignettes, such as the bored bears at a board meeting – nearly 3,000 teddies in all. Admission is $5 for adults, $3 for seniors and teens, $2 for children ages 4-12. The museum is open 10-5 Wednesday-Saturday and 1-5 Sunday.

For a plunge into Naples' warm cultural climate, check with **Philharmonic Center for the Arts** at 5833 Pelican Bay Blvd, ☎ 597-1900. The 77-piece Naples Philharmonic is based at "The Phil" and the Miami City Ballet performs there three times a year. It hosts audiences of up to 1,222 for Broadway productions, touring orchestras, chamber music, and children's shows. Its art galleries host changing exhibitions and guided tours of renowned works.

In its four-acre historical park, **Collier County Museum**, at 3301 Tamiami Trail E, ☎ 774-8476, displays a Seminole Indian village, a classic swamp buggy, an archaeological lab, a Children's Discovery Cottage, native Florida gardens, and a steam locomotive, plus indoor exhibits, including prehistoric artifacts. Hours are 9-5 weekdays. Donations are accepted.

FISHING & BOATING

Naples' charters take you to Rookery Bay (see *Marco Island*, below) and Ten Thousand Islands for the best back bay fishing. Some go into deep waters and haunt the passes. From land, piers and passes offer best access to fish congregations, including snook, sheepshead, lady fish, trout, and snapper.

Naples Fishing Pier (see *Sights & Attractions,* above) at 12th Ave S, ☎ 434-4696, in the heart of old Naples, is Florida's longest free fishing pier, extending 1,000 feet into the Gulf. Facilities include bait shop, snack bar, restrooms, and showers, with metered parking. Hours: concession, 7:30 am-6 pm; parking until 11 pm. For other fishing supplies, see listings under *Shopping,* below.

The *Lady Brett,* at Tin City on Highway 41, ☎ 263-4949, departs twice daily for half-day fishing trips aboard a 34-foot powerboat. Fish in deep water about 12 miles from shore. Cost is $45 per adult, $40 per child under age 12. Tax is not included in prices.

If fly fishing is your thing, contact Capt. Tom Shadley at **Mangrove Outfitters**, 4111 E Tamiami Trail, ☎ 793-3370. He conducts classes in fly tying Tuesday evenings in season, 7-9 (no reservations required; $5 for supplies), and holds casting clinics by prior arrangement. Guides charge $350 for full day, $250 for half-days, and take you to the Everglades, Rookery Bay, Pine Island Sound, Estero Bay, and other local backwaters.

Port-O-Call Marina, off Hwy 41 E, ☎ 774-0479, rents deck (pontoon) boats and power boats from 17-23 feet in length, to accommodate six to 12 persons. Rental rates for half-days are $95-$160; for full days $145-$245, gas and tax extra.

Boat owners can launch their vessels into Vanderbilt Channel at **Delnor-Wiggins Pass State Recreation Area** (see *Sights & Attractions,* above) at 11100 Gulf Shore Drive N, ☎ 597-6196. There's an entry fee into the park. A free ramp is located at **Cocohatchee River Park** off Vanderbilt Drive The park has picnic tables and a playground.

Find *Sweet Liberty,* at the Boat Haven off of Hwy 41, ☎ 793-3525. The 53-foot catamaran departs daily for shelling, sightseeing, and sunset trips. Cost is around $20 for adults, $10 for children. Call ahead for reservations.

Odyssey Boat Tours, at Crayton Cove City Dock, ☎ 566-6557, advertises the same agendas as above, but faster. Powerboat cruises for up to six passengers cost $25-$35 each, plus tax, for shelling, sightseeing, and sunset-gazing in Rookery Bay.

Most famous for its Dolphin Watch Nature Cruises, **Double Sunshine**, at Tin City on Hwy 41, ☎ 263-4949, is a two-decked vessel that departs five times daily for 1½-hour narrated sightseeing cruises, and at 10 daily for the dolphin excursion. Cost is $15 per adult, $10 per child under age 12. Tax is extra.

The Naples Princess, at 1001 10th Ave S, ☎ 649-2275, is the premier dinner cruise vessel in the area. Its excursions are $20-$35 per person, plus tax and gratuity, and include a Conservancy-Narrated Nature

Cruise with continental breakfast, Island Buffet Lunch, Mid-Afternoon Sightseeing, Sunset Hors d'Oeuvres, Sunset Dinner, and Sunday Brunch. Call ahead for times and to make reservations.

Hiking and Sea Kayaking Adventures, ☎ 353-7269, has designed half-day, full-day, and overnight trips into the local wilderness. Cost is $35-$250 for single kayak, $45-$250 tandem. Meals and transportation are included. Kayak lessons cost $25 an hour, two-hour minimum.

The Conservancy of Southwest Florida, Merrihue Drive at 14th Ave N, ☎ 262-0304, (see *Downtown Sights & Attractions*, above) leads free 45-minute on-site boat tours through mangrove forest.

OTHER WATER SPORTS

Go parasailing, kayaking, waverunning, windsurfing, sailing, or paddleboating with a tour or rental from **Naples & Bonita Beach Watersports**, at Vanderbilt Inn (see *Where to Stay*, below), ☎ 591-2839. Parasail rides cost $50 and up. Waverunner rentals begin at $40 for a half-hour. Other prices: half-hour sailing lessons, $25; one hour Hobie Cat rental, $30; single hour kayak rental, $10; guided backbay waverunner tour, $90 for a single, $110 for a double.

Diving on the West Coast appeals to die-hard divers only, because of low visibility and lack of natural reefs. However, local operators teach scuba courses, usually taking students out of the region for open-water dives. For information and supplies in Naples, contact **Scubadventures**, 971 Creech Rd at Seabreeze Plaza on Hwy 41 N, ☎ 434-7477.

HIKING & BIKING

Five miles of hiking trails intertwine with pine flatwoods and oak and palm hammock terrain at the edge of **Corkscrew Marsh** on Corkscrew Rd, ☎ 332-7771. The trails are open free to the public daily during daylight hours. Free guided tours are offered the second Saturday of every month.

Hiking and Sea Kayaking Adventures, ☎ 353-7269, organizes custom hiking tours to Big Cypress Preserve, east of Everglades National Park, and other natural sites. Cost: $45 for half-day, $90 for full day, including transportation from hotel.

At **The Conservancy of Southwest Florida**, Merrihue Drive at 14th Ave N, ☎ 262-0304 (see *Downtown Sights & Attractions*, above), naturalists take you on a free guided hike through a sub-tropical hammock. You can also hike the two trails unguided.

Naples lays out a start-and-stop loop of metropolitan bike paths. One favorite route of local cyclists' runs through Pelican Bay, a development at the north end of town with a 580-acre nature preserve. **Bicycle Shoppe of Naples** at 813 Vanderbilt Beach Rd, ☎ 566-3646, rents conventional bikes for $7 plus tax per day.

OTHER SPORTS

You'll find avid shellers combing local beaches. The most devoted head to **Key Island**, a barrier island at the mouth of the Gordon River at Naples' south end, almost entirely owned by local conservation agencies and the state. Local charters will take you there to go shelling and birding. You'll also hear the island referred to as Keewaydin Island.

For high-flying adventure, take to the air in the open cockpit of an authentic 1941 Boeing Stearman biplane with **Naples Barnstormers**, located at the Naples Airport, ☎ 774-4773. For about $100 per hour, you can tour above the Everglades, the Gulf Coast, or wherever (nearby) is your fancy.

WHERE TO EAT

Naples has a well-deserved reputation for its restaurants, which come in all varieties, but are heavy on fine cuisine. It has enough old-style fish houses, however, to balance the fancy.

One of the oldest favorites, **The Dock at Crayton Cove**, at 12th Ave S, ☎ 263-9940, sits outside on Naples Bay and attracts swarms in season. It's very casual, but you'll find a lot of Naples' wealthy population gracing its wooden tables. The menu gives you a little of the old mixed with a bit of the new, selections the likes of grilled tuna cheesesteak, blackened shrimp tacos, and fish and chips. It's open daily for lunch and dinner. Dishes are $7-$13.

For a taste of Naples' cutting edge, try **Annabelle's**, downtown at 494 Fifth Ave S, ☎ 261-4275. Its clever artsy avant-garde decor spills onto the sidewalk. Sandwiches, salads, pasta dishes, and other entrées are creative combinations of baby greens, goat cheese, grilled meats and seafoods, and other such trendy ingredients. It's open Monday-Saturday for breakfast, lunch ($3-$11), and dinner (entrées $15-$25).

Go to **St. George and the Dragon Restaurant**, at 936 Fifth Ave, ☎ 262-6546, to enjoy a great steak and to see the eccentrically decorated ladies' room (even if you're a man)! The rest of the restaurant's rich nautical decor, along with the great food, is also worth the visit, and it's close to shopping. There's somewhat of a dress code for dinner, but lunch is casual. Main courses are $11-$30. In season it is open daily for dinner, Monday-Saturday for lunch, with reduced hours off-season. Reservations recommended.

Close to another shopping front, at 1300 Third Street S, **Terra**, formerly The Chef's Garden, ☎ 262-5500, is a landmark. It's a perfect setting for a special occasion, with new continental specialties and fresh roses on the table. It's open daily for lunch and dinner in season; closed for lunch off-season. A la carte entrées such as yellowfin tuna and grilled veal chops are $15-$25.

For something less formal, you may want to hike upstairs to its companion restaurant, **Truffles**, ☎ 597-8119, where you can get well-made sandwiches, pastas, seafood, salads, and dreamy desserts. Try the Truffles Crispy Fish and the key lime pie. Prices are $7-$20. It's open daily for lunch and dinner, and serves a great Sunday brunch.

Not far away from Naples' spendy, trendy neighborhoods, **Whistle Stop Steakhouse**, at Waterloo Station, 200 Goodlette Rd S, ☎ 263-8440, offers dependably good homecooked food for reasonable prices: $7-$9 for hefty sandwiches, $12-$17 for steaks, seafood, and other entrées. It's known for its great salad bar. Around the restaurant, you'll discover a bit of local railroad history. The restaurant is open Monday-Saturday for lunch and dinner.

WHERE TO STAY

Naples lodging doesn't come cheaply, as a rule, although it does have its off-ramp chains and older motels for budget travelers. Rates listed below do not include 8% sales and bed tax.

Vanderbilt Beach, the Gulf-side community at Naples' north side, has two fun beach resorts in different price ranges. The ever-popular **Vanderbilt Inn**, 11000 Gulf Shore Drive N, ☎ 597-3151 or 800-643-8654, has been around for decades to keep beach- and water-lovers happy. Locals know it for its happening chickee (thatched roof) beach bar. It also has a nice restaurant and pool, and a variety of watersports rentals (see *Other Water Sports*, above). High-season rates are $170-$280. Throughout the rest of the year, the range is $85-$220.

La Playa, 9891 Gulf Shore Drive, ☎ 597-3123 or 800-237-6883, recently made-over in high style, exudes a privileged tropical air. Rooms are

Caribbean-style gorgeous, and tennis courts are plentiful. Expect to pay $145-$235 (excluding penthouse suites) off-season, $195-$345 in season.

The Ritz-Carlton, 280 Vanderbilt Beach Rd, ☎ 598-3300 or 800-241-3333, is the grande dame of Naples hotels. Book there if you want a splurge on the wild side, because aside from its inherent good manners, the Naples Ritz has a nature-loving proclivity that starts with its mangrove preserve and ends with its eco-tourism concierges. Rates in season begin around $310; off-season, the low end runs $150-$250, depending on time of year.

Great for all manner of sportslovers, **Naples Beach Hotel & Golf Club**, at 851 Gulf Shore Blvd N, ☎ 261-2222, recently celebrated its 50th anniversary. Lining the beach at the heart of Olde Naples, the 135-acre resort is especially popular with golfers. It also offers extensive watersports, a pool, tennis courts, and a fine kids program. Complete with restaurants, bars, and shops, the hotel has recently renovated accommodations in old Florida-style buildings and high rises. Rates in season are $195-$425 for rooms and suites. Packages available.

In the midst of Naples' historic shopping district, and a short walk from the beach, **Inn by the Sea**, at 287 11th Ave S, ☎ 649-4124 or 800-584-1268, exudes the charm one expects from a B&B. Built in 1937, its six rooms are named for local islands and are showcase-decorated according to their individual seaside themes. Rates in season are $85-$165, off-season $50-$95.

For an affordable stopover option near the interstate, consider **Budgetel Inn**, at 185 Bedzel Circle, Davis Blvd and Rte. 951, ☎ 352-8400 or 800-4-BUDGET. New and modern, the hotel has a swimming pool, comfortable rooms, and is located close to several chain restaurants. Cost in high season, which includes continental breakfast, is $100-$106; $40-$80 in off-season months.

SHOPPING

Naples' renowned shopping has spread throughout the city, in old restored downtown areas and new, fashionable shopping plazas. Art galleries are abundant, as are jewelry, antique, home decor, and fashion shops and boutiques.

For the best in window shopping, head to Olde Naples' **Fifth Street** district and **Third Street South Plaza and the Avenues,** or to the new, spectacular plazas: **The Village of Venetian Bay**, at Gulfshore Blvd N and Park Shore, and **Waterside Shops at Pelican Bay**, Seagate Drive and Tamiami Trail N. Sportsmen will want to stop at **Everglades Outfitters**, 779 Fifth Ave S, ☎ 262-8117 and, at the same address, **Naples Sporting Goods**, ☎ 262-6752. They're open Monday-Saturday.

More touristy, but also more affordable are **Old Marine Waterfront Marketplace** at **Tin City** off Highway 41 S, and **Dockside Boardwalk**, 1100 Sixth Ave S. You'll find nice wildlife-themed shops at both.

To buy the unaffordable at more affordable prices, vie for the cast-offs of the rich at upscale consignment shops, of which there are a wealth. Some of the best include **Collector's Studios**, at 555 Fifth Ave S, ☎ 643-1355, open Monday-Saturday 10-5; **Conservancy Upscale Resale Shoppe**, at 732 Tamiami Trail N, ☎ 263-0717, open Monday-Friday 10-4 and Saturday 10-2; **Kid's Consignment**, at 4444 N Tamiami Trail, ☎ 261-9596, open Monday-Friday 10-5 and Saturday 10-4; **New To You Consignments**, at 933 Creech Rd and Hwy 41, ☎ 262-6869, open Monday-Saturday 10-5; and **Encore** at 3105 Davis Blvd, ☎ 775-0032, open Monday-Saturday 10-4. They sell clothes, furniture, and decorative items.

Marco Island

Floating offshore in the middle of nowhere, Marco Island is surprisingly developed. Outdoors lovers may at first be put off by its skyscraping row of beachfront resorts and condos, but upon closer inspection you'll find the island thoroughly steeped in waterbound sports. As chief among the Ten Thousand Islands stretching to the south, Marco Island provides great oppor-

Marco Island.

tunities for serious fishermen, bird-watchers, and outdoors folk in general.

Away from its glamour front, you'll find charming time-stilled communities, waterfront fish houses, and thriving marinas. Here is a civilized departure point for deep adventure in the Everglades.

BASICS

Marco Island consists of several communities. The least known, Isles of Capri, is a series of interconnected islands at Marco's northern threshold. It has been developed for residential use. You can't get to Isles of Capri from Marco Island proper, but must turn off Route 952 onto Capri Boulevard before Marco (watch for signs). Capri Boulevard continues through the community.

To get to Marco Island proper from Highway 41 or Interstate 74, take Route 951 (interstate exit 15). Two bridges span the bay waters known as Marco River to reach the island. The main high bridge lies at the island's north end and gets you closest to Olde Marco and the island's resort area. Follow it south to Marco Island.

The south-end bridge is a better access if you're approaching from the east along Highway 41 or if you want to get straight to Goodland, the fishing community at that end of the island. Turn southwest off of Highway 41 onto Route 92 to cross the south bridge.

Collier Boulevard (Route 951) crosses the north bridge and continues through the island's commercial section and along the Gulf front. Crossroad Bald Eagle Drive (953) heads north-south to Olde Marco and mid-island. It connects to San Marco Drive (92), which crosses the south bridge.

 *Try the **Marco Island Trolley Tour**, ☎ 394-1600, It makes stops throughout the town of Marco, and issues passes for one-day reboarding. Cost is $10.*

INFORMATION

For more information, contact the **Marco Island & The Everglades Convention & Visitors Bureau**, 1102 N Collier Blvd, Marco Island 33937, ☎ 394-3061 or 800-788-6272.

SIGHTS & ATTRACTIONS

One of the area's most vital attractions sits at Marco Island's doorstep. **Rookery Bay Estuarine Reserve & Briggs Nature Center** on Shell Rd off Rte. 951, ☎ 775-8569, is 8,000 acres of prime wilderness that looks much the way it did before this rough-and-tumble land was settled. Go there to gaze at birds, alligators, and manatees. A stroll along the 2,500-foot boardwalk reveals the wonders of mangrove ecology (admission $3 adults; $1 children). You can hike Monument Trail around the bay for free. An exhibit hall interprets the environment, and hosts boat, canoe, and birding trips. The bay is popular with fishermen, and there's a small boat ramp on premises. The center is open 9-5 every day except Sunday.

One public access allows visitors onto Marco Island's beautiful sands. Hence, **Tigertail Beach**, Hernando Drive, ☎ 353-0404, is a popular place. Go early in nice weather to find a parking spot. Or take the trolley there. Facilities include a concession stand, picnic tables, sailboat and personal watercraft rentals, volleyball, restrooms, playgrounds, and showers. Its hours are 7-dusk. Parking is $3 per car.

The neighboring residential community of Isles of Capri has no strong tourist attractions, but does offer visitors a nice menu of seafood restaurants (see *Where to Eat*, below) and marina services (see *Fishing & Boating*, below).

FISHING & BOATING

Marco's fishing preoccupation is self-evident. An abundance of marinas offer charters, rentals, docking, bait and tackle shops, and other facilities. They include **Marco River Marina** at 951 Bald Eagle Drive, ☎ 394-2502; **Factory Bay Marina** at 1079 Bald Eagle Drive, ☎ 642-6717; **Misfits Marina** at 231 Capri Blvd in Isles of Capri, ☎ 642-9666; and **Goodland Bay Marina** at 604 Palm Ave, ☎ 394-2797.

Fishing charters concentrate on the fish-full waters of Marco Islands' many waterways. Rookery Bay is a favorite, especially in winter. Gordon and Caxambas passes have a reputation as hot summer fishing spots.

Capt. Russ Gober, ☎ 394-5513, has long-time experience fishing local waters. You can have you catch prepared at his father's place, Stan's Idle Hour (see *Where to Eat*, below). His rates for charters of one to four people are $250 for a half-day, $350 for a full day.

Sunshine Tours out of Marco River Marina, ☎ 642-5415, takes fishermen aboard a 32-foot boat with bathroom for offshore excursions ($325 for half-day, $550 for full day, parties of five or less). Backwater fishing and shelling trips cost $36 and $25, respectively. For current local fishing information, call its **Fishing Hotline** (☎ 941-642-8888).

The longest running tour boat is *Rosie* at 1083 Bald Eagle Drive, ☎ 394-7673, a paddlewheel double-decker that goes on lunch, dinner, and sightseeing excursions. Closes in summer.

For all varieties of water excursions – sightseeing, shelling, fishing, snorkeling, dolphin spotting, and nature tours – connect with **Captain's John and Pam Stop** at Stop's Marine in Goodland's Calusa Island Marina, ☎ 394-8000. Modes of transportation include a 26-foot luxury vessel and a 30-foot tri-hull pontoon. Rates start at $35 per person ($30 for children under age 12) for 2½ hours of backwater fishing. Call 7-9 for reservations.

Moran's Barge Marina at the Goodland Bridge on San Marco Rd (Rte. 92), ☎ 642-1920, rents 18-foot consoles ($100 for full day, $70 for half-day), 22-foot pontoons ($110 and $75) and waverunners ($65 per hour).

Factory Bay Marina (1079 Bald Eagle Drive, Marco; ☎ 941-642-6717) rents pontoons, center consoles, and Grady Whites for $65-$99 half-days and $99-$169 full days. It also conducts approximately two-hour airboat tours into the Ten Thousand Islands for $20 per adult, $10 per child under age 12.

Marco Island's only public boat ramp, on Roberts Bay at the island's south end, is accessible from **Caxambas Park** on S Collier Ct. Restrooms, bait and fuel are available. Small boats can use free-of-charge the shell ramp at **Rookery Bay Reserve** on Shell Rd off Rte 951 on the way to Marco Island, ☎ 775-8569.

Beach Sports Surf & Tackle at 571 S Collier Blvd, ☎ 642-4282, covers a variety of adventure needs. It sells live bait, tackle, and fishing licenses. It rents sea kayaks and launches you on a self-guided adventures for $35 a day single or double. It instructs in PADI scuba and has the island's only compression chamber.

OTHER WATER SPORTS

Marco Island Jet Ski & Water Sports operates out of Marriott's Marco Island Resort (see *Where to Stay*, below), ☎ 394-6589, and provides 10-15 minute parasail rides ($60 with photo) and towed tube rides ($15). It rents waverunners for $55 single, $65 double for 35 minutes. Waverunner Ten Thousand Islands excursions last one hour and cost $100 for singles, $125 for doubles.

HIKING & BIKING

Bike paths run along Collier Boulevard, Marco Island's resort road, and in other parts of the island. **Beach Sports Surf & Tackle** at 571 S Collier Blvd, ☎ 642-4282, rents a wide variety of bikes starting at $8 a day (hourly and weekly rates available) and in-line skates for $16 a day. It's open daily 8-6 and delivers equipment free-of-charge.

WHERE TO EAT

Restaurants are rife on Marco Island, everything from the utmost casual to tiptop elegance. Seafood reigns, particularly stone crab claws, a Florida delicacy encased in a rock-hard shell – hence the name. They are in season from mid-October to mid-May and can be quite costly, depending upon availability. To keep restaurant tabs down, try them as an appetizer, prepared steamy hot or iced with drawn butter or tangy mustard sauce.

To obtain a sense of Marco Island's salty demeanor, savor the seafood and seaside atmosphere of **Snook Inn** at 1215 Bald Eagle Drive, ☎ 394-3313. It fronts the Marco River, and has a lively outdoor chickee bar. Those who can't watch boat traffic from a window can peer into an aquarium. The food is typical Old Florida style – beer-battered grouper, breaded shrimp, plus steaks, chicken and a salad bar, entrées ranging from $9 to $18. Lunches are $7-$9. The restaurant is open daily.

For a brush with island tradition, dine grandly at **Olde Marco Inn,** 100 Palm Street, ☎ 394-3131. Built in 1883, it has been restored to its original gracious Southern style. Its six rooms display distinctive personalities – from fully formal to veranda style. The international/seafood menu has a German accent, offering such specialties as weinerschnitzel, shrimp scampi, and stone crab claws at $15-$36 for a complete dinner. It's open daily for dinner; reservations are accepted.

The finest French classic cuisine graces the tables of intimate and bright **The Dining Room** at 1000 N Collier Blvd, ☎ 394-2221. A la carte entrées such as chicken veronique, grilled lamb chops, and fresh salmon are $15-$23. The restaurant is open daily except Sunday for dinner only; call ahead for reservations.

Goodland has its share of good-eating restaurants, primarily fish-house types. Most notorious is **Stan's Idle Hour Seafood Restaurant** at 221 W Goodland Drive, off Rte. 92, ☎ 394-3041. Named for its colorful owner, the restaurant embodies Goodland's spirit with fresh seafood, done mostly old-Florida style (fried). The house features all-you-can-eat stone crabs and will prepare your catch after a day's fishing with Stan's son, Russ Gober (see *Fishing & Boating*, above). Pies are homemade and delicious. You can dine outdoors on the canal front or indoors in a modern setting of light wood. Go Sunday afternoons for Buzzard Bash dancing and country crooning. It's open daily except Monday for lunch and dinner, and closes the month of August. Sandwiches and dinner entrées are in the $6-$18 range. Reservations accepted for dinner.

Little known to the outside world, but well known to locals, **Little Bar** at 205 Harbor Drive, ☎ 394-5663, outdoes its modest name with lots of dining space, some on a screened porch dockside, some in a room decorated with the remains of a historic boat, some in rooms paneled with oak pipe organ pieces. Cuisine goes beyond old-Florida style with tropic flair, everything from Buffalo frog legs and blue crab balls to meatloaf with mushroom gravy, red beans with kielbasa, shrimp pesto on linguine, and *tournedos au poivre*. The soft shell crab sandwich is tops. Lunches are $4-$7; dinners $10-$16, depending on the market price of fish. It serves lunch and dinner daily; reservations suggested for dinner.

Isles of Capri has restaurants both fine and casual. On the finer side and with a German flavor, **Alexander's Shrimp Boat Restaurant** at 203 Capri Blvd, ☎ 394-0252, is open for dinner daily and accepts reservations. Continental and seafood selections run $11-$22.

On the casual side of the Isles, **Bub's Sunset Bar & Grill** at 231 Capri Blvd, ☎ 394-8767, serves wings, burgers, salads, shrimp, and stone crabs in a screened chickee at Misfits Marina. It's open daily for lunch and dinner with the same menu, prices ranging from $5 to $15.

WHERE TO STAY

Marco Island proper lays out a strip of high-reaching resorts and condos along its crescent beach. This is the Marco Island most know about. To find something less Miami Beach-ish, head to the north and south ends of the island.

Marriott is the monarch of Marco beach resorts. **Marriott's Marco Island Resort and Golf Club** at 400 S Collier Blvd, ☎ 394-2511 or 800-GET-HERE, is a large property offering all manner of outdoor activities. It has its own miniature golf course, playgrounds, more than three miles of beach, and a great program for kids. For big kids, there are watersports rentals, a shopping arcade, swimming pools, an off-property golf course, tennis, and a fitness center. Guests have several dining options. The resort also organizes tours to the Everglades and other nearby attractions. Rates in season are $260-$365 for rooms, $550 and up for suites. Off-season, you pay anywhere from $135-$290 for rooms, $325 and up for suites.

Radisson Suite Beach Resort, 600 S Collier Blvd, ☎ 394-4100 or 800-814-0633, also occupies Marco's golden beach with an array of accommodations, watersports rentals, restaurants, and activities. It has two tennis courts, a basketball court, a large pool and Jacuzzi, and shuffleboard. Popular with families, it engages children in a well-planned recreational program. Rates for a room in season start at $199, suites at $259; off-season rates are as low as $99 for a room, $129 for a suite. Packages available.

At the island's north end, in Olde Marco, **The Boat House Motel**, 1180 Edington Place, ☎ 642-2400, provides a more secluded, boating-oriented option. In season, rooms are $70-$95, off-season, $45-$65. There are also condos to rent. The operation rents bicycles, paddle boats, waverunners, pontoons, and fishing boats, and offers docking to boat owners. It is situated on the Marco River, with a wood deck and pool stretching along the water.

In Goodland, **Mar-Good RV Park**, 321 Pear Tree Ave, ☎ 394-6383, rents cottages and RV sites in its self-sustaining community with its own marina and restaurant. RV sites cost $25 per two persons per day, with full hook-ups and cable TV. Cottages rent for $50-$70 per day. Weekly and monthly rates available.

Everglades City/Chokoloskee Island

At Naples' backdoor lies Florida's proudest possession, the Everglades. The term Everglades has two frames of reference. Generically, it refers to the type of environment that spreads from Naples to Miami, Lake Okeechobee to Cape Sable, including the 721,000 acres of nearby Big Cypress National Preserve. Specifically, it means that territory bought by the United States Park Service in the 1940s, and protected to this day against development. This vast region was saved from the ravages of man's greed by the writings of Marjorie Stoneman Douglas, though it still teeters on the brink of destruction. It is the second largest national park, after Yellowstone. Its appeal is more subtle than that of most national parks, so it often gets ignored.

These massive wetlands – home of the endangered Florida panther and American crocodile – cover 2,100 square miles and shelter more than 600 types of fish and 300 bird species. Its land of Ten Thousand Islands holds the largest mangrove forest in the world; its shores have pine and hardwood forests, cypress stands, and wetland prairies.

The best known Everglades features are its mangrove islands and its so-called River of Grass, the slowest moving river in the world. Both are fertile wildlife incubators. The region puts on the best bird show

In the Everglades.

around, hosting wood storks, white pelicans, ospreys, sanderlings, frigates, great white herons, tri-color herons, bald eagles, and other species both rare and common. In the water, dolphin come to feed, mullet jump, manatees mow the sea grasses, and alligators ogle. This is also the home of more reclusive animals, most notably the seriously endangered Florida panther, along with the Florida black bear and the bobcat.

The best way to explore the 'Glades is by water, but some hiking and biking opportunities also exist. Here is a whole other world from the kingdom of Florida beyond. This world holds Florida's heart. If it stops beating, so will the arteries that lead out of it. So will a wealth of wildlife.

To base your exploration on this side of the Everglades, you will want to head to one of the major camping areas, or to the slightly redneck island towns of Everglades City and Chokoloskee Island.

BASICS

To penetrate the Everglades from the West Coast, you can either approach from Highway 41 or take exit 14A off the stretch of Interstate 75 known as Alligator Alley (75¢ toll). The exit takes you down Route 29, a narrow, lightly traveled road from which you get snapshot glimpses of what awaits ahead.

Everglades City lies at the juncture of Highway 41 and Route 29. To get to Chokoloskee Island, follow the signs in Everglades City that direct you to turn right at Captain's Table. After driving around the circle that is the town hub, you'll head across the Chokoloskee Causeway.

The Everglades gave birth to two unusual modes of transportation, adapted to its shallow, swampy waters. Swamp buggies are modified Jeep-like vehicles built for any number between two and a crowd. They were developed by early 'Glades hunters and today are used widely for touring wetlands.

Air boats are fast, shallow-draft, noisy boats that zip across the water's surface.

Although not exclusive to the Everglades, pontoon boats – flat, shallow-draft vessels – are popularly used in the area's skinny waters. They allow passage where v-shaped hulls deny it.

INFORMATION

Contact **Everglades Area Chamber of Commerce,** P.O. Box 130, Everglades City, FL 33929, ☎ 695-3941. It has a welcome station at the corner of Hwy 41 and Rte. 29, open daily 9-5. For information about **Everglades National Park**, contact US Department of the Interior, National Park Service, Everglades National Park, P.O. Box 279, Homestead, FL 33030.

EVERGLADES SIGHTS & ATTRACTIONS

Collier-Seminole State Park at 20200 E Tamiami Trail, ☎ 394-3397, is one of the most newcomer-friendly ways to access the Everglades environment. The park entails more than 6,400 acres, of which 4,760 is wilderness mangrove preserve. You have options to camp, picnic, hike, bike, canoe, and boat around the encompassing area to be-

Canoeing the Everglades.

come better acquainted with the plants and animals that dwell in the pinelands, salt marsh, and cypress swamp. It features a wildlife interpretation center and a historic walking dredge that was used to build Tamiami Trail out of the mosquito-swarming muck. Entrance to the park, open sunrise to sunset, is $4 per car of up to eight passengers or $2 per vehicle with single occupant. Admission by bike, by foot, or per extra passenger is $1.

Fakahatchee Strand State Preserve, ☎ 695-4593, protects a stretch of land north of the national park, but offers limited access. You can walk along a 2,000-foot boardwalk at Big Cypress Bend, off Hwy 41, in dry weather to experience the eerie beauty of the swamp. In rainy season, wear galoshes. Experience native royal palms, cypress trees, and other rare vegetation. No admission.

Despite its natural temperament, the Everglades is tainted with inevitable commercialism. You'll find alligator wrestlers and air boats and panthers in cages. Those places announce themselves; some offer tours. For more information on airboat rides, see *Fishing & Boating* below.

EVERGLADES CITY & CHOKOLOSKEE ISLAND SIGHTS & ATTRACTIONS

The islands slowly develop their historic past into tourist sites. A historic museum is underway in Everglades City. The first and main attraction is **Smallwood Store** in Chokoloskee, ☎ 695-2989. Not so long ago, the barn-red building served as an Indian trading post. It remained a store and post office until it closed in 1974, and part of it retains the general store atmosphere while one room is given to exhibits on the Everglades' pioneer days. Its most sensational claim and homespun yarn centers around the gundown of outlaw Ed Watson, subject of a bestselling novel by Peter Matthiessen. The store is open 10-4 daily. Adults pay $2.50 for admission, seniors $2, children under 12 are admitted free when accompanied by an adult.

FISHING & BOATING

You can spend several hours in the water here without seeing another boat or other sign of humanity. With all that water, water everywhere, Ten Thousand Islands and River of Grass afford the aqua-inclined opportunities unparalleled anywhere in Florida. It is recommended that you explore the area in cool weather, late October through March, to avoid the battalions of mosquitos. Boating requires a shallow draft and local knowledge of the labryinthine waters. For first-timers, it's best to hire a guide.

Fishing guides are plentiful. **Captain Max Miller**, ☎ 695-2420, specializes in light tackle backbay fishing. Rates for one to three people are $200 for a half-day, $300 for a full day.

For sightseeing tours of Ten Thousand Islands, you can find private charters or hop aboard two available group tours. **Everglades National Boat Tours**, located on the Chokoloskee Causeway, Rte 29, ☎ 695-2591 or 800-445-7724, conducts naturalist-narrated tours through Ten Thousand Islands and its teeming bird and water life. Tours depart daily every 30 minutes 9-4:30 or 5, depending upon what time the sun sets. They last about an hour and a half. Cost is $11 for adults and $5.50 for kids age 6-12.

For a more intimate wildlife experience, try **Majestic Everglades Excursions** in Everglades City, ☎ 695-2777. A pontoon boat takes up to six passengers on a tour of the Ten Thousand Islands, their nature, and their history. Narrated by owners Frank and Georgia Garrett, the trip reveals obscure places and lore that may be new to even the most knowledgeable bird- and wildlife-lover. Binoculars are provided. Depending upon the day, you may get a dolphin show that beats any theme park, a peek at ospreys setting up housekeeping, or a tour along the route taken by the murderers of the Everglades' favorite outlaw, Ed Watson. Tours depart twice daily when weather and tides permit, and last about four hours, costing $65 each. Morning tours include a light lunch; afternoons, fruit and cheese. This is the way to go if you want to learn more than surface prattle about the islands.

Airboats can load you up with only one other person or a boatload. You won't have to look very far to find someone who will take you sightseeing in this uniquely Floridian fashion. Some add alligator shows and other land-borne attractions to the trip. If you don't like noise and commercialism, try another mode of exploration. To give it a go, contact **Everglades Private Airboat Tours**, located one mile west of Rte 29 on Hwy 41, ☎ 695-4637 or 800-368-0065. Rates are $60 for 1-2 passengers, $25 for each extra adult, $10 for children ages 4-12.

By canoe and kayak, you can reach the region's most hidden places. Strike out on your own or follow a guided tour through the Ten Thousand Islands' 98-mile **Wilderness Waterway** canoe trail. Canoeists must register with park rangers. You can paddle portions of the trail; the entire length takes at least a week. Chickee (Indian-thatched) hut landings provide primitive shelter for campers.

For canoe rentals, call **Everglades National Park Boat Tours** at ☎ 695-2591 or FL 800-445-7724. Canoe rentals cost $18 a day, including shuttle service. The facility is open daily 8-5. Several outfitters run guided tours within the park. Canoeists must bring all of their own gear unless outfitted by one of these businesses.

A list of canoe rentals, outfitters, and recommended gear, plus necessary charts, guidebooks, and complete information are available from US Department of the Interior, National Park Service, Everglades National Park, P.O. Box 279, Homestead, FL 33030.

Huron Kayak & Canoe, located just before the Chokoloskee Causeway, ☎ 695-3666, does guided trips from a half-day ($35 each) to six days ($540 each, meals included). Some trips are seasonal. Tours are led by two canoeing champions. Instructions and rentals also available.

North American Canoe Tours/Everglades Canoe & Kayak Outpost, ☎ 695-4666, rents 17-19 foot aluminum canoes for $18-$30 a day. Kayaks come in four sizes and rent for $35-$55 a day. The service also rents equipment and complete outfitting, and provides shuttle service. Its tours range from one-day guided adventures for $40 each to seven-day Everglades paddles for $800 each, including meals, equipment, and two nights at Ivey House B&B (see *Where to Stay,* below).

You can rent canoes at **Collier-Seminole State Park** (see *Sights & Attractions,* above), 20200 E Tamiami Trail, ☎ 394-3397, for use in the park's 13-mile canoe trail into the wilderness preserve. Primitive overnight camping is available to canoeists. Canoe rentals are $3 an hour, $15 a day.

HIKING & BIKING

The 6½-mile trail at **Collier-Seminole State Park,** 20200 E Tamiami Trail, ☎ 394-3397, ribbons through pine flatwoods and cypress swamp. Plus you can walk a self-guided board trail to experience life in a salt marsh.

Bike paths traverse Everglades City and cross the causeway to Chokoloskee Island. W.J. Janes Memorial Scenic Drive branches off of Highway 29 north of Everglades City to lead you along a gravel-paved road into Fakahatchee Strand (see *Everglades Sights & Attractions,* above). Most of the road is gravel-paved. Its forest of royal palms, cypress trees, and air plants provides pristine scenery and bird habitat. Stillness is the drive's greatest asset; you feel completely removed from the everyday world.

In Everglades City, you can rent from the **Ivey House B&B,** ☎ 695-3299, for $3 per hour, $15 per day. Guests are allowed free use when available.

OTHER SPORTS

To see the Ten Thousand Islands from cloud-level, go flight-seeing with **10,000 Island Aero-Tours,** ☎ 695-3296. Prices start at $45 per person, minimum of two per flight.

WHERE TO EAT

This part of Florida more closely approximates Southern culture than any other area of the Southwest coast. Accents are twangy and food typically fried. Frog legs, stone crab, blue crab, and grouper appear on most menus.

Captain's Table Restaurant, ☎ 695-2727, serves standard Everglades fare – blue crab, shrimp, oysters, and freshly made hushpuppies – on a screened veranda overlooking the water, or in a cypress ship motif. Lunch dishes are $5-$9; dinner entrées, $11-$27.

With its tin roof, columned front porch, cypress-lined lobby and mangrove view, the venerable **Rod and Gun Club**, 200 Broadway, ☎ 695-2101, firmly grasps its Southern roots. Inside the lobby, an alligator hide stretches along a wall behind a copper-topped center fireplace. Built circa 1889 as a home that grew into an inn for hunters, fishermen, and yachters, it once entertained presidents and dignitaries within its pecky cypress walls. Today the Rod and Gun Club still feeds intrepid sportsfolk who arrive by boat or car. The main dining room feels like a sportsman's lodge, wooded and clubby. A screened porch dining room invites leisurely dining. Sample Dixie-Florida fare: fried fresh fish, seafood platter, frog legs, shrimp, stone crab, Southern peanut butter pie (if you don't have room, get a piece to go), and Key lime pie. It's open daily for breakfast, lunch ($8-$11) and dinner (entrées $10-$20). No credit cards accepted.

WHERE TO STAY

The islands are known for their RV parks more than any other type of lodging. They do have several inexpensive motels, including some located in RV parks. One of the largest, best maintained of these is **Outdoor Resorts of Chokoloskee Island, ☎ 695-2881** (motel) or 695-3788 (RV resort). It has what's important to vacationers in these parts: a marina, boat rentals, a bait and tack shop, and guide service for fishing and touring. Pull into one of 283 full-service sites or stay in the motel. Either way, you can take advantage of the resort's three pools, health spa, lighted tennis and shuffleboard courts, and restaurant. Site use for two people runs $30-$40 a day year-round (monthly rates available). Motel efficiency and rental trailers are $65-$75 (weekly rates available). Boat rentals are $85 a day; canoes, $25.

Aside from the camping resorts, Everglades City boasts one hotel that has gained attention for its historic, Southern charm. The **Rod and Gun Club** at 200 Broadway, ☎ 695-2101, offers nothing fancy but complete escape from what irks us out in the real world. Cottages are basic, perhaps in need of a bit of repair, but loved by a devoted following. There's a pool and restaurant (see *Where to Eat*, above) on premises, plus docking and other boating amenities. Rates at their summer lowest are $50 a night; at their winter highest, $85.

Outdoor enthusiasts find **Ivey House B&B**, 107 Camellia Street in Everglades City, ☎ 695-3299, to their liking. Lodge-like, the hostelry has 10 rooms, small but clean and cooled. Cold breakfast is included, and family-style dinner available for $10-$15 each. It guides tours into the Ten Thousand Islands by canoe, kayak, or boat (see *North American Canoe Tours* under *Fishing & Boating*, above), and rents equipment. Bike use is complimentary. Lodging rates are $50-$60 per night for a room; $90-$130 for a cottage.

CAMPING

Five miles east of Rte. 29 on Hwy 41, **Big Cypress Trail Lakes Campground,** ☎ 695-2275, lets you camp by tent or RV in Big Cypress National Preserve, a magnificent sanctuary adjacent to Everglades National Park. Tent sites cost $12 per night. Two RV campers pay $15 per night, electric and water included. Weekly and monthly rates available.

Collier-Seminole State Park (see *Everglades Sights & Attractions*, above) at 20200 E Tamiami Trail, ☎ 394-3397, has more than 100 sites for tent- and RV-campers, plus canoeing and hiking trails. Sites without electricity cost $14.17 per night, $16.29 with electricity. Reservations are accepted.

Index

Adventure Guide to Northern Florida & the Panhandle

by Cynthia & Jim Tunstall

A beautifully written guide to the northern regions of the Sunshine State, with a focus on the many outdoor adventures you can enjoy while visiting. Whether you want to swim with manatees, dive underwater caverns, bike the 47-mile Rails to Trails path, or try your hand at waterskiing in the warm waters of the Gulf, this book has it all. Starting with the region's history – from native Indians to Spanish explorers – the book gives a solid background on Northern Florida & its panhandle. The *Travel Strategies & Helpful Facts* section offers tips on dealing with the wildlife and insects, the tropical climate, clothing and gear you may need and driving and road conditions. The Tunstalls then offer an introduction to the nature of adventure, briefly describing the many recreational opportunities such as sea kayaking, biking, snorkeling, diving, fishing, horseback riding, parasailing and hiking. Breaking the area into regions, the guide then starts traveling in earnest, giving the specifics of each town and city. Pensacola, Panama City, Gulf Breeze, Tallahassee, Jacksonville, Gainesville and Fort Walton are just a few of the interesting towns covered. For each region, the authors start with a *Touring* section, which looks at getting around and taking in all the sights, from museums and galleries to state parks, theaters and historical buildings. Then comes the real backbone of coverage – the adventures. Every opportunity for recreation is discussed, listing the best places for each, along with contact names and numbers of local tour operators. The final section gives a huge selection of places to stay and eat, whether you're looking for a beachside villa with all meals served by a full staff, or an in-town B&B where you can relax in the morning, then dine out and sample the nightlife later.

Entertainment to suit all tastes is also covered. Maps and directions ensure that you won't get lost, and a full index helps you locate particular sports, sites and destinations with ease.

$15.95/280 pp/ISBN 1-55650-769-0

Other Florida Books From Hunter Publishing

Adventure Guide To The Florida Keys & Everglades

2nd Edition

by Joyce & Jon Huber

A highly informative guide to the best of South Florida's natural wonders. Most visitors define themselves by what they do. A few just wanting to lie back and do nothing – there's a section for them at the back of the book that lists all the great resorts – but the true flavors of this special area can be tasted only by those who venture out. Scuba diving, snorkeling, canoeing, birdwatching, sea kayaking, deep-sea fishing, aerial tours, swamp hiking, nature trails and fly-fishing are the way to go! From Key Largo, Islamorada and Marathon all the way down to Big Pine Key, Little Torch Key, Sugarloaf Key and fun-packed Key West, this sun-splashed region is full of adventures for the active traveler. This guidebook puts them into catagories – parasailing, swimming with dolphins, cycling, etc. – then tells you where to find them. In addition, you'll find a comprehensive list of outfitters and tour operators ready to help. Practical advice abounds, with tips on where to rent equipment, what to wear for a cycling trip, a nature hike or an hour's parasailing, and how to charter a boat. To insure future generations some fun, too, the book has EcoTips, a small collection of earth-friendly ways to leave the area a little better than you found it. These include catch-and-release tactics, wild bird rescue tips, desilting techniques for corals and sponges, and news on the all-natural fish food now available for divers. A selection of colorful accommodations and restaurants is given for each town, based on repeat visits by the authors. Color photos and numerous maps.

"... a great book – practical and easy to use. The perfect traveler's guide to these two beautiful and ecologically sensitive areas." *Wilderness Southeast*

"The Everglades will always be mysterious, but finding them? This book makes it easy to discover the whole region, even the secret places like Corkscrew Swamp." *National Audubon Society*

"Vastly informative, absolutely user-friendly, full of information that makes me want to leave immediately to investigate those places so well described... from trails to historic sites to underwater adventure, it's all there." *Society of Aquatic Veterinarians*

$14.95/220 pp/ISBN 1-55650-745-3

Florida: A Camping Guide

By Blair Howard

There's nothing like the glow of a campfire on a remote beach. Or the clutter of RVs near a noisy highway! On the theory that camping is what (and where) you make it, order a copy of this invaluable book to camping in the Sunshine State.

Over 150 campgrounds are profiled, each with details on facilities, security features, nearby services and attractions, rates, directions and opening seasons; contact numbers are provided. But what about the atmosphere? Howard gives you the lowdown on the feel of each establishment, telling which are the most secluded and perfect for a quiet weekend break and which are family-oriented, offering heaps of playgrounds, activities and campfire programs.

The book is divided into regions – the South, the Panhandle, Central Florida, Central West Coast, the Northeast, the Southwest and the Central East Coast – and a special locator map identifies each site by number. Photos add spark to the informative text.

$13.95/192 pp/ISBN 1-55650-721-6

Where To Stay In Florida

By Phil Philcox

Should you make reservations at the chain hotel nearest the airport and hope it has adequate rooms for your presentation? Where will you find a hotel with a health club so you can keep up your fitness routine? *Where to Stay in Florida* offers thousands of accommodations to choose from. The state is broken down into an alphabetical listing of towns, and under each town is a comprehensive listing of every place offering a roof over your head for a night, a week, a month or longer – B&Bs, motels, resorts, vacation cabins, chain hotels. Also included are accommodation finders, offices set up specifically to help find lodgings to suit each person's needs. A special section is dedicated to chain hotels and the deals they offer to educational groups, business travelers, government/military staff, senior citizens and weekend travelers.

"Probably the most extensive listing of accommodations in Florida you will find, this guide covers 4,000 places to stay - renting from $20 to $1,000 a night." *Atlanta Journal*

$12.95/380 pp/ISBN 1-55650-682-1

Charming Small Hotels - Florida

Think of a Florida vacation and an image of towering hotels, crowded beaches and poorly-maintained motels springs to mind. But imagine finding smaller hotels off the main strip where the staff caters to your every need, the food is excellent and the nicely decorated rooms are kept clean. Now you want to go, right?

Here is a selection of smaller establishments that offer something special to their guests. Perhaps they are set in a historic building, or maybe the owners are gourmet chefs willing to whip up a five-course dinner for you.

With this book, you'll be able to choose the perfect hotel, whatever your price range. All of the 300+ places listed have been chosen by independent inspectors, and no one can pay to have a hotel included.

Along with a color photo, you'll find a detailed profile of the hotel, with the authors' comments on atmosphere and surroundings. A "Fact File" gives contact names and numbers, credit card policy, rates, dining options, and amenities in an easy-to-read format, so you can see at a glance what's on offer. Regional maps show hotel locations.

This is the latest volume in a best-selling series that includes volumes on New England, Italy, Great Britain, France, Paris, South of France, Austria, Germany, and Tuscany/Umbria.

"Each of these easily portable pocket books gives photographs and capsule descriptions of more than 400 properties, covering practicalities and salient features." *Gourmet Magazine*

"Ooooh! Wait til you see this guide." *The New York Daily News*

"I have used the Spain and Italy volumes to find delightful, inexpensive hotels with such good results that I would trust their recommendations." *The Washington Post*

$12.95/224 pp/ISBN 1-55650-757-7

Look for these at your local bookstore or order from Hunter Publishing, 130 Campus Drive, Edison NJ 08818. (732) 225 1900; (800) 255 0343. To order by mail, send a check for the price indicated, plus $3 shipping/handling, to the address shown above. Or order from our Web site at www.hunterpublishing.com.